A Spacious Path to Freedom

A Spacious Path to Freedom

Practical Instructions on the Union of Mahāmudrā and Atiyoga

by

Karma Chagmé

with commentary by

Gyatrul Rinpoche

translated by

B. Alan Wallace

Snow Lion
Boulder

Snow Lion
An imprint of Shambhala Publications, Inc.
4720 Walnut Street
Boulder, Colorado 80301
www.shambhala.com

9 8 7 6 5 4 3

Printed in the United States of America

♾This edition is printed on acid-free paper that meets the American National Standards Institute Z39.48 Standard.
♻This book is printed on 30% postconsumer recycled paper. For more information please visit www.shambhala.com.
Snow Lion is distributed worldwide by Penguin Random House, Inc., and its subsidiaries.

The Library of Congress catalogues the previous edition of this book as follows:
Karma-chags-med, 17th cent.
[Thugs rje chen po'i dmar khrid Phyag Rdzogs zuṅ 'jug thos pa don ldan. English.]
A Spacious path to freedom: practical instructions on the union of Mahāmudrā and Atiyoga/by Karma Chagmé; with commentary by Gyatrul Rinpoche; translated by B. Alan Wallace.
p. cm.
Includes bibliographical references and index.
ISBN 978-1-55939-071-2 (1st ed.)
ISBN 978-1-55939-340-9 (2nd ed.)
1. Avalokiteśvara (Buddhist deity)—Cult. 2. Mahāmudrā (Tantric rite)
3. Rdzogs-chen (Rñiṅ-ma-pa) I. Gyatrul, Rinpoche. II. Wallace, B. Alan.
III. Title.
BQ4710.A83K3813 1997
294.3'444—dc21
97-33447
CIP

Contents

Preface by Sangye Khandro 7
Translator's Note 13

1 A Treasury of Oral Transmissions 15
2 The Stage of Generation 39
3 The Cultivation of Quiescence 63
4 The Cultivation of Insight 85
5 Identification 103
6 Practice 125
7 Mahāmudrā 149
8 Atiyoga 171
9 Sealing with the Dedication 191

Notes 215
Glossary of Terms 219
Glossary of Names 221
Index of Texts Cited by the Author 225
General Index 239

Venerable Gyatrul Rinpoche
photo: Deborah Korman/Vimala Archives

Preface

by Sangye Khandro

Karma Chagmé Rinpoche was born in the Nyomtö region of Zalmo Gang in the Do-Kham area of the snowy land of Tibet. In exact accordance with the prophecies given by the illustrious Vajrayāna master Guru Padmasambhava, he appeared as a Nirmāṇakāya in this world in the year 1613. His father was the well-known Mahāsiddha Padma Wangdrak, and his mother was an apparent wisdom Ḍākinī known as Chökyong Kyi. Curiously enough, at the very moment he was born, his father gave him the longevity empowerment from the *termas* of Tertön Ratna Lingpa. His father also gave him his first name, Wangdrak Sung. His father was his Lama until he was eleven years of age, during which time the young Wangdrak Sung learned to read and write, perform spiritual ceremonies, memorize texts, and sit in silent meditation for extended periods of time.

The young child was a brilliant learner and went on to master everything that was presented to him. In his eleventh year, he met one of his important karmic Lamas from past lives, the hidden contemplative Prawashara. After receiving many of the important empowerments, transmissions, and pointing-out instructions at the feet of his teacher, he went out to wander in sacred lands and power spots to perform and accomplish the inner practices. In short, he actualized each one of the deities to which he had been initiated and attained authentic signs of realization. After this he received the important transmissions for Avalokiteśvara and the lineage of the Mahāmudrā from Kün-ga Namgyal of Drungpa Tserlung.

At the age of nineteen, Wangdrak Sung resolved to abandon the lifestyle of a householder and journeyed to the seat of the Karmapa, Tsurphu Monastery, to receive the vows of ordination. There he took the vows of refuge, novice ordination, and full ordination. Becoming a fully ordained monk, he then joined the Saṅgha at the Thupten Nyingling Monastery of the Zurmang tradition. Now known by his ordination name, Karma Chagmé, he served the monastery with forthright honor and diligence, while simultaneously mastering all the major and minor texts on logic.

In the year of the dragon, the Karmapa and his two spiritual sons came to the Zurmang Monastery. During their stay, Karma Chagmé received from the Karmapa many important empowerments, transmissions, and pointing-out instructions, among which were the teachings for the co-emergent Mahāmudrā. Then Karma Chagmé accompanied the Karmapa for the next year and a half, remaining with him in retreat and receiving further instructions. Karma Chagmé became famous throughout the land of Tibet, and in his twenty-first year he was given a public examination during the Great Prayer Festival of the Karma Kagyü before a gathering of twelve thousand monks. Following this, his fame increased when he offered two of his fingers as butter lamps. This occurred first at the passing of the Karmapa and later in front of the Jowo Rinpoche image in the central cathedral in Lhasa while receiving the Bodhisattva vows.

After performing many miraculous deeds, Karma Chagmé resolved to actualize the form of Avalokiteśvara known as Gyalwa Gyatso as his principal meditation deity. He entered into a strict thirteen-year retreat, during which he wrote many of his important commentaries. Close to the conclusion of his retreat Karma Chagmé recognized and enthroned the young *tertön* Min-gyur Dorje. At the same time, he offered to the treasure-revealer the essential empowerments and transmissions, which awakened the indwelling awareness through which blessings began to well forth as a trove of treasures from his lifetime spent in the company of the great Guru Padmasambhava. Recalling countless past lifetimes, the young *tertön* Min-gyur Dorje began having visions of innumerable deities, which unleashed a storehouse of precious transmissions. Karma Chagmé, as the treasure-keeper, was the scribe who recorded them.

After concluding his retreat, Karma Chagmé went on to lead many great and important accomplishment ceremonies that blessed the minds of everyone present. In addition, he bestowed the empowerments for the *Namchö*, or "Space Dharma," revelations of *tertön* Min-gyur Dorje, and the revelations of the great *tertön* king, Ratna Lingpa. He wrote an important commentary, *Buddhahood in the Palm of the Hand*, that combines these two great treasure lineages, elucidating the subjects of the outer and inner preliminaries, the vital energies, the channels and fluids, mystic heat, blissful emptiness, cutting through to original purity, and crossing over into spontaneous presence. In addition, he wrote the text partially translated here, which combines the practical instructions he had received on Mahāmudrā and Atiyoga. The founder of the Payül tradition of the Nyingma order, the Vidyādhara Künzang Sherap, received all of these important transmissions directly from Karma Chagmé. Notably, this particular lineage of practice has become the very heart of the Payül tradition and has been practiced continuously to the present time.

The Mahāsiddha Karma Chagmé Rinpoche, who was an authentic emanation of Avalokiteśvara in this world of phenomenal existence, passed away in the year 1678 after announcing to thousands of his disciples that the time had come for him to change realms. With astonishing signs he dissolved his mind into the heart of Buddha Amitābha. For seventeen consecutive days extensive after-death ceremonies were performed by scores of Lamas and monks who gathered to honor their precious Lama. Among the many countless signs of marvels that occurred before, during, and after the cremation were many images of Avalokiteśvara Gyalwa Gyatso that were found to be embossed on the very bones of this great practitioner.

Tertön Min-gyur Dorje was one of the great one hundred and eight treasure-revealer incarnates prophesied by Guru Padmasambhava. In the treasures that came into this world before him, such as those revealed by the treasure-revealer Ratna Lingpa, Düdül Dorje, and others, there are many references to the coming of Min-gyur Dorje. Born in 1645 in the Ngom Tö Rola region of the snowy land of Tibet, the young incarnate child made no mistake in choosing his virtuous parents. His father was of the unbroken ancestral heritage of Lord Buddha Śākyamuni, and both mother and father had remarkable dreams of their child before, during, and after conception.

In accordance with all the prophecies about him, his right hand was marked with a most extraordinary blue mole, signifying the sole essential nature of the Dharmakāya. Throughout his childhood, he displayed signs and gestures that were unlike anything he could have seen or learned from anyone else; and as soon as he could speak, he told everyone who he was in his previous life. He learned how to read and write through a vision of Guru Loden Chegsé (one of the eight emanations of Guru Rinpoche), who instructed him. When he was seven years old, he perceived many Ḍākinīs in visions, and they gave him pith instructions on the importance of relying upon a Lama. Immediately, he had a perfect vision of his future root Lama, Karma Chagmé Rinpoche, who was in a strict retreat at the time. The young *tertön* developed a burning, insatiable desire to meet him as soon as possible.

When he was ten years old, with the help of the Dharma Protectors, Min-gyur Dorje finally met his Lama, Karma Chagmé, who recognized him to be an unmistakable manifestation of Guru Rinpoche. Chagmé Rinpoche proceeded to bestow upon him *The Synthesized Quintessence of the Realization of Enlightened Awareness* in five stages of development. He was instructed to meditate on the clear light Mahāmudrā in successive meditation sessions. Karma Chagmé then led the young *tertön* through a series of techniques that caused him to lucidly remember all of his past lifetimes, everything he had received, and his profound familiarity with the pantheon of enlightened wisdom manifestations.

As he began to reveal his profound *termas*, he also continued to receive many transmissions and teachings from Karma Chagmé Rinpoche. As the fame of this young saint spread far and wide, fortunate disciples came from all regions of Tibet to receive these transmissions. Although the treasure-revealer Min-gyur Dorje had many disciples who were also Dharma-keepers and lineage-holders of his treasures, the principal one was Karma Chagmé Rinpoche.

Min-gyur Dorje was destined to reveal earth-treasures as well; unfortunately, the merit of sentient beings was deficient at the time and, due to this, his presence in this world was cut short. In 1667, when he was only twenty-three years old, he began showing signs of an illness that got progressively worse. With a full vision of the eight *herukas* and their *maṇḍalas*, Min-gyur Dorje's mind stream of enlightened awareness dissolved into the empty sphere of truth. His body remained upright in the perfect meditation posture for three days.

The great Vidyādhara Künzang Sherap, the founder of the Payül tradition, was one of the *tertön's* main disciples and treasure-keepers. Künzang Sherap was now the perfect upholder of the lineages of both Karma Chagmé Rinpoche and Tertön Min-gyur Dorje. His lineage has been transmitted through the succession of Payül lineage-holders to the present time.

The Venerable Gyatrul Rinpoche, also referred to as Payül Gyatrul, is a Lama who holds this lineage in the present day. Born in Tibet in 1925, he was recognized by Jamyang Khyentse Lodrö Tayé to be the incarnation of Sampa Künkyap, a Payül lineage meditator who spent his life in retreat and later gave empowerments and transmissions from his retreat cave to multitudes of disciples. After being brought to his Payül Dhomang Monastery, the young Gyatrul was educated by his tutor Sangye Gön. Sangye Gön received his name as a newborn baby from the famous Gili Tertön (Dudjom Lingpa), who singled out the child while passing through his village, named him, and predicted his future.

During the many years that the young Gyatrul spent with his Lama, he remembers him having regular visitations from a white man (Avalokiteśvara), and he recalls that Sangye Gön's own white hair turned black and he grew new teeth, replacing those that were missing. Most of Gyatrul Rinpoche's basic training occurred under his teacher Sangye Gön, including his training in the lineage of Karma Chagmé's *Buddhahood in the Palm of the Hand, The Union of Mahāmudrā and Atiyoga,* and in much supplementary material that he studied with his teacher for three consecutive years. Later Gyatrul Rinpoche entered retreat with the miraculous activity emanation of the Dudjom incarnations, Tulku Natsok Rangdröl, who became his root Lama. Tulku Natsok Rangdröl's root Lama was Lam Dolo, who was the tutor of Dudjom Lingpa as a young boy. Again he received these important transmissions while simultaneously practicing them in retreat. On yet another occasion, Gyatrul Rinpoche received the transmissions directly from the great Payül Chogtrul Rinpoche, the root Lama of H.H. Penor Rinpoche, the present head of both the Payül lineage and the Nyingma Order as a whole. He received these and countless other transmissions again from the great Apkong Khenpo. He spent much of his life in Tibet before the Chinese occupation in the presence of these and many other great teachers, receiving the important transmissions and accomplishing the practices.

Since arriving in the West, among the many great deeds and acts of kindness that Gyatrul Rinpoche has displayed is his organization of two historic Dharma tours of H.H. Penor Rinpoche to the United States. During that time the lineage of Mahāmudrā and Atiyoga was firmly established through the transmissions of the essential empowerments and pointing-out instructions bestowed at various locations around the country. Later, the Venerable Gyatrul Rinpoche took the time to give the necessary instructions and lead students in the practices. Many of the principal practices from the cycle of *Buddhahood in the Palm of the Hand* have been translated into English, and numerous retreats have already taken place under Rinpoche's direction. In the past year and a half, Rinpoche has been teaching extensively from the *Practical Instructions on the Union of Mahāmudrā and Atiyoga,* including instructions on identifying the essential nature of awareness and all the supplementary chapters.

The profound blessings of the lineage of practice and realization make their authentic mark in the West through the kindness of the Venerable Gyatrul Rinpoche and the great lineage-holders and founders of the past. This account is but a mere drop of potent nectar to moisten the minds of those who will go on to turn the pages of this precious book of authentic practical instructions. More extensive accounts of the life stories of both Karma Chagmé Rinpoche and Tertön Min-gyur Dorje can be found in the *Garland of Immortal Wish-fulfilling Trees,* the history of the Payül Tradition of the Nyingmapa. As for the Venerable Gyatrul Rinpoche, he continues to turn the wheel of Dharma, elucidating many great lineages, inspiring many students to translate the precious teachings into English for the benefit of generations to come, and tirelessly encouraging practitioners on the path.

Tashi Choling, 1995

Translator's Note

Karma Chagmé presented his classic work *Meaningful to Behold: The Essential Instructions of Avalokiteśvara on the Union of Mahāmudrā and Atiyoga,*[*] in its entirety as an oral teaching lasting thirty days. This is a more elaborate treatise than his work translated as *Union of Mahamudra and Dzogchen* (Hong Kong: Rangjung Yeshe Publications, 1994), with a commentary by Tulku Chökyi Nyima. The portions of *Meaningful to Behold* that are translated here are those on which the Venerable Gyatrul Rinpoche gave oral commentary at his Buddhist center Orgyen Dorje Den in San Francisco during 1994 and 1995. At that time, Gyatrul Rinpoche gave teachings on the first chapter and the concluding eight chapters of this text, which cover the main practices of Mahāmudrā and Atiyoga, but he chose not to give a commentary on the intervening chapters, which discuss the preliminary practices. Thus, these chapters have not been translated here. However, similar versions of this same subject matter are presently available in numerous other English translations, including the above-mentioned *Union of Mahamudra and Dzogchen*, the Ninth Karmapa's *Mahamudra: Eliminating the Darkness of Ignorance* (Dharamsala: LTWA, 1978), Patrul Rinpoche's *Words of My*

[*]*Thugs rje chen po'i dmar khrid phyag rdzogs zung 'jug thos ba don ldan* by Kar ma chags med (Bylakuppe: Nyingmapa Monastery, 1984). The title of this work, *A Spacious Path to Freedom,* does not correspond to that of Karma Chagmé's work, as it designates only a part of Karma Chagmé's work, together with Gyatrul Rinpoche's commentary.

Perfect Teacher (San Francisco: Harper Collins, 1994), and Khenchen Thrangu Rinpoche's *The Four Ordinary Foundations of Buddhist Practice* (Delhi: Sri Satguru Publications, 1994).

I have also translated the supplementary chapters of *Meaningful to Behold*, along with a commentary that Gyatrul Rinpoche presented during 1995 and 1996; this will appear in a subsequent volume. Gyatrul Rinpoche comments that teachings on the six transitional processes, or *bardos*, which I have translated in the book *Natural Liberation: Padmasambhava's Teachings on the Six Bardos*, with Gyatrul Rinpoche's commentary, should be regarded as ancillary to these teachings.

I have translated this text in close collaboration with the Venerable Gyatrul Rinpoche, who went through it with me line by line. Afterwards, he gave teachings on this treatise at Orgyen Dorje Den, his Buddhist center in San Francisco, for which I served as interpreter. This oral commentary was transcribed by a number of his students in California and Oregon and was then edited by Rinpoche's students Neal King and Lindy Steele. To the best of our knowledge there is only one edition of this text, which was published in India. Written in the *dbu med* script, many words are abbreviated, and the spelling is loose, to say the least. This made the translation particularly challenging, and I would not have taken on the task but for the constant encouragement and assistance I received from Gyatrul Rinpoche.

Karma Chagmé states that he composed this treatise so that many old mendicants and recluses may accomplish their eternal longing for happiness by practicing the union of Mahāmudrā and Atiyoga. He speculates that no advanced scholars will be interested in this work, though they may gratified by its many citations. Karma Chagmé concludes this work with his apology to scholars for any possible errors in the order of some of the citations. Despite our best efforts, there may still be errors in the translation. If these are detected by other scholars, I hope they will bring them to my attention. As Gyatrul Rinpoche strongly emphasized, this work is intended chiefly for those wishing to practice Mahāmudrā and Atiyoga in order to realize the essential nature of their own minds. It is our earnest prayer that our efforts will help make this profound contemplative path accessible to people in the modern world.

B. Alan Wallace
Santa Barbara, California
Spring, 1997

CHAPTER ONE

A Treasury of Oral Transmissions

Namo guru lokitara deva ḍākinī sarva siddhi hūṃ

Not composing this out of my own mental constructs, I bow at the feet of Amitābha, Avalokiteśvara, Padmasambhava, and my gracious spiritual mentor, a Nirmāṇakāya who has taken human form in these degenerate times. I shall set forth advice concerning the essential instructions on the union of Mahāmudrā and Atiyoga. May the assembly of Three Roots,[1] the Lords of Dharma, and the Guardians grant their permission and blessings.

On this occasion when there is a confluence of circumstances of the teaching, an audience, a place, and time, as soon as I sat down upon the Dharma throne, I visualized myself in the form of Avalokiteśvara, the Great Compassionate One, and cultivated the *samādhi* of immeasurable loving-kindness. So that there may be no hindrances in this monastic courtyard, recite this *mantra* to vanquish the power of *māras*, as taught in *The Sūtra of the Questions of Sāgaramati*. Recite it three, seven, or twenty-one times or as much as you can. This should not be recited so [loudly] that it can be heard in the marketplace:

> *Tadyathā śame śamavati śamitaśatru aṅkure maṃkure mārajite karote keyūre tejovati aloyani vivṛttanirmale mama panaye khukhure khakhagrase grasane amukhi pāraṃmukhi amukhi śamitāni sarvagrahabandanane nigṛihītva sarvaparasravādina vimuktamārasaśa svātita vṛddhamūtra anurgatitva sarvamāre sucaritaparivṛddhe vigacchantu sarvamāra garmaṇi.*

> Sāgaramati, utter these syllables of the *mantra*. If you speak of Dharma, within a radius of a hundred *yojanas*, no kinds of *māras* will come to harm the gods. Those who do come will not be able to create obstacles. Then explain the words of Dharma coherently, clearly, and mindfully.

Then an offering assistant offers a *maṇḍala*.

– Whether the teachings take place in a monastic courtyard or inside the monastery, it is best to recite this *mantra* fairly quietly. Both the recitation of the *mantra* and the offering of the *maṇḍala* are preparations for giving and receiving the teaching. –

Homage to Avalokiteśvara!

These are the profound instructions of Avalokiteśvara. In presenting the essential instructions of the union of Mahāmudrā and Atiyoga, I shall first discuss the qualifications of a spiritual mentor. *The Three Hundred* by Śākya Ö states:

> Possessing ethical discipline and knowing the rituals of the *vinaya*,
> With merciful compassion for the ill, and having a pure retinue,
> Eager to serve by means of the Dharma and material goods—
> Those who stand out as such are praised as spiritual mentors.

– It is best to devote oneself to a spiritual mentor with the following qualifications: A fully qualified spiritual mentor must be well-versed in both the *sūtras* and *tantras*. In particular, a Mahāyāna teacher should be motivated by the spirit of aspiring for awakening and the spirit of venturing towards awakening. Furthermore, a Vajrayāna spiritual mentor must have accomplished the stages of generation and completion, and have extensive experience in terms of oral transmissions, explanations, and empowerments. The Lama must know the purpose of each element of the empowerment, and the disciples should know how to receive an empowerment. Otherwise, it will be nothing more than an empty ritual. This is also true for the vows of refuge. By understanding their meaning and rejoicing in having received them, there will later be less danger of your letting these vows degenerate. This will be of benefit to you in this and in future lifetimes. Otherwise you will be like an alcoholic who gives up drinking for a few days, but then goes right back to it because of not recognizing what truly needs to be done. –

The Twenty Precepts states:

> Accept a spiritual mentor who abides by his precepts,
> Who is knowledgeable and capable.

– In Tibet, occasionally people took novice or full monastic precepts without even knowing what they were, and some of them never did learn. Whatever precepts you take, whether lay vows, novice vows, or full ordination, it is important to know what they are, so that you truly arrive at their essence. Similarly, the cultivation of the spirit of aspiring for awakening leads to the spirit of venturing towards awakening. Moreover, tantric practice becomes meaningful only if you learn about the generation and completion stages. Engaging in such practices or taking precepts without understanding makes it difficult to penetrate to their real significance. –

The Ornament for the Sūtras states:

> A teacher of supreme beings
> Is one who is gentle, free of arrogance and depression,
> Whose knowledge and understanding are lucid and broad-ranging,
> Who goes everywhere without material compensation,
> Who is endowed with the Spirit of Awakening and great learning,
> Who sees the truth, is skillful in speaking, and is merciful.
> Know the greatness of this sublime being,
> Who is not despondent.
> Expansive, having cast off doubts,
> And revealing the two realities, he is worthy to be accepted.
> This one is called a superb teacher of Bodhisattvas.
> Devote yourself to a spiritual friend who is peaceful, subdued, and utterly calm,
> With superior qualities, zeal, and a wealth of scriptural knowledge,
> With realization of thatness and with skill in speaking,
> A merciful being who has cast off depression.

– Great teachers of the present and the recent past, such as His Holiness the Dalai Lama, Dudjom Rinpoche, Gyalwa Karmapa, and Kalu Rinpoche, were never known to boast about their qualities or to put on airs. A spiritual mentor should not show signs of depression. Without thinking about material compensation, the Lama should serve the needs of sentient beings. For example, as a young Lama in Tibet, I frequently went to places where beggars lived so that I could be of service to them. Many, many times, I would go accompanied by monks to recite prayers for them. We would take our own food so we would not have to ask them for any. Eventually, the Chinese communists took over the area where we lived, imprisoning all of the monks and Lamas who had not previously fled. But I was overlooked, for the beggars had petitioned the government, requesting that I be left alone because I had taken care of them and had asked for nothing in return. Although I did not flee until later, people thought I had died or had been imprisoned. It was only due to these beggars that I was not. –

Nāgārjuna says:

> Devote yourself to one possessing twelve qualities:
> Much learning and great wisdom,
> Not aspiring for material goods or possessions,
> Possessing the Spirit of Awakening and great compassion,
> Enduring hardships and having little depression or fatigue,
> Having great practical advice, liberated from the [mundane] path,
> And possessing knowledge and erudition and comprehension
> of the signs of warmth.[2]

Atīśa's *A Lamp on the Path of Enlightenment* states:

> Know a good spiritual mentor to be one
> Who is knowledgeable of the precepts and rituals,
> A spiritual mentor who abides by the precepts,
> And who endures granting precepts and is compassionate.

I personally do not have such qualifications of a spiritual mentor, but in degenerate times it is rare to find mentors who are faultless and who are imbued with excellent qualities. Therefore, it is appropriate to devote yourself to a spiritual mentor whose virtues are equal to his faults or to one whose virtues even slightly outweigh his faults. *Worship of the Ultimate* states:

> Due to degenerate times, the faults and virtues of spiritual
> mentors are mixed,
> And there are none who are totally free of sins.
> Upon well examining one who has greater virtues,
> Disciples should devote themselves to him.

– Spiritual mentors are not the only people with shortcomings or faults. Disciples and students are in the same situation. We must recognize our flaws and by reading books on Dharma, we can learn not only how to listen to the Dharma but determine which defects are to be eliminated. This is true for everyone because each of us, whether rich or poor, from the West or East, is seeking enlightenment. So we need to abandon our faults and learn how to receive teachings.

I have taught Dharma in the United States for many years. In one high school where I taught, I saw students sitting with their legs propped up, barely listening while they fooled around with other things. On one hand, you can't blame them because they didn't comprehend the significance of what I was teaching. But unfortunately, they were not able to receive any blessings. You don't show reverence for the sake of the Dharma or for another person. You show reverence solely to receive the benefits and blessings of the teachings. –

Lord Gampopa says of the tradition of the practice lineage[3]:

> If a spiritual mentor lacks realization, it does not help even if his disciples act with reverence and devotion. As an analogy, although the clay may be good, if its mold has no indentations, it will not form into a statue. If the disciples have no reverence or devotion, it does not help even if the spiritual mentor has realization. This is like a cow having milk, but its calf having no palate.

– A fully qualified spiritual mentor should have not only the qualities of learning, thinking, and meditating, but also experiential realization that results from spiritual practice. As a result of such practice and realization, one's own mental afflictions are pacified. Today people tend to spend many hours working on computers rather than gaining the inner quality of experiential realization. A computer may have a tremendous amount of information loaded onto it, but we have yet to see a computer that has attained liberation or omniscience. The pacification of mental afflictions is what the practice of Dharma accomplishes and what a computer cannot achieve. The great Mahāsiddhas of India and Tibet followed this tradition. To subdue their own mental afflictions and attain the state of liberation and enlightenment, they applied themselves to Dharma. For this very reason, Buddha Śākyamuni turned the wheel of the Dharma. This is the avenue that all of the Buddhas of the past followed. In Tibet, specifically, the twenty-five disciples of Guru Padmasambhava and the many great beings of each of the traditions attained their states of realization by putting the teachings into practice.

If a calf has no palate it will be unable to suck milk from its mother's teat. To give a similar example, after serving the Buddha for twenty-five years, Devadatta thought he had the same qualities as the Buddha. He acknowledged that the Buddha had a crown protrusion and an aura of light extending all around him. But apart from those qualities, he believed himself to be the equal of the Buddha, so he saw no reason to revere him. As a result he took birth in a miserable state of existence as a great *preta.*

To avoid that pitfall we need faith. By the power of faith, we are able to eliminate the two types of obscurations. Through the power of faith both ontological and phenomenological knowledge arises. It is also by the power of faith that both the common and uncommon *siddhis* arise. –

Nevertheless, according to the general tradition of the teachings, even though I have no fine experiential realizations, if you listen with faith, realizations will arise. In the past there lived in Nepal an intelligent, literate man who killed both his parents. Thereafter, while he was out roaming, he secretly killed an Arhat who was living in a vacated temple. Putting on the robes of his victim, he pretended to be the slain Arhat. Everyone thought that he was that Arhat, and with faith and devotion they asked him for Dharma. By reading the scriptures to them and explaining the Dharma, he gathered a following of a hundred thousand disciples, including monks. Those with good karmic momentum[4] attained Arhatship, and many acquired extrasensory perception and paranormal abilities. Those Arhat disciples who could see with extrasensory perception saw that their spiritual mentor was a sinful man, and they tried to guide him. However, they did not succeed, and he went to hell. This account is explained at length in Dharma histories, and it is called *The Account of Bhikṣu Mahādeva*.

Sakya Paṇḍita implied the same thing in his remark, "Even if someone has many disciples, there is no guarantee that he is good." With respect to the stream of oral transmissions and so forth, even if the lineage is impure, this is no problem. If a hole in an irrigation channel is blocked even with a garment of a corpse, the water still helps the fields. It is like that. Drogön Chöpak received an empowerment from a shepherd, and he received a *sādhana* of *The Perfect Expression of the Names of Mañjuśrī* from the widow of a liturgist. The reason he did so was that he was afraid that the lineage of that empowerment and oral transmission might be cut. With that in mind, the Kadam spiritual mentors say, "People's faults do not taint the Dharma."

– Certain people speak very highly of their own accomplishments, even claiming that they are emanations of the Buddha. Such people often attract a following, and indeed, they may be able to display certain outward signs. However, such signs may actually be due to blessings of a malevolent spirit.

For example, in Tibet, there was a Lama called the Black Horse Lama. With an exclamation of *phaṭ* and a snap of his fingers, he was reputed to be able to send people's consciousness to a pure realm. These outer signs were not due to realization, so when he died, he did not enter a pure realm himself. Shortly after his death, an enormous fish was found in Lake Kokonor in the Amdo region of Tibet. Parasites were devouring this huge fish bit by bit. A clairvoyant Lama recognized that this fish was, in reality, the incarnation of that Black Horse Lama.

Some time ago, an indigent man made his way to Lhasa. Upon reaching the outskirts of the city, he leaned against a boulder for a nap. While asleep, a malevolent spirit possessed him. Suddenly, he was endowed with extrasensory perception and other *siddhis*. Exploring his abilities, he discovered that he was able to thrust his foot right through stone and could mold rock as if it were dough. Quickly, word spread that he was an accomplished being.

The previous incarnation of Tonglen Rinpoche, who truly had extrasensory perception, realized that this poor man had simply been possessed. So he invited him to his monastery and greeted him with much pomp and ceremony. After greeting him, he put a rock in the man's hand and asked him to demonstrate his power. Before making this request, Tonglen Rinpoche had exorcised him. No matter how hard the man tried to knead the rock, nothing happened, and he realized he possessed no special qualities. He no longer had extrasensory perception; he couldn't explain the Dharma. He had nothing.

Then he asked the Lama what had happened. Tonglen Rinpoche told him he had been possessed by a spirit, but that it had been exorcised. Upon hearing this, with tears rolling down his face, he prostrated to the Lama and requested advice. The Lama said, "In order to be sure that all of these people don't lose faith in you, I suggest that you go into retreat and practice Dharma." The man did so, but he had to start from the beginning stages of practice, because in reality he had accomplished nothing.

With respect to oral transmissions, even if the lineage is impure, it is not a problem. Dilgo Khyentse Rinpoche often sought out and received any oral transmission he thought was on the verge of disappearing. It made no difference who was giving it. He would receive it and, in turn, pass it on to make sure that the lineage remained unbroken. –

Even if those who listen to the Dharma lack faith, do not know how to listen, and do not understand the meaning, they benefit from merely hearing the sound of Dharma. In the past, a female dog heard the sound of Bhikṣu Upakuta teaching Dharma. As a result, her obscurations were attenuated, and as soon as she died, she was reborn as a Paranirmitavaśavārtin god. In India a pigeon heard a *bhikṣu* reciting *The Condensed Perfection of Wisdom*. As a result, its obscurations were attenuated, and after it passed away it was reborn as a man. Thereafter, he took monastic ordination and remembered all of *The Condensed Perfection of Wisdom* that he had heard before. Moreover, a frog heard a *bhikṣu* teaching Dharma from the sky, its obscurations were attenuated, and upon its death was born in the Trayastriṃśa Heaven. Upon examining the cause of its rebirth, with a flower in hand, that *devaputra* went to make prostrations to the Buddha. The Buddha uttered a verse of Dharma beginning with "All composites are impermanent," and that being saw the truth.

The crucial, primary qualification of a spiritual mentor is stated by Naropa, "The qualification of a spiritual mentor is that he possesses the lineage." *The Single Meaning of the Vajra Speech* states, "There is great profundity in the connection within the lineage of the holy Dharma." The real lineage of the realization of this Dharma, which transfers blessings, is the unbroken rosary of Buddhas: Vajradhara, Tilopa, Naropa, Marpa, Milarepa, Dagpo, Düsum Kyenpa, Rechenpa, Pomdragpa, Karma Pakṣi, Orgyenpa, Rangjungwa, Yungtönpa, Rölpey Dorje, Kachö Wangpo, Dezhin Shegpa, Ratnabhadra, Tongwa Dönden, Jampal Zangpo, Paljor Döndrup, Chödrak Gyatso, Sangye Nyenpa, Mikyö Dorje, Könchok Yenlak, Wangchuk Dorje, and Chökyi Wangchuk, who is Amitābha in human form.

From Chökyi Wangchuk, I, Rāga Asey, received the *pratimokṣa* vows of going forth, the novice vows, the *bhikṣu* vows, the Bodhisattva vows of the Spirit of Awakening, and one month of instructions on mind training and the Kadam stages of the path. I also received three times the complete four empowerments of Secret Mantra, one month of instructions on Mahāmudrā, and two weeks of instructions on *The Single Meaning*, entailing an extensive explanation of the fivefold practice. In addition, I received many oral transmissions on the inner meaning and so forth of the *Five Dharmas of Maitreya* and *A Guide to the Middle Way*. In short, I devoted myself to that spiritual mentor for three years. Just as a receptacle may be poor while the strap is fine, so [while I am a poor vessel] this is a superb lineage. All real lineages of realization of other Dharmas are included in this lineage. Tilopa heard the Dharma directly from Vajradhara and Vajravārāhī. By again devoting himself to spiritual mentors of the lineage of the Four Doctrines, he received teachings belonging to the four unsurpassable classes of *tantras*. The Bodhisattva Lodrö Rinchen and the son Rāhula, bearing the secret name Déwé Gönpo, both granted the teachings on Mahāmudrā to Saraha. Then the lineage runs from Nāgārjuna, Śawaripa, and Maitrīpa to Marpa.

From Mañjuśrī and Nāgārjuna stems the lineage of the profound view. From Maitreya and Asaṅga runs the lineage of vast activities.

From Mañjuśrī, Śāntideva, and Serlingpa runs the lineage of mind training. They were brought together in Atiśa. That lineage came through Dromtön, Gyalsey, Kumché, Jayülwa, Gyachakri, Kangkawa, and so on to Dagpo. That is called the nondual union of the streams of the Kadampa and Mahāmudrā. It also runs from Sharawa to Düsum Kyenpa. Düsum Kyenpa heard *The Great Perfection Aro Oral Lineage* from his spiritual mentor Dragkarwa, so the real lineage of the Great Perfection is also synthesized there.

Karma Pakṣi received *The Sūtra of the Synthesized Meaning, The Tantra of the Net of Magical Displays*, and *The Great Perfection of the Supreme Mind* from Katogpa Jampa Bum, and he gained expertise in them. His compositions concern the union of Mahāmudrā and Atiyoga. *The Pith Instructions of the Ḍākinīs* received by Rangjung Dorje from Padma Ledreltsal came to be known as *The Yellow Document*. For six months Rangjung Dorje prayed to Orgyen Rinpoche, who then granted these instructions to him directly; they are called the *Pale Document on The Pith Instructions of the Ḍākinīs*. He was given the meaning of the union of Mahāmudrā and Atiyoga.

In the region of Ugpa, Yungtönpa skillfully trained in the threefold treatises on the *sūtras*, apparitions, and the mind, so his view was chiefly the Great Perfection. Rölpey Dorje had a vision of Vimalamitra, who then dissolved into his forehead. As a result, realization of the Great Perfection arose in him, and he composed spiritual songs and instructions. Therefore, the real lineage of the Great Perfection is also synthesized in this lineage.

Identifying the Three Embodiments: Essential Instructions of the Great Compassionate One, which existed in the oral lineage stemming from Marpa, Milarepa, and Dagpo, was written down by Rangjung Dorje. *The Essential Instructions of the Mahāsiddha Maitrīpa* was heard from Maitrīpa himself by both Lord Dezhin Shegpa and Chödrak Gyatso. Furthermore, *The Treasure of Siddhis: The Hundred Thousand Teachings on the Maṇi* gradually made its way from Ngadak Nyang to Rangjung Dorje. Tongwa Dönden heard Sangye Lingpa's treasure *The Unsurpassed Innermost Secret of the Great Compassionate One* and *The Essential Instructions on the Refreshment of the Mind-itself* from the Sey Lama Yeshe Dorje. Chödrak Gyatso heard *The Tantra of the Synthesized Mysteries of Avalokiteśvara* and *The Essential Instructions of Avalokiteśvara* from Ratna Lingpa himself. Paljor Döndrup heard *The Essential Instructions of the*

Palmo Tradition, The Essential Instructions of the Tsembu Tradition, and *The Essential Instructions of the Bodhisattva Dawa Gyaltsen.* Thus it is said that there were no empowerments, oral transmissions, or teachings in Tibet that he did not receive.

Chökyi Wangchuk heard from Kün-ga Namgyal *The Three Zhijé Cycles,* the twenty-five volumes of *The Path and Fruition,* the twelve volumes of *The Synthesized Essence of the Intended Meaning,* and *The Three Cycles of the Oral Lineage.*

Mikyö Zhap received from Khenchen Chödrup Seng-ge the *pratimokṣa* vow lineage stemming from Kache Paṇchen. Mikyö Dorje received from Karma Trinley both the oral transmission lineage and the explanation lineage of the five treatises of dialectics. Lord Chökyi Wangchuk and Chöying Dorje received from Norbu Gyenpa *The Rainbow Treasure: A General Synthesis of the Jewels of the Great Perfection* and *Avalokiteśvara's [Instructions on the] Natural Liberation from the Miserable States of Existence.* They also sat through the entire oral transmission of the Kangyur.

The root of the meaning of all those is synthesized in *The Great Instructions on the Ocean of Definitive Meaning.* Therefore, so that it may be well received, the union of the real lineage and the blessing lineage of transference are synthesized in this successive lineage.

Lord Tilopa's emanation, the Mahāsiddha Masey, first received *The Great Perfection Quintessence of the Ḍākinīs* from Sangye Zhagchenpa, and signs of accomplishment then appeared. Later on, he received the oral lineage from Dezhin Shegpa. Then I, Rāga Asey, received from the Dharmakāya Özer Seng-ge, the realized Lodrö Dragpa, the realized Döndrup Tsenchen, the venerable Legshé Drayang, and the Mantradhara Rinpoche Tserlung Drungkyi Kün-ga Namgyal the vows of refuge, the vows of dwelling in devotion, the lay vows, the oral transmission of the meditation of Avalokiteśvara, and an eighteen-day teaching on Mahāmudrā. The real lineage of all those stages of instruction, which comes from an unbroken lineage of *siddhas,* is synthesized in that.

The proximate lineage is described by Karma Pakṣi, "It makes no difference whether or not there is any other lineage between Karmapa, whose name is renowned, and Avalokiteśvara." From the Tenth Incarnation of Lord [Karmapa] I received the oral transmission of the meditation of Avalokiteśvara, *guruyoga,* Mahāmudrā, and the introduction [to awareness], and he prophesied that Min-gyur Dorje would be a Dharma Master and a Master of Treasures. While spending three years in the same house, I received from him the Space Dharma, including

Buddhahood in the Palm of Your Hand: Instructions on the Great Perfection, The Seven Seeds of Dharma: Essential Instructions of Avalokiteśvara, and so on. From Düdül Dorje I received general instructions on the *yānas* and many empowerments and oral transmissions related to the Great Perfection. He prophesied that I would be a Dharma Master and gave me sacred substances marked with the syllable "A." He gave me much advice concerning the importance of my own practice of the Great Perfection, of teaching it to others, and so on. Those are the lineages of these instructions.

Other empowerments, oral transmissions, and Dharma connections came from forty-nine spiritual mentors, including Situ Chökyi Gyaltsen, Gyaltsap Dragpa Chog-yang, Lama Drung Yigpa, Rinchen Könchok Paljor, Taglung Tashi Paldrup, Drikung Könchok Trinley Namgyal, Drugchen Karma Tenpel, and Drubgyü Tenpa Namgyal. The limitless, inexpressible, gradual lineages I have received from them are clearly set forth in my account of oral transmissions.

The essential meaning of all those is synthesized in these instructions. Specifically, in terms of the Mahāmudrā cycle, synthesized here are *The Three Treasuries of Dohas, The Three Treasuries of Mysteries, The Eight Treasuries of Dohas, The Extensive and Concise Elucidations of the Primordial Wisdom of Milarepa,* Dagpo's *Jewel Ornament of Liberation* and *Ten Dharmas, The Fivefold Practices* of Drikung Dharmarāja, Gö Tsangpa's *Great Reverence* and *The Summarized Meaning of the Equal Taste,* Rangjung Dorje's *One Word of Essential Teachings,* Orgyenpa's *Great Introduction,* Yang Gönpa's *Support,* Wangchuk Dorje's *Pointing Out the Dharmakāya,* and Gyatönpa's *Hundred Thousand Teachings.* The meaning of those oral transmissions I have received is also synthesized in these instructions.

I have also received many lineages of Great Perfection oral transmissions, including *The Great Perfection Quintessence of the Ḍākinīs, The Pith Instructions on the Clear Expanse,* and *The Natural Emergence of the Peaceful and Wrathful from Enlightened Awareness;* their meaning is synthesized here. I have received the oral transmissions of *The Essential Instructions of Avalokiteśvara* according to the Tsembu tradition, the Palmo tradition, and the Maitrīpa tradition, Avalokiteśvara Jinasāgara's *Introduction to the Three Embodiments,* Avalokiteśvara's ultra-secret, unsurpassed instructions *The Refreshment of the Mind-itself,* the essential instructions on *The Tantra of the Synthesized Mysteries of Avalokiteśvara, The Hundred Thousand Teachings on the Maṇi,* and the synthesis of ultra-secrets, *The Natural Liberation from the Miserable States of Existence;* their meaning is also synthesized here. Therefore, these are not fragmented oral transmissions of partial teachings. Rather, these are connected to lineages of holy Dharma.

Düdül Dorje also said that I, Rāga Asey, was to be among the Dharma Masters, for I have received many treasures including Vidyādhara Longsel Nyingpo's *The Complete Synthesis of the Three Roots*, *The Pith Instructions on the Clear Expanse*, and *The Pith Instructions of Vimalamitra*. He gave me the text of *The Complete Synthesis of the Three Roots*, holy substances, and a long-life blessing, and he granted me the empowerments and oral transmissions of all his Dharma treasures. He wrote, "It is not necessary to meet me directly. Engage in your own practice and cause it to flourish among others." At the time that I received that letter, excellent signs occurred. The lineage of teachings given by Ḍākinīs is also completely present in this.

Regarding the real lineage of transmitted teachings, Sachen Künga Nyingpo had a vision of Mañjuśrī, who gave him four phrases of Dharma; and on that basis he composed the *Instructions on Parting from the Four Cravings*. Tsangpa Gyarey had visions of the seven Buddhas, who gave him several verses. On that basis he composed instructions on his own tradition concerning dependent origination. Pagmo Drüpa and other Kagyü patriarchs disseminated many teachings, including *Dreams of the Spirit of Awakening*, *Zhijé Dreams*, and *Dreams of Secret Activity*.

Although there is no one to compare with them, during Rāga Asey's thirteen-year commitment to Avalokiteśvara practice, one evening I had an experiential vision: in the space in front of me appeared a turquoise-maned lion like a gathering of clouds. Riding bent over upon that lion was a terrifying, naked, brown, cannibal demon, with his lower fangs reaching up to his eyebrows and his upper fangs reaching to his chest. Upon him was Orgyen Rinpoche, his body brown and naked. His left wrist was adorned with a radiant golden bracelet, and he held the upper arms of the cannibal demon with both his hands so that it could not move. His face was frowning, and he was baring his teeth; and on his head he wore a saffron-colored lotus cap. I saw him vividly. Then as soon as he disappeared, he placed a text in my hand. Thinking I was hallucinating, I did not examine it. As it appeared before my eyes, its pages were the color of a conch shell, with its opening words written in red dye, with exquisite calligraphy. Gazing at it, I saw four *vajra* lines, which are the primary words of these instructions. The next morning I wrote them down, and I understood that they synthesized the meaning of *The Essential Instructions of Avalokiteśvara* as well as both Mahāmudrā and Atiyoga. Later on in a dream I encountered Dong Kachöpa, who gave me an introduction to Mahāmudrā. I presume those to be a blessing lineage of transmitted teachings, and they are the root of these instructions. Those are accounts of the lineages to demonstrate the noble origins of the Dharma.

– Karma Chagmé is able to trace the lineage up to himself, but three hundred years have intervened since his time. You may wonder how the lineage continued on to me. In terms of the immediate lineage, I received these teachings from three sources. First of all, I received these teachings from Sangye Gön. Sangye Gön wore patched clothing, and looking at him, you would think that he had no inner realization at all. But in fact, he encountered Avalokiteśvara directly. He would speak to him and receive teachings from him as if he were another person in the same room. He gave many prophecies and constantly recited *Oṃ maṇi padme hūṃ*. As he grew older, his hair turned white and his teeth fell out. But as he continued to practice, his wrinkles disappeared, a set of teeth grew, and his hair turned black again. Outwardly, he still looked like nothing special.

Secondly, I received these teachings from my primary spiritual mentor, Natsok Rangdröl, who was an embodiment of the enlightened activity of Dudjom Rinpoche. You can learn more about Natsok Rangdröl in the biography of Dudjom Rinpoche and of Ratna Lingpa, who is the same being as Dudjom Rinpoche.

Thirdly, Palyül Chogtrul Rinpoche gave me these teachings. Palyül Chogtrul Rinpoche's story can be found in *A Garland of Immortal Wish-fulfilling Trees* by Tsering Lama Jampal Zangpo.[5] Additionally, I have received all of these transmissions from His Holiness Penor Rinpoche. –

The qualifications of disciples who listen to the Dharma are stated in *The Vajra Garland Explanatory Tantra*:

> Just as the milk of a lioness
> Is not to be placed in an earthen container,
> So is the Mahāyogatantra
> Not to be given to those who are not suitable vessels.

– This injunction pertains to teaching Mahāyāna, Vajrayāna, and to Atiyoga in particular. Those without faith who are completely involved in the eight mundane concerns are not suitable vessels, and they should not be taught these kinds of Dharma. –

The Sūtra of the Ten Grounds states:

> It is said: If unsuitable vessels of the Śrāvakayāna hear explanations of the Mahāyāna, they will become frightened and nihilistic,

> and they will fall to miserable states of existence. Therefore, examine the faculties [of your listeners] and then reveal the Dharma.

The Five Stages states:

> Those who are devious and slothful,
> Who, due to their mental afflictions, see the faults of their spiritual mentor but not his virtues,
> And who disparage their spiritual mentor,
> Those who receive empowerments and become pompous,
> And have inferior attitudes will not attain the primordial wisdom of omniscience.

The Five Stages also states:

> Upon seeing their spiritual mentor in public, they ignore him.
> Then they make prostrations to him in private.
> Even if he is your own son, such an inferior, bad-natured disciple
> Is to be rejected like anyone else.
> Even if he is born of the royal class, noble class, or priestly class,
> He should never be accepted in one's midst.

– In the Tibetan region of Kham there was one Lama who was the disciple of another Lama. The senior teacher was, in fact, an extremely fine practitioner, spending all of his time in retreat and living like a beggar, while the other Lama, his student, gained a reputation as a great teacher. One time when the student was teaching a large group of his own disciples, including many monks, his Lama came out of retreat and sat among the students. The other students, recognizing their Lama's Lama, immediately prostrated, while the younger Lama pretended that he did not see him and began teaching. After the teachings, all of the other disciples dispersed, but the senior Lama stayed. Only when everyone had left, while feigning great surprise at seeing him, did the disciple come over and prostrate himself. "Oh, you did not see me?" asked the senior Lama. "No, I didn't see you," replied his student. As soon as the words were spoken, both of his eyes fell out. Immediately, recognizing the error of his ways, he began to do prostrations with great reverence. Then he confessed, "I did see you, but I was embarrassed because you look like a beggar. Please forgive me. I was completely at fault." Instantly, his eyes jumped back into his head.

You should not even allow an inferior disciple in your midst let alone teach such a person. Beyond that, it is said in certain Tibetan texts that if you live downstream from a person with broken vows, you shouldn't even drink the water that flows from the stream. –

Elsewhere *The Five Stages* states:

> The stages of teachings are not for those
> Who have contempt for their spiritual mentor and lack faith,
> Who have the conceit of being tantric practitioners and become inflated at the sight of texts,
> And who have no faith and no empowerments.

A disciple who is a suitable vessel is described in *The Tantra of the Charnel Ground Ornament*:

> Give to one who is courageous, subdued, and intelligent,
> Patient, honest, and candid,
> Faithful, of good breeding, and generous,
> And who has much learning and maintains his pledges.

The first section of *The Tantra of the Net of Magical Displays* states:

> A disciple is one who has the qualities of
> Delighting in virtue and meditation,
> Being always reverent towards the spiritual mentor,
> And constantly making offerings to the deities.

Do not give teachings to such a disciple as soon as you are asked to teach Dharma. *The Moon Lamp Sūtra* states:

> If you are requested
> To make the gift of Dharma,
> First of all say, "I shall not teach."

That is not a mere ploy, but rather allows for an examination of the disciple's mind-stream. If the Dharma would be of benefit to the public, it is all right to teach it even if it is not requested.

– If a Lama obstinately refuses to grant instruction to a qualified disciple, this constitutes an infraction of the Lama's *samaya*. It is proper for the Lama to show some hesitation by not consenting on the first request in order to arouse and examine the disciple. It is not a ploy to see if the amount of offerings can be increased, but rather provides time to examine the student's mind-stream. –

The above *sūtra* states:

> Proceed after you have examined the mind-stream to see if this person is a suitable vessel.
> If you know that the person is a suitable vessel,
> Teach even if you are not requested to do so.

Then when you are explaining the Dharma, the acts of sitting upon a Dharma throne and wearing a fine cap and clothing are not a case of putting on airs or showing off; rather, they are to honor the Dharma. *The Holy Dharma of the White Lotus Sūtra* states:

> In a clean and pleasant area
> Arrange a spacious seat
> Draped with various dyed cloths;
> And let it be on a raised throne.

The Sūtra of the Questions of Sāgaramati states:

> A propounder of Dharma should maintain good hygiene, behave with dignity, bathe well, and dress in finery.

– In Tibet, Lamas didn't wash very often, sometimes sponging off only once a year, so it is not surprising to find instructions like these. In the West, people often dress in their finest clothes when they attend church, synagogue, and so on. Of course, I am not sure whether they do this to show devotion to their objects of refuge or because they are looking for a boyfriend or girlfriend. If a Lama dresses up, this certainly shouldn't be motivated by wanting people to think he is a very fine Lama. It shouldn't be for any of the eight mundane concerns, but purely for the sake of honoring the Dharma.

The real ornament that one should bring to the teaching is the purification of one's own mental afflictions. This is the true ornament, the great wealth, not diamonds or gold. This ornament is the best indication that excellent qualities have been generated. The finest ornament to wear is that of the transmutation of the five poisons into the five primordial wisdoms. Cultivating these inner qualities and inner purity is better than the closest shave.

The proper way to receive teachings is taught very well in the Patrul Rinpoche's classic text *Words of My Perfect Teacher*. These instructions are very important, because once we observe our behavior, we can transform nonvirtue to virtue, dishonor to honor, unrestrained conduct to restrained conduct, and unbeneficial conduct to beneficial conduct. –

The benefits of teaching Dharma in that way are greater than filling incalculable galaxies with the seven royal symbols, various jewels, oil lamps, and incense, and offering them to all the Buddhas. *The Great Mound of Jewels Sūtra* states:

> One who bestows a verse [of Dharma] to one sentient being is making an enormous gift more precious than filling with jewels galaxies as numerous as the grains of sand of the Ganges and offering them with a mind of supreme virtue to the Jinas. That gift of verse brings forth compassion, and that cannot be measured or counted.

A *sūtra* states:

> More than flowers, incense, and oil lamps, the offering of teaching my Dharma accurately in order to be of service is the true offering to the Jina.

And:

> If Dharma is taught, this is superior to filling the entire universe with various precious substances such as gold and silver and making a gift of them.

The Great Lion's Roar of Maitreya Sūtra states:

> One may completely fill Buddha realms as numerous as the grains of sand of the Ganges with the seven kinds of precious substances and offer them to the Jinas with great delight. But one who bestows a single verse to one sentient being makes a precious and enormous gift, a gift of verse that brings forth compassion. That cannot be measured or numbered. How could one imagine [the benefits of] giving this to two or three people?

The Sūtra of the Holy Golden Light states, "Śāriputra, among gifts, the gift of Dharma is said to be supreme." *The Sūtra of the Questions of Sāgaranāgarāja* states, "Due to the gift of Dharma, there arises pure extrasensory perception of the extinction of defilements." *The Sūtra of the Questions of Siṅha* states, "Due to the gift of Dharma, one recalls [past] lives," and "In degenerate times there is greater benefit in explaining one verse of Dharma than there is in filling the whole universe with gold and giving it away."

– The gift of Dharma applies not only to teaching Dharma. For example, if people invite a Lama to teach, the very extension of this invitation is a gift of Dharma. Arranging a location for others to hear the Dharma, whether in a Dharma center, renting a room or using your own home, too, is such a gift. The person who acts as interpreter is also giving the gift of Dharma. These act to purify hindrances as long as they are performed with faith.

After accepting an invitation, if the Lama comes to the teachings wondering, "How rich are they? Which is the prettiest? Which is the most handsome?" his teaching is reduced to a mere mundane activity. If those who are arranging for the teachings are really selling the Lama and the Dharma, their nonvirtuous actions will give rise only to miserable results. In contrast, if all of the participants' motivation is virtuous, then this is the greatest of offerings.

These days it is difficult to find good patrons of the Dharma and good interpreters. It is certainly difficult to find fully qualified spiritual mentors. To create such a situation is really creating the opportunity for the Dharma in a dark age. Therefore, if you can participate in the gift of

Dharma in one way or another, it is most beneficial to do so with the thought that there is great merit here. To participate in the gift of Dharma with faith, with the motivation that it may alleviate the suffering of others, and with an attitude of rejoicing, is the perfect gift. –

The Great Lion's Roar of Maitreya Sūtra states:

> In bad times the benefit of filling with gold
> Galaxies as many as the grains of sand in the Ganges
> And giving them away does not compare
> To that of uttering a single verse [of Dharma].

A spiritual relationship is more profound than any congenial, mundane relationship. *The King of Samādhi Sūtra* states:

> In the case of one person relying upon another,
> There may be no mutual respect.
> The Buddhas, the wise who have fully eliminated latent propensities,
> Do not praise that devotion.
> One who reveals the Dharma in order to benefit living beings
> Is an extraordinary teacher.
> He is a friend who does not create divisiveness between one person and another.
> Ten million *māras* cannot separate one from him.
> People who rely upon mundane, material things
> Become totally involved in the affairs of this life.
> People who rely upon the Dharma without material things
> Find great meaning.
> The mind free of material things settles down.
> Teaching Dharma without material remuneration,
> Those who are happy without material things
> Swiftly become awakened.

There are incalculable benefits in explaining the Dharma. *The Sūtra of Bringing forth the Extraordinary Resolve* states:

> Maitreya, bestowing the gift of Dharma without desiring wealth or honor is bestowing the gift of Dharma without material things. [Such people enjoy] twenty benefits: they are [1] mindful, [2] aware, [3] intelligent, [4] reverent, [5] wise, [6] they realize transcendent wisdom, [7] they have little attachment, [8] little hatred, [9] little delusion, [10] *māras* cannot harm them, [11] the Buddhas, the Bhagavāns, hold them in mind, [12] non-human spirits guard them, [13] the gods imbue their bodies with luster, [14] their enemies cannot harm them, [15] they are not parted from their friends, [16] their words are worth memorizing, [17]

> they attain fearlessness, [18] their minds are filled with many joys, [19] they are praised by the wise, and [20] their gift of Dharma is remembered. Maitreya, those are the twenty benefits.

Even if one is very learned and intelligent, if one does not receive the Dharma, one does not recognize virtue and sin, just as one does not see in the dark without a lamp, no matter how clear one's vision. *The Compendium on Hearing* states:

> Upon entering a building
> That is engulfed in darkness,
> One does not see the presence of visual forms
> Even though one has eyes.
> Likewise, a person of good breeding,
> Even one who is intelligent,
> Does not know sinful and virtuous things
> Until he hears of them.
> Just as one with eyes and a lamp
> Sees forms,
> So are virtuous and sinful things
> Known due to hearing.

– We can see from our own experiences that people with no understanding of Dharma often have an exalted sense of their own personal identity. Those whose minds are inseparable from Dharma easily engage with anybody, whether in high or low positions, men or women. I'm not speaking of people who enter into shallow relationships with everyone. An excellent example of the former is the case of His Holiness the Dalai Lama. Whether he meets a man or woman, Tibetans or foreigners, he is at ease. Sometimes women come up to him, and he may either give them a hug or very warmly take both of their hands in his. He is not putting on an act. It is simply a spontaneous expression of his own inner compassion as well as an indication of the subdued nature of his own mind. In contrast, those with no knowledge or practice of Dharma feel there is distance between themselves and others. Moreover, some people still feel alienated even after having heard teachings and having acquired knowledge of Dharma. This is a sign that they have not fathomed the Dharma, and that they are still subject to self-grasping. This sense of distance felt between ourselves and others—between subjects and objects—is a merely sign of our own limitation. –

The Great Mound of Jewels Sūtra states:

> Virtuous and sinful things
> Are not known without hearing of them.
> Phenomena are known after one has heard.
> One commits no sin after one has heard.

Sin is rejected after one has heard.
Nirvāṇa is attained after one has heard.
Wisdom increases after one has heard.
Wisdom analyzes meanings,
And upon seeing the meaning, joy is attained.
Due to attaining the meaning, the mind becomes attentive
And there is *nirvāṇa* in this life.

Other benefits of hearing the Dharma are stated in *The Bodhisattva Corpus Sūtra*:

Phenomena are known as a result of hearing.
Sin is averted as a result of hearing.
That which is meaningless is rejected as a result of hearing.
Nirvāṇa is attained as a result of hearing.

Birth Accounts states:

Due to hearing, the mind becomes lucid,
Joyful and stable;
Wisdom arises, and delusion vanishes.
Even if you know this, it is worth acquiring.

The Sūtra of the Questions of Prince Candra also says this:

Hearing is the lamp that dispels the darkness of delusion.
It is the best possession that cannot be carried off by thieves
and so on.
It is the weapon that vanquishes the enemy, stupidity.
It is the best of friends who gives advice on how to act.
It is the steadfast friend even if you become poor.
It is the harmless medicine for the illness of grief.
It is the best of armies that conquers the host of great evils.
And it is the best of treasures of fame and glory.
When meeting honorable people, it is the best of beings.
In public it delights the learned.
To opponents it is like the light rays of the sun.

– Learning, which is the best of friends, advises us in terms of both skillful means and wisdom. It is the friend on whom you can rely, who will neither deceive nor trick you. It is the medicine for the illness of grief, and unlike ordinary medicines, it has no detrimental side effects. If you want to earn praise, first learn the Dharma and use that knowledge to subdue your own mind. To your opponent in debate, hearing will be like the light rays of the sun. –

And:

> One becomes disciplined and vivid confidence arises.
> It gives immediate renown.
> It is a special cause of eloquence.
> By becoming accustomed to the glory of hearing, reality is clearly known.
> Those with learning dwell on the path of the three spheres[6] without inconsistencies.
> Disciples of learning take the essence of practice,
> And they easily escape from the fortress of rebirth.

The Sūtra of the Questions of Nārāyaṇa states:

> Son of good breeding, if you have learning, wisdom will arise. If you possess wisdom, your mental afflictions will be calmed. With no mental afflictions, *māras* will be unable to harm you.

And:

> Learning has a stainless majesty.
> Due to hearing, evil is averted.

– Without learning, we are not able to recognize our own mental afflictions. If we can't do this, how can we know what needs to be eliminated and what steps to take so that excellent qualities will arise?

Erudite people are found the world over. But for the most part, they fail to apply their knowledge to their own minds. I have found this to be true in most countries in the West, and it is frequently true in Tibet. After many years go by, these people may decide to practice something, so they dig through all their acquired knowledge to find something to practice. This is not a very useful route to follow. The practical route is to practice from the beginning, discovering what needs to be eliminated. This is the route our spiritual mentors advise us to take. Without postponing this to sometime in the future when circumstances will be better, right now, little by little, practice eliminating these harmful mental afflictions.

It is important to apply our knowledge internally. The Buddha attained enlightenment in this way. The pure lands are internal; the mental afflictions are internal. The crucial factor is to recognize the mental afflictions. Only by recognizing their nature can we attain Buddhahood.

By practicing at our own level step by step, doubt is gradually removed like clouds vanishing in the sky, and certainty develops. Some of us are fortunate to be raised in the Dharma. For example, both of my parents were practitioners, so I was raised in the Dharma. But whatever your background, do not let your Dharma be like the rice in a bowl, always remaining separate from the container. Rather, apply Dharma by means of hearing, thinking, and meditating. One of these alone is not enough. All three must be practiced. If you lack hearing and thinking, you are not in a good position to meditate effectively. Such meditation is like trying to climb a mountain without your hands. However much you learn of the Dharma, practice it with faith and compassion. Apply it to your own mind. –

The way to devote yourself to your spiritual mentor while you are listening to the Dharma is taught in *The Sūtra of the Questions of Śrīsambhava*:

> Son of good breeding, Bodhisattvas who are supervised by a spiritual friend never fall to miserable states of existence. Like intelligent children, they constantly look to the face of the spiritual friend. Like dogs, they do not become indignant at the spiritual mentor's scolding. Like boats, they come and go without depression. Like bridges, they stand up to felicity and adversity. Like a blacksmith's anvil, they bear all the pains of heat and cold. You should bring forth the sense of yourself being a patient and the spiritual friend being a physician.

A *sūtra* states:

> Devote yourself to your spiritual friend, obeying his words with the sense of being like a servant. Devote yourself to your spiritual friend with the sense of being like a garment that gently covers the skin. Devote yourself to your spiritual mentor with a sense of being like a sweeper who has abandoned pride. Devote yourself to your spiritual mentor with a sense of being like a bull with his horns cut off and who has abandoned conceit.

The way to listen to the Dharma is taught in *Birth Accounts*:

> Sitting on a low level,
> Bring forth the splendor of discipline.
> Watch with your eyes filled with delight,
> And take in the words like drinking nectar.
> Reverently and single-pointedly
> Bring forth lucid and stainless attention.
> Like a patient listening to the words of a healer,
> Devoutly listen to the Dharma.

Concerning the object of your attention while listening to the Dharma, imagine your spiritual mentor as Mañjuśrī, the King of Speech, gold in color, with both hands at his heart in the *mudrā* of the wheel of Dharma, holding the stems of two blue *utpala* lotuses. The open blossoms above both shoulders hold emblems, one with a sword and the other with a treatise. He is adorned with silks and jewels, and he is seated in the Maitreya posture upon a lion throne. In front of him imagine yourself as Green Tārā, with her palms pressed together, holding an *utpala* that has just blossomed. She is sitting with her knees on the ground. From the spiritual mentor's mouth the words of Dharma emanate in the form of the seed syllables of vowels and consonants. They enter both your ears, visualized as sixteen-petalled, blue *utpalas*, and they gently dissolve into your heart. Imagine that all the meanings of the Dharma you hear are being vividly understood and realized. Meditate like that until the end of tomorrow's Dharma session. This completes the introduction to the Dharma and the topics of teaching and listening.

CHAPTER TWO

The Stage of Generation

Homage to Avalokiteśvara!

These are the profound instructions of Avalokiteśvara on the cultivation of the stage of generation, which is a means of swiftly attaining enlightenment. This is a unique characteristic of the secret Mantra[yāna], and as such it surpasses the *sūtra* tradition. *A Lamp on the Three Avenues* states:

> For those with no confusion regarding even a single point,
> Having no difficulty in a multitude of techniques,
> And for those of sharp faculties,
> The Mantrayāna is superior.

– "A single point" refers to the mind. This is what needs to be examined, subdued, and liberated. Apart from that, there is no other Buddhahood, because the attainment of Buddhahood depends upon liberating your mind. By understanding that single point, you will have no difficulty with the multitude of techniques. However, if you lack insight into this single point, you possess only the qualities of the scholar. –

The Great Tantra of Sampuṭa states:

> In short, the Buddhahood
> That is attained after countless billions of eons
> May joyfully be achieved by this sacred means
> In this very lifetime.

> You will attain the state of Vajradhara,
> Or that of a world emperor,
> Or the eight great *siddhis*,
> Or whatever you desire.

The Tantra of the Orb of Primordial Wisdom states:

> Or it may even be accomplished effortlessly
> As soon as this body is abandoned.

– By means of this practice, it is possible to attain enlightenment in this lifetime. If that doesn't happen, then enlightenment may be attained in the intermediate state immediately following this life, after the body has been abandoned. –

The Primary Tantra of Kālacakra states:

> Those who have come to be executioners and so on,
> And those who have committed the five deeds of immediate retribution
> May become awakened in this very lifetime
> By following the conduct of the Mantra[yāna].

– Even after having committed the five deeds of immediate retribution,[7] in the best of circumstances, enlightenment can be attained in this lifetime by entering into the Mantrayāna with faith, cultivating pure vision, and enthusiastically applying yourself to practice. In this way you may gain insight into the nature of the mind. Even if you do not attain enlightenment in this lifetime, this may be achieved during the intermediate state following this life. –

The Guhyasamāja Tantra states:

> Even sentient beings who have committed such great sins
> As the five deeds of immediate retribution
> May become accomplished by means of the ocean of the Vajrayāna,
> The supreme vehicle.

The Tantra of the Equal Union with All the Buddhas states:

> With the technique of this Secret Mantra[yāna]
> You will become accomplished in this very lifetime.

The Tip of the Vajra states:

> In this and all other lifetimes
> The bearer of the *vajra* will strive diligently,
> And upon the completion of sixteen lifetimes,
> The serenity of awakening will be attained....

And:

> Ordinary beings will achieve awakening,
> But not otherwise.

Thus, by means of the Path of the Perfections there is no way to achieve spiritual awakening in less than seven, five, or three countless eons. By means of the Secret Mantra tradition, awakening is attained at best in this life; middling is to attain it in the intermediate state; and at least one attains it in no more than three, seven, or sixteen lifetimes. As an analogy, by achieving swift-footedness one may cover in one day a distance that would otherwise take months and years to traverse. Likewise, this is due to the power of meditating on the indivisibility and equality of your chosen deity and yourself.

– By following the Path of the Perfections, with its five paths and ten Bodhisattva grounds, it is not possible to achieve perfect enlightenment in less than three, five, or seven countless eons. On the Vajrayāna path, however, which is here likened to the *siddhi* of swift-footedness, awakening may be attained in sixteen lifetimes at the most.

In Tibet the mundane *siddhi* of swift-footedness was occasionally accomplished. In fact, fairly recently in the Sertar region of Golok, a nun by the name of Dzongtö Kandroma accomplished extraordinary realization and gave many prophecies. There is a mountain in that area which normally requires two or three days to circumambulate. However, having accomplished swift-footedness, Dzongtö Kandroma could circumambulate it in only one hour. Many nomads living in this region saw her display this *siddhi*. After she passed away, a stone *stūpa* containing her relics was built, and on various auspicious days rainbows and other wondrous events appeared there. –

Ācārya Jñānasakara says:

> As an analogy, one who has accomplished swift-footedness
> May in days or a month
> Reach a destination
> That would take a weak person
> Or a bullock-drawn wagon a long time to reach.
> Likewise, that which is reached after a long period
> In reliance upon the Path of the Perfections
> Or other paths,
> Is reached in this lifetime by means of the Mantra[yāna].
> This is due to reliance upon the power of equality.

Although deity meditation is also found in the Kriyātantras, Caryātantras, and Yogatantras, that is not called the stage of generation. In the Anuttarayogatantras four stages of generation are taught on account of the *yogas* pertaining to the four modes of rebirth. The womb-born generation by way of the Six-phase Yoga, the generation by way of the Five Purifications, and the generation by way of the Three Techniques cannot be practiced except by a spiritual friend who knows those techniques by heart. Thus, Mahāsiddha Karma Pakṣi says, "Those who are illiterate [should practice] the *yoga* of instant total recall."

Clearly and without grasping, meditate on such a deity, like a design in the sky, as appearing but having no intrinsic nature. The colors [of the deity] are unmixed, like a rainbow in the sky; the features are clear like reflections in a mirror; the appearance is pervasive, like the reflections of the moon in water. Recognize this in accordance with the three or twelve chief metaphors.

– When you visualize the deity, you should not visualize it like a statue or like an image depicted in a *tanka*. Rather visualize it like a drawing in the sky, appearing yet having no intrinsic nature. This does not mean that it is hazy or indistinct, for it should be visualized clearly. Distinctly and clearly imagine the entire form of the deity complete with all ornamentation, but without grasping. It is grasping that has perpetuated our existence in *saṃsāra* for countless eons. Therefore, this meditation must be free from all grasping, whether virtuous, nonvirtuous, or ethically neutral. –

Ācārya Nāgārjuna says:

> You have no thieves in [your] empty house;
> And though you lack flesh, bone, and blood,
> Like a rainbow in the sky
> You reveal your body.

– In this passage, Nāgārjuna is speaking to Avalokiteśvara. He remarks that Avalokiteśvara's body, like an empty house, has no intrinsic nature. It is without flesh, bone and blood, and yet he reveals his body like a rainbow in the sky. –

The Vajra Pavilion Tantra states:

> One who meditates on my body—
> Either as an illusory body
> Or as being like a dream—
> Will see me directly
> As a result of earnest meditation.

The glorious Pagmo Drüpa says:

> Meditate on the body of the deity as being like a rainbow.
> Get rid of your ordinary notion.

– Here the "ordinary notion" to be eliminated is grasping onto phenomena as being substantially existent. –

Meditate single-pointedly, without grasping, on the empty appearance of your chosen deity. Whatever chosen deity you meditate on, it is the same, but meditating on the Great Compassionate One, Avalokiteśvara, is praised as being the best.

– All male and female deities, whether they perform pacifying, enriching, subjugating, or ferocious activity, are the same in nature. Nevertheless, it is said that if an ordinary person meditates on Avalokiteśvara, this brings the greatest blessings, and this practice is praised by all of the Buddhas. –

The Tantra of the Lotus King states:

> Suffering stops simply by hearing of the characteristics
> Of the body of the Protector Avalokiteśvara,
> And one is led to bliss with mindfulness and veneration.

– "Mindfulness" in this instance especially means reverently recalling the Protector Avalokiteśvara, which leads one to bliss. –

And:

> Among all his four hands,
> The palms of the first are pressed together at the heart.
> He is white, radiating a blue sheen,
> The purest of all colors.
> His vast purity is known to all.
> By meditating while bearing him in mind,
> The obscurations of sins of immediate retribution are purified.
> In relation to yourself and others,
> Cherish his *maṇḍala* alone.
> Many thoughts and appearances are purified.
> If done well, this alone [suffices].

Orgyen Rinpoche says, "By actualizing the Great Compassionate One, all the Sugatas are actualized." In the section on the assembly of four deities, *The Kadam Volume* praises Avalokiteśvara, saying:

> The serene Compassionate One is without compare.
> His bounty of compassion is incalculable.
> That is the essential nature of Avalokiteśvara.

– By actualizing Avalokiteśvara, the Compassionate One who is none other than the nature of all the Buddhas, they are all actualized. –

And:

> He is the palace
> Of all the Jinas and their Children.
> In a single pore, incalculable realms of Jinas
> Are gloriously displayed.

– The palace—which is to say, the body—of the Buddhas is the body of Avalokiteśvara; the speech of Avalokiteśvara is the speech of all the Buddhas, and the mind of Avalokiteśvara is the mind of all the Buddhas. Therefore, by actualizing the body, speech, and mind of Avalokiteśvara, the body, speech, and mind of all the Buddhas are actualized. –

And:

> If well examined, it is like this:
> He alone is the *maṇḍalas* of all the Buddhas
> Of the four embodiments
> And the assemblies of peaceful and wrathful Vīras and Vīrās.

The Tantra of the Lotus King states:

> The Lord said:
>
> > This is meditation on the one *maṇḍala* of the body
> > Of all the Buddhas of the three times.
> > The synthesis of all the Buddhas
> > Is the body of the Protector Avalokiteśvara.
> > Simply by recalling him,
> > All thoughts of the cycle of existence are stopped;
> > And the entire essence of all *nirvāṇas*
> > Well emerges.

The Holy Dharma of the White Lotus Sūtra states:

> Recall with no doubts
> The pure being Avalokiteśvara.
> When you are dying and when you are assaulted by mental afflictions,
> He will be a pure protector, refuge, and friend.

– As you are experiencing the suffering of dying or when you are afflicted by anger, attachment, ignorance, and so on, recall Avalokiteśvara with faith and you will be liberated from that suffering. –

In terms of *mantras*, there are none that have benefits comparable to those of the six syllables. *The Tantra of the Lotus King* states:

The Lord said:

> Free of doubts, apply yourself to this,
> Which is the condensed essence of
> All the Buddhas of the three times.
> If you reverently utter one time
> *Oṃ maṇi padme hūṃ,*
> Which is like a jewel in the ocean,
> Sentient beings will be freed from the malady of the hells.
> By uttering it twice,
> The door to the realm of *pretas* is closed.
> Reciting it three times closes off the realm of animals.
> Even while indulging in the five sensual pleasures,
> One who is not separated from this remains pure.
> By recalling these [syllables], there is no fault
> In one's food, clothing, or drink.
> This is like taking the essential kernel
> From inside a husk of rice.
> It is like taking a flower
> From a wish-fulfilling tree.
> Gods, *nāgas, yakṣas,*
> *Gandharvas,* the fire-god, Yama,
> Brahma, Indra, Kumbhāṇḍa,
> And all outer and inner malevolent beings
> Are pacified by the recitation of the king of *mantras.*
> Its excellent qualities are beyond reckoning,
> For the Āryas [alone] can calculate them.

– Simply by reciting the six-syllable *mantra* while eating, drinking, and dressing, any faults that may be accrued can be purified. This is something we can easily do. You need no external machines or technology, and it costs nothing. Moreover, reciting *Oṃ maṇi padme hūṃ* either at the beginning or end of a meal has great benefit. Malevolent or obstructive forces may be purified, and the diseases they cause may be dispelled. Only the Buddhas can calculate the great benefit of reciting this *mantra.* –

The Hundred and Eight Names of Avalokiteśvara states:

> The Lord said, "If a son or a daughter of good breeding brings Ārya Avalokiteśvara to mind and recites *Oṃ maṇi padme hūṃ,* that person will not be born in a miserable state of existence and will not go to Avīci. Those who recite or chant that upon rising in the morning will be freed from leprosy, abscesses, rashes, boils, skin diseases, idiocy, respiratory diseases, and all other illnesses.

> They will recall it wherever they are born, and when they die, they will be born in Sukhāvatī. Wherever they are born and wherever they dwell, they will never be separated from Ārya Avalokiteśvara. If this is recited constantly, one will be clear-minded, one's voice will be melodious, and one will become knowledgeable in all sacred literature."

The Sūtra of Basket Weaving states:

> Buddha Dīpavara said, "If any son or daughter of good breeding recites this six-syllable knowledge-*mantra,* that person will be imbued with inexhaustible ability. Your aggregate of primordial wisdom will be purified. You will be endowed with great loving-kindness and great compassion. Day by day, the Six Perfections will be completely perfected. In terms of your status, you will attain the state of a world-emperor. You will not fall back from the state of a Bodhisattva. You will be manifestly awakened in the state of unsurpassable, truly perfect enlightenment. Those who utter this six-syllable knowledge-*mantra* and who constantly apply themselves to its recitation will be endowed with merit. Reciting this assembles as many Lord Buddhas as there are grains of sand in the Ganges. Ten million Tathāgatas are present in each pore of that child of good breeding. Dwelling there, O child of good breeding, you attain such a wish-fulfilling jewel. Child of good breeding, it is good that your progeny will be liberated. Child of good breeding, even the organisms that live in your stomach will become irreversible Bodhisattvas, and they will offer their gratitude."

The Sūtra of Basket Weaving states:

> Lord Śākyamuni said, "Lusting for another's wife and committing adultery, the act of killing, murdering one's father and mother, slaying an Arhat, causing a *bhikṣuṇī* to lose her ordination, destroying a *stūpa,* destroying a temple, maliciously drawing blood from the body of a Tathāgata, and the obscurations of the acts of immediate retribution are all utterly purified with these six syllables of *The Sūtra of Basket Weaving.*"

Songtsen Gampo gave this advice to his minister of foreign affairs:

> The pinnacle of the Great Compassionate One is found in the six syllables *Oṃ maṇi padme hūṃ.* It is these six syllables that purify obscurations for your own sake, and it is these six syllables that purify the abodes of the six states of existence for others' sake. It is these six syllables that give rise to the common *siddhis* in this

> life, and it is these six syllables that give rise to the supreme *siddhi* of Mahāmudrā in the future. Recite these six syllables *Oṃ maṇi padme hūṃ*. Count them, actualize them, teach them, and explain them. This is the way followed by the Buddhas of the past, it is revealed by the Buddhas of the present, and it is the path of the Buddhas of the future.

To the people of Tibet he gave this advice:

> This is the quintessential Dharma of the Great Compassionate One. There is nothing superior to *Oṃ maṇi padme hūṃ*. This is the unmistaken essence for attaining supreme enlightenment.

The emanation king taught:

> This essence *Oṃ maṇi padme hūṃ*is a wish-fulfilling jewel, so all supreme and common *siddhis* arise from this. Recite this! Earnestly apply yourself to this!

When Orgyen Rinpoche was about to leave for the continent of Cāmara, he left this final testament:

> The benefits of the six syllables cannot be expressed or reckoned even by all the Buddhas of the three times. Why? Because it is the quintessence of the Bodhisattva Avalokiteśvara's mind that constantly, compassionately surveys the six types of sentient beings; and because it liberates all sentient beings from the cycle of existence. Therefore, kings and subjects of future generations, hold fast to the Great Compassionate One! Recite the six syllables! Have no anxiety about going to the miserable states of existence. This is the tutelary deity of this snowy land of Tibet, so offer prayers of supplication with faith, reverence, and veneration. Blessings will directly be experienced. Do not be of two minds or foster doubt. None of the Buddhas of the three times has taught any Dharma more profound than this. Nor do I, Ācārya Padmasambhava, teach or know of anything more profound. Let all the kings and subjects of Tibet who are living now and who will come in the future bear this in mind.

Songtsen Gampo, the emanation king, spoke these words as his last testament:

> There will come an evil time when the merit of all people will decline. In that era, if you wish to create joy and happiness, offer prayers of supplication to the Great Compassionate One, Avalokiteśvara. Recite the essential six syllables *Oṃ maṇi padme hūṃ*. All joy, happiness, needs, and desires of this life will be

> realized due to this, so it is like making supplications to a [wish-fulfilling] jewel. In the future it is certain that your obscurations will be purified and you will attain enlightenment. Do not foster doubt or be of two minds about this!

Machik Labdrön says:

> Now I have widely emphasized both Avalokiteśvara and the venerable Tārā. It appears that these two are the general protectors of us who dwell in the snowy land of Tibet, and they are certainly our tutelary deities. In that respect, from the time that they know how to speak, little children know how to recite the six syllables, and that is certainly a sign of their mind-streams being blessed by Ārya [Avalokiteśvara]. We should all definitely recognize Ārya [Avalokiteśvara] as our tutelary deity.

And:

> The essential six syllables are the synthesis of the 84,000 collections of the Dharma, the foundation of all the profound collections of *tantras*, and the synthesized essence of both the *sūtras* and *tantras*. Like butter that emerges from churning milk, they are the essence of the ocean-like teachings. In terms of their efficacy, they overcome all kinds of unfavorable influences such as illness, malevolent spirits, and obstructive forces. In terms of a substance, they are like a diamond. As they swiftly fulfill all one's desires, the six syllables are like a wish-fulfilling jewel.

The signs of meditating on this deity and reciting the *mantra* are stated in *The Tantra of the Questions of Subāhu*:

> When you have recited like that and the *mantra* comes close,
> At night you will see these dreams while sleeping:
> A mansion, a tree, a brahmin, a lion, a horse,
> A mountain, a radiant chariot, clouds and wind,
> Joyfully riding in the dream
> Upon a tiger, a rhinoceros, and a mighty elephant,
> A garland of flowers, perfumes, and clothing,
> Meat, beer, fish, rice, and treatises,
> Forms of deities and red *utpala* flowers,
> A full chariot or a milk cow with a calf,
> A white parasol, a fan, shoes, a sword,
> A yak-tail fan with a golden handle and a rosary,
> Jewels, pearls, oyster shells, conches, and silver,
> A beautiful woman and a girl,

Ornaments graced with various precious substances,
Receiving a white bed and a cushion,
A stream and a great river at dawn,
A waterfall, an ocean, and a pond,
Dreaming of a spring, drink, or a sea,
Or bathing your body with blood,
A deity, and the form of a Jina in the presence of a *stūpa*,
Bodhisattvas and Pratyekabuddhas,
The taintless Saṅgha of *bhikṣus*, *bhikṣuṇīs*,
And *upāsakas*, earth-spirits, and gods,
Brahmins making offerings, attractive people,
Humans, kings, wealthy and talented boys,
Your father, mother, friends, relatives, and *yakṣas*,
Actualized deities, groups of young women,
Devouring the sun and moon,
Going inside the earth and consuming all the seeds,
Treading on people and eating meat,
And seeing a woman enter inside your body.
Whoever sees these fine dreams
Will soon become accomplished.
In a single month, a fortnight, one day,
And with each instant they come closer.

It is important to check your dreams. *The Tantra of Fine Accomplishment* states:

Even in dreams *siddhis* are seen,
And *siddhis* occur there as well.

In general, it is necessary to receive an empowerment to practice the secret Mantra[yāna], and it is wrong to do so if that is not received. However, according to Mahāsiddha Karma Pakṣi, as for this public Dharma of Jinasāgara, which was prophesied and granted by Avalokiteśvara, it is all right even if you have not received an empowerment. For those who have not received an empowerment, who have not been granted the oral transmission, and who have not completed the Dharma training from a master, may the blessing be equal to that of the Great Compassionate One. This is stated in Karmapa's *Sadhana of Jinasāgara, the Great Compassionate One*:

Everyone copy this. Practice it. Grant the empowerment. Vastly serve the needs of others with this public Dharma. By the blessings of the spiritual mentors, the chosen deities, and Ḍākinīs,

> even without receiving the oral transmission, may all those who write this down and see it have their own and others' needs fulfilled like the rising sun.

The public Dharma of the Blessed Lord, the Great Compassionate One, is to be cultivated as the stage of generation after having cultivated the Spirit of Awakening. Imagine a white syllable *Hrīḥ* as the seed of your consciousness. From the *Hrīḥ* are emanated white rays of light in the ten directions, striking all sentient beings and thereby purifying their sins and obscurations. Then vividly imagine the realm of the external universe and all the sentient beings who inhabit it as the Great Compassionate One. Drawing the light rays back in, they dissolve into the syllable *Hrīḥ*. As a result, the *Hrīḥ* on a lotus, sun, and moon seat melts into light, from which you vividly imagine yourself as the Great Compassionate Lord.

How are you present? Your body is white, with one face and four arms. You are smiling like a blossoming lotus. The locks of your hair are bound up in braids, and they are adorned with a crown of five kinds of precious substances. You wear a silken diadem. The palms of your first two hands are joined at your heart. In your lower right hand you are turning a pearl rosary, and in your lower left hand you hold the stem of a lotus. You are adorned with a collarband, neckband, and necklace composed of various precious substances. You are seated in the cross-legged position. If viewed from the outside, you are inwardly luminous, and if viewed from the inside, you are outwardly luminous. Imagine that various rays of light are shining forth from your body. That visualization is the generation of the *samayasattva*.

As for the visualization of the *samādhisattva*, imagine a white *Hrīḥ* on a moon-disk at your heart, and imagine [the syllables] *Oṃ maṇi padme hūṃ* circling it in a clockwise direction. That is the *samādhisattva*.

With the recitation of *Oṃ maṇi padme hūṃ*, imagine that the Buddhas and Bodhisattvas of the ten directions and all the Sugatas of the three times, in the nature of the Great Compassionate One, unceasingly descend upon you and all sentient beings like snowflakes. That is the dissolution of the *jñānasattvas*.

With respect to phenomena as the presentation of the divine body, think of the outer environment and the sentient beings who inhabit it as being the Great Compassionate One, just as you have imagined yourself. With respect to sounds as the presentation of the divine speech, imagine them as the sounds of the six syllables. With respect to memories and thoughts as the presentation of the divine mind, recognize them as self-arisen primordial wisdom, the union of appearances and emptiness. You will gain mastery over the reality of the one taste of the many intellect-transcending presentations of the phenomena of the divine body, speech, and mind. This wish-fulfilling jewel *sādhana* is to be taught as a public Dharma to all the six kinds of beings. When the father spiritual mentor and his spiritual sons don their crowns, they grant this as a public Dharma.

– The "intellect-transcending presentations" of the body, speech, and mind of the deity transcend the conventional intellect, and they are no longer distinguished as separate from one another. They appear, but are devoid of intrinsic nature.

The above is a clear account of the meditation on the stage of generation, and though the stage of completion is not discussed, for the time being these instructions alone will suffice. You will reap enormous benefit if as you breathe you are able to recite the six syllables throughout the course of the day. Maintaining this recitation in the dream state is also very good. –

These verses written down by Lord Könchok Yenlak were received by Rāga Asey more than forty times from the father spiritual mentor and his two spiritual sons, so they have an extraordinarily great blessing.

– The following verses begin with a reference to the Spirit of Awakening. Bear in mind that the Spirit of Awakening encompasses much more than saying, "I love you," which is so easy to say. There are two stages in cultivating the Spirit of Awakening. The first is the cultivation of the spirit of aspiring for awakening, together with the four immeasurables of loving-kindness, compassion, empathetic joy, and equanimity. Those are the foundation. Secondly, you cultivate the spirit of venturing towards awakening. However, if you have not cultivated the spirit of aspiring for awakening and the four immeasurables, there will be no benefit in trying to bring forth the spirit of venturing towards awakening. It will not arise. This would be like listening to many Dharma teachings without engaging in the preliminary practices. Without penetrating into the meaning of the Four Thoughts that Turn the Mind, you will not yearn to turn away from *saṃsāra*. Without that yearning, you may attempt to practice the Great Perfection, but there will be no benefit, because your practice will be superficial.

The whole of Buddhist Dharma is designed to counteract the mental afflictions. As you engage in the practice, it's helpful to think of your mind as being like a field strewn with rocks, weeds, and gravel. You cannot reap a harvest until the land has been cleared and made suitable for planting. Similarly, we must first subdue our own mind in order to become genuine Buddhist practitioners. The spirit of aspiring for awakening and the four immeasurables are like clearing the field, because they lay the foundation for the possibility of the harvest—the spirit of venturing towards awakening.

We must aspire for supreme enlightenment for all sentient beings without discrimination, for they, like ourselves, are ignorant of what to abandon and what to follow. Cultivate the aspiration to turn every sentient being away from the suffering of delusion and to lead each one to supreme enlightenment. Follow this by entering into the practice of the Six or Ten Perfections. –

Bring forth the aspiration for supreme enlightenment
And [imagine] your consciousness as the white syllable *Hrīḥ*.
Rays of white light are emitted,
Purifying the sins and obscurations of all sentient beings.
The outer universe is a palace and its inhabitants are deities.
The light rays are withdrawn and dissolve into the *Hrīḥ*.
Upon a lotus, sun, and moon seat
The syllable *Hrīḥ* melts into light,
Which transforms into yourself as the Great Compassionate One.
The color of your body is white, and you have one face.
Like a blossoming lotus, you are smiling radiantly.
The braids of your locks are bound up,
Adorned with a crown of five precious substances
And a silken diadem.
The first of your four hands are pressed together at your heart.
The lower right holds a pearl rosary,
And the lower left holds a lotus.
You are beautifully adorned with a throat ornament,
A collarband, neckband,
Necklace, and semi-necklace of various precious substances.
You are luminous, with no outer or inner obscurations.
You are seated with both legs crossed.
Various rays of light shine out.
That is the nature of the *samayasattva*.
Upon a moon-disk at your heart
The six syllables circle clockwise
Around a white syllable *Hrīḥ*.
That is the *samādhisattva*.
By the power of verbally reciting
Oṃ maṇi padme hūṃ,
All the Sugatas of the three times
Become of the nature of the Great Compassionate One
And dissolve into you like raindrops.

That is the fully perfected *jñānasattva*.
The whole universe and all its inhabitants become the deity.
Phenomena are the presentation of the divine body.
All sounds and voices are the six syllables.
Sounds are the presentation of the divine speech.
The mind is the self-arisen union,
And memories and thoughts are the presentation of the divine mind.

– Each of the six states of existence has a corresponding seed syllable. We, as impure human beings, have the seed syllable of *Nriḥ*. Even *devas*, both peaceful and wrathful, possess a seed syllable. In particular, the white seed syllable *Hrīḥ* symbolizes pure primordial wisdom unstained by the cycle of existence. It is the seed syllable of Avalokiteśvara. Imagine that your consciousness as the seed syllable *Hrīḥ* emits rays of white light that strike every sentient being without exception, purifying the sins and obscurations of each one. This purifies not only sins and obscurations, but also the grasping onto the bodies of others and ourselves as impure. Thus, all physical, verbal, and mental nonvirtues are purified.

To counteract ordinary grasping onto the environment in which you dwell, view it as a palace. Once you have purified ordinary grasping onto sentient beings and view them as forms of Avalokiteśvara, you must next purify the ordinary grasping onto your own body, speech, and mind by visualizing them in the pure form of the Great Compassionate One, Avalokiteśvara. You smile radiantly to express your joy at the purificatory power that Avalokiteśvara has over the mental afflictions. Do not merely imagine yourself as beautiful and smiling, but include every sentient being. This beauty is an inherent, natural beauty, not the type of beauty that comes from applying cosmetics.

Avalokiteśvara's form and ornaments symbolize his complete freedom from all that is to be eliminated and his complete accomplishment of all that is to be realized. As Avalokiteśvara, your body is luminous due to being free from any obscurations of the mind. Your awareness is utterly unimpeded and indestructible. In fact, it is worthwhile to learn the symbolic meaning of every aspect of the deity because each is a sign of a particular inner quality and realization.[8]

At the beginning of the practice, visualize the syllable *Hrīḥ*, which then transforms into Avalokiteśvara. The nature of your awareness is already Avalokiteśvara and is primordially enlightened. The essence of your awareness is the Dharmakāya of Avalokiteśvara; the nature of your awareness is the Sambhogakāya of Avalokiteśvara; and the pervasive compassion of your awareness is the Nirmāṇakāya of Avalokiteśvara. Don't think that all emanations of Avalokiteśvara outwardly manifest all of the signs and symbols, such as one thousand arms and eyes. Nor should you think that the emanations will necessarily be male or female.

If it is true that the nature of your awareness is already enlightened, why do you need to meditate? If you can genuinely dwell in total trust in the enlightened nature of your awareness, it is okay not to meditate. If you practice this meditation without such absolute trust, it is like hitting yourself on the head with a hammer.

Imagine possessing a treasure-trove of jewels, but not knowing it. You may be completely destitute simply because you don't know you possess this treasure. Our Buddha-nature is like the hidden and unknown treasure-trove, and we must have someone point it out to us. Yet even that isn't enough. We must trust this person and trust what is being pointed out. Just having a wish-fulfilling jewel is not sufficient, and even recognizing that you have one is not enough. In order to reap any benefit, you must cleanse it, make offerings, and make supplications to the gem. Only then will it fulfill your needs. Each of us is endowed with the wish-fulfilling jewel of our own nature, and it, too, must be cleansed. Firstly, we engage in Hīnayāna practice for the sake of cultivating the spirit of emergence—the aspiration to be free of the cycle of existence. Then we must eliminate that which needs to be eliminated and practice that which needs to be practiced—purifying obscurations and accumulating merit. Only when we discover our own spiritual wealth will we truly be wealthy.

Awhile ago, I heard that some people discovered diamonds in a house. There's nothing amazing about that. Even if you discover many houses filled with diamonds, they won't give you Buddhahood. What is truly amazing is that each of us is imbued with a Buddha-nature—each of our minds is already enlightened. What is even more amazing is having this and not recognizing or using it. That is stunning!

The visualization of your form as Avalokiteśvara is the *samayasattva*. *Samaya* means pledge, and *sattva* means being. This *samayasattva* symbolizes the commitment to engage in this practice with a pure view of the body, speech, and mind from this time forward. This is a solemn vow. To engage in the practice one day, drop it the next, and perhaps later get around to it again is to toy with the Dharma, and that is not genuine practice.

The visualization of the moon-disk at your heart with the six syllables circling around the white *Hrīḥ* is the *samādhisattva*, the *samādhi* being. By the power of your motivation and visualization, with concentration and verbal recitation of the *mantra*, you imagine all *jñānasattvas*, or primordial wisdom beings, of the three times dissolving into yourself. The pledge beings and the primordial wisdom beings become nondual. You may ask again, if the very nature of our present awareness is primordially that of Avalokiteśvara, why must we perform this visualization? Truly, there is no need. So why do we do it? Because it is auspicious.

For all practices of the stage of generation, this process is the same. The essential point is to purify our grasping onto impurity so that pure vision can arise. This purification process takes place by employing skillful means, which include the two stages of generation and completion. These stages are, of course, based upon the prior development of a spirit of emergence. Through such sequential practice, there arises a sense of confidence. When confidence arises, you see the pure nature of your environment, other sentient beings, and yourself.

Does this purity arise in dependence upon your practice, or do you discover a primordial purity? Ultimately, there is no difference. But for those on the path, whether of small, medium, or great capacity, it may seem that they see things as pure as a result of progressing along the path. With this pure vision, imagine all appearances as the display of the divine form of the body of the chosen deity, which in this case is Avalokiteśvara. Imagine that all sounds are the speech of your spiritual mentor and your chosen deity. View all that arises in the mind as the pure presentation of the divine mind of Avalokiteśvara. When you hold all appearances as the body of Avalokiteśvara, all sounds as the speech of the deity and all mental contents as the mind of Avalokiteśvara, this constitutes the culmination of the stage of generation.

Is this fundamentally different from Great Perfection practice? Please be aware that it is not. You can speak of the Dharmakāya, Sambhogakāya, and Nirmāṇakāya of the body and the speech. Likewise, there are the three divine embodiments of the mind. The whole thrust of Great Perfection practice is primordial reality. This has always been the case; it is not something that we fabricate or imagine. Rather, it is a reality to be discovered. The various divine embodiments are all qualities of a single awareness—your own. Moreover, all the qualities of the Buddha, which far surpass our imagination, are qualities of our present awareness. It's astonishing that we fixate on the eight mundane concerns by pinning our hopes on them and ignoring our own treasure-trove of awareness.

When I was in Tibet, sometimes people had visions and dreams that they thought were amazing, and, of course, they wanted to tell other people. What's so amazing about this? Since we are in *saṃsāra,* naturally various things appear to us. When we dream, sometimes unusual dreams occur. There is nothing amazing about these either. If on the other hand, whatever appears to the mind can be recognized as its own pure nature, that is truly amazing. When we recognize the actual nature of our dreams as the pure display of the Dharmakāya, that, too, is amazing. But what is truly the most astonishing is that we are amazed by things that are not at all astonishing, and fail to be amazed by that which is truly worthy of amazement and is inherent within each of us. The wise recognize our situation, and, although they may laugh at us, they truly have compassion for us. -

The Mahāsiddha Maitrīpa says:

> The outer recitation according to the *sūtras* is to chant it distinctly with a loud voice while focusing on your divine body and the *Hrīḥ* at your heart.
>
> The inner recitation according to the Mantra[yāna] entails imagining a moon-disk in the center of an eight-petaled red lotus at your heart. Upon it, the six syllables circle clockwise around a *Hrīḥ* with a *visarga*, emitting five kinds of light rays, filling the

interior of your body. Again rays of light are emitted outwards, striking the external universe and transforming it into the pure realm of Sukhāvatī. Striking all the sentient beings who inhabit the universe, the light rays transform them into Avalokiteśvara. Imagine the *mantra* being recited by everyone, and you recite it just loud enough so that it can be heard within your room.

The secret, soundless recitation entails reciting with the tip of your tongue while maintaining clear *samādhi*.

The recitation of thatness entails clearly imagining yourself as Avalokiteśvara. The rays of light are emitted from the *Hrīḥ* at your heart, filling the entire exterior and interior of your body, including your pores, with the Great Compassionate One. By striking the realm of the external universe, they transform it into Sukhāvatī. They strike all the sentient beings who inhabit the universe, and all turn into Avalokiteśvara. In short, all appearances of forms become the body of Avalokiteśvara, and you recite mentally while imagining all sounds as the six syllables.

– The outer recitation entails visualizing and chanting the six-syllable *mantra* loudly and continuously. According to the inner recitation, from the *Hrīḥ* and the *visarga* (the two circles on the right side of that Sanskrit or Tibetan syllable) light rays emanate and strike all sentient beings subject to the three poisons. Imagine that all are purified and turn into the form of Avalokiteśvara. You as Avalokiteśvara then recognize the primordial purity of each sentient being.

The secret, soundless recitation is so quiet as to be almost inaudible. For the recitation of thatness, imagine that Avalokiteśvara fills your entire body out to the pores. Imagine the five elements of your body and all other appearances in the form of Avalokiteśvara. Because we are not able to dwell in the knowledge that all beings are of the nature of Avalokiteśvara, we must rely on the support of visualization to affirm and retain this awareness.

One of the major themes of the stage of generation is the purification of rebirth in *saṃsāra* by way of purifying the four ways of taking birth (instantaneous birth, birth due to heat and moisture, birth from an egg, and birth from a womb). Corresponding to the four ways of birth are four practices within the stage of generation, each of which serves as an antidote for a particular type of birth. For example, birth into the god and hell realms is instantaneous. As a god, one instantly takes birth in a lotus, without the support of parents or a womb. Similarly, beings are instantly born into the hell realms. Likewise, within the stage of generation, you arise from a seed syllable, instantly appearing as your chosen deity. This stage of practice is designed as an antidote to ordinary, instantaneous birth. By engaging in this practice, you are able to purify your habitual propensities for this type of birth. –

The Primary Words of Essential Instructions of the Great Compassionate One, which were presented by Vajravārāhī to the Siddha Tsombupa, state:

> To achieve awakening in one lifetime and with one body, you must have strength of mind like this. Everyone else meditates on one chosen deity after another. That results in adopting and rejecting chosen deities, so there will never come a time when they achieve *siddhis*. Imagine all chosen deities as being included in your own body. Wherever you live, that is a palace. This is a cause of the pristine pure realm when you are awakened. Everyone else meditates on one spiritual mentor after another. That results in adopting and rejecting spiritual mentors, so there will never come a time when they achieve *siddhis*. Moreover, by imagining your spiritual mentor as a human, blessings do not arise. Imagining your primary spiritual mentor in the form of Buddha Amitābha, seated in the manner of the Lord of the [Buddha] Family, invite the lineage spiritual mentors. They nondually dissolve into your primary spiritual mentor, like snowflakes coming in contact with a hot stone. Thus, think of this being as the synthesis of all spiritual mentors.
>
> Visualize yourself as the Great Compassionate One, the synthesis of all chosen deities. Upon a lotus and moon at your heart imagine the six white syllables circling around a white *Hrīḥ*. Recite them as if you were reading them. Whoever you are with, think of them as your chosen deity, and imagine all sentient beings as your chosen deity. Eventually when you are enlightened, that will be a cause for your attaining a perfectly pure retinue of disciples.
>
> Everyone else dispenses with a *mantra* after reciting a single rosary and wonders if it will result in a *siddhi*. There will never come a time when they carry through with a propitiatory retreat. By transforming all sentient beings into your chosen deity, think of them as helping with the *mantra*. Such a practice is said to result in immeasurable or incalculable benefits, and you develop great enthusiasm for your spiritual practice.
>
> The transformation of the universe and its inhabitants into the pristine nature is the presentation of appearances as the divine body. Recognizing all sounds as the empty sounds of the speech of your chosen deity, or recognizing them as the sound of the *mantra*, is the presentation of sounds as the divine speech. Recognizing all occurrences of memories and thoughts in your mind as the empty awareness of the mind of your chosen deity is the presentation of memories as the divine mind.

– Observing Tibetans' habit of roaming from one practice to another, Atiśa commented, "Although Tibetans meditate on a hundred deities, they fail to actualize even one; Indian contemplatives meditate on only one deity, but they actualize a hundred." We can see that some people move from one tradition to another, never taking any practice to its culmination. They rove from one deity practice to another, just as people go from one girlfriend or boyfriend to another—or even go from one spouse to another. This type of fickleness brings no benefit in the long run, but only results in adopting and rejecting deities without ever actualizing any of them.

Imagine the nature of the deities as present in your own body. Your body, speech, and mind are the nature of all of the Buddhas. Visualize your house as a palace, not necessarily like the palaces depicted in Tibetan iconography, but one of your own vision. Visualizing your environment in this utterly pure fashion lays a foundation for the time when you actually attain enlightenment.

Hold a pure view of your spiritual teacher, but do this only if your teacher is an authentic spiritual mentor. If the Dharma teacher is a disgrace to the Dharma and leads people to the lower realms and not to enlightenment, then pure vision is not needed. On the other hand, there is no benefit if we have doubt about our spiritual mentor. An aphorism states that hope destroys the Tibetans, while the Chinese are overcome by uncertainty. It is clear that Americans, too, are subject to much uncertainty. This brings no blessing. Don't think that you have to superimpose excellent qualities on your spiritual mentor when you imagine him or her in the form of the Buddha. You are solely affirming the enlightened nature of the mentor.

Next, imagine inviting all of the *kama* and *terma* spiritual mentors of the lineage. At this point you may wonder what to do if you have connections to different traditions. Bear in mind that in fact they are not different, and there is no fault in mixing one tradition with another. In the beginning, it may seem very artificial to look upon your spiritual mentor as an actual Buddha. Even if this is contrived and strained in the beginning, eventually it will come naturally and effortlessly.

Developing a pure vision of other beings results in their becoming your excellent disciples when you manifestly obtain Buddhahood. Imagine them joining you in reciting the *mantra*. In fact, think that all sounds that arise from the earth, water, fire, and air are the sound of the *mantra*. –

Those of you with little intelligence who cannot visualize this should come to the certain conviction that you are the Great Compassionate One, whose body is white, with one face, four arms, ornaments, and clothing. Upon a moon at your heart imagine the six syllables circling clockwise around a white *Hrīḥ*. From it rays of light are emitted in all directions, and those light rays make offerings to all the Buddhas and Bodhisattvas of the ten directions. They all turn into bodies of the Great Compassionate One, and imagine them coming and dissolving into you like falling raindrops. Again, upon being struck by your light, all sentient beings also turn into bodies of the Great Compassionate One, and imagine them murmuring the six syllables. From time to time observe the mind that is doing the meditation.

– People who have little or no education or who have not spent time thinking about the teachings may not be able to engage in the full meditation, but it would be a shame for them to ignore this practice altogether. So for such people Karma Chagmé suggests a simpler visualization. Imagine from the *Hrīḥ* in your heart light rays emanating in all directions, making offerings to the Buddhas and Bodhisattvas of the ten directions. Pleased with your offerings, they take on the form of the Great Compassionate One. In all sizes, some vastly large and others very tiny, they merge into you. Then, like falling raindrops, the six-syllable *mantra* and the ritual hand implements dissolve into you. –

The Hevajra Tantra states:

> There is no meditation nor a meditator.
> There is no deity, nor a *mantra*.
> In the nature that is devoid of conceptual elaboration
> The deities and the *mantras* are perfectly present:
> The beings Vairocana, Akṣobhya, Amoghasiddhi,
> Ratnasambhava, and Amitābha.

– For someone practicing genuine meditation, there is no sense of "I" doing the meditation, no action of meditating, no deity, and no qualities of the deity. Yet, one is not left with a nihilistic, sheer vacuity. Rather, all inexpressible and inconceivable excellent qualities of the body, speech, and mind of all of the Buddhas are included in a single awareness.

In the above passage, the reference to the five Buddhas implicitly includes the three and five embodiments of the Buddha, as well as all of the peaceful, enriching, subjugating, and ferocious forms. The qualities of the Buddha's mind are the two types of knowledge, ontological and phenomenological. The Buddha's speech has sixty qualities of enlightened speech, and his body has the thirty-two signs and the eighty marks symbolic of enlightenment. This is true not only of Buddha Śākyamuni, but of all the Buddhas.

At times our motivation may be altruistic as we try to engage in helpful activities, but in fact it is very difficult to serve sentient beings effectively. Although we yearn to be of service to others, we cannot be fully successful until we have brought forth the genuine spirit of venturing towards awakening in which pure altruism has been generated and self-grasping has been completely banished. Through hearing, thinking, and meditating, we gradually come to spiritual maturation. As we free ourselves of our faults, the purity of our own minds will shine forth like the rays of the sun. But it is very difficult to be without some trace of self-interest. Often, even when we are trying to be of service to others, our actions are mixed with our own self-centered desires.

The short treatise *Parting from the Four Cravings* states that if you still crave for your own self-centered goals, you lack the Spirit of Awakening. To counteract this, listen to the Dharma, ponder it, and put it into practice. We may be less than successful if we are impatient and want to be of service immediately without devoting ourselves to spiritual practice. In order to have a pure sense of altruism and be focused solely on the interests of others, we must have already abandoned clinging to our own interests.

Let's observe our own behavior. For example, if we offer a cup of tea to someone and that person accepts graciously, we are content. However, if the person doesn't respond as we think appropriate, we become irritated and offended. What is the source of this attitude? It comes from grasping onto the "I." Some Dharma teachers do their best to teach students, but when the students don't practice as they are instructed, the teachers get irritated. Why is that? Again it is due to grasping onto the self.

When people would tell His Holiness Dudjom Rinpoche that they had done something virtuous, he frequently would cheerfully respond, "Yah, Yah, Yah!" And if they told him of something really bad, he gave the same response. At first I thought this was weird, as if he didn't care whether or not people behaved virtuously. But as I thought about it further, it occurred to me that it was really an expression of his own abandonment of grasping. Maybe it was an expression of his awareness of the illusory nature of this entire cycle of existence—his insight into the complete lack of truth of everything in *saṃsāra*, in which everything is deceptive and misleading. Once this grasping onto the self has been eliminated, the door is opened to engage in pure service, unmixed with self-interest.

Years ago, when I lived in India after fleeing from Tibet, I saw some monks who lived like beggars. They had virtually no possessions, yet all day long they were always cheerful. You would never hear them speaking about mundane things. Their speech was always related to the Dharma, and all of their waking hours were filled with Dharma. In contrast, outside in the marketplace, the merchants were not at all happy. They were engaged in jealousy, trying to get this and avoid that. They had none of the simple happiness of those monks. Even certain Lamas who made great claims about wanting to preserve the Dharma and serve sentient beings did not have that simple sense of good cheer. The Dharma practice of those monks effectively counteracted their five poisons. By listening to and pondering the Dharma, they were able to cure themselves of the illness of the five poisons, which leads to the realization of the truth of cessation of suffering and its source.

Whether you want to accomplish your own interest or serve the needs of others, you must first acquire knowledge. But if you don't put it into practice, your knowledge is like a patch slapped on old clothes. If you don't sew it on well, it will come off very easily. First gain good understanding, then put it into practice. Upon putting it into practice there arises realization, and from this, confidence arises. When this happens, you can then effectively serve the needs of yourself and others.

Whenever you travel on an airplane, the flight attendants demonstrate what to do in an emergency. They tell you to put the oxygen mask over your own nose before putting it over your child's nose. That's not because you should be selfish, but because if you pass out, you won't be able to help anyone at all. So you see, the essential point is that we must first subdue our own minds before we can effectively serve others.

If you have failed to subdue your own mind, even if a thousand Buddhas surround you, they will be of no benefit. If you want to subdue your enemies, you must subdue your own mind. If you want to bring about world peace, subdue your mind. A subdued mind is the Lama. A subdued mind is the Ḍākinī, the chosen deity, and the Buddha. A subdued mind is the pure land. You are already imbued with the Buddha-nature. This is your inherent nature. What actual benefit have you gotten from the essential nature of your mind? –

The Primary Treatise on the Fivefold Practice states:

> If an immutable fortress—your own body as the deity's
> body—
> Is not secured for the king,
> The assemblies of Ḍākinīs will not gather.
> So diligently regard your body as your chosen deity.

This completes the instructions on the stage of generation.

– A king has confidence and pride because, inside his mighty fortress, he feels invulnerable. If you take away his fortress, he is out on his own. In this passage the fortress refers to maintaining your body as the deity's body. Without this the Ḍākinīs will not gather. To do this practice, regard your body, speech, and mind as the body, speech, and mind of the deity. Regard others' bodies, speech, and minds in the same way.

Even without the oral transmission, empowerment, and instructions, this particular Avalokiteśvara practice can be practiced and great benefit can be derived, especially at death. This is due to the extraordinary qualities of Avalokiteśvara. Moreover, this practice is not confined to a specific monastic order or spiritual tradition within Tibet. All schools of Tibetan Buddhism equally revere Avalokiteśvara and engage in this practice. –

May there be virtue!

CHAPTER THREE
The Cultivation of Quiescence

Homage to Avalokiteśvara!

The profound practical instructions of Avalokiteśvara on the method for subduing your own mind are for cultivating quiescence.

– The topic of this chapter is quiescence. What is it that is being quieted? Principally, the five poisons: delusion, attachment, hatred, pride, and jealousy. These are the primary mental afflictions, but as we know from our own experience, there are many secondary afflictions.

The Tibetan term translated here as "quiescence" is "zhiney" (*zhi gnas*). The first syllable means "to pacify," for in the state of quiescence the five poisons are pacified. For this to be truly beneficial, the meditator must remain in that state in which they are subdued, otherwise they will swiftly re-emerge. Thus, the second syllable means "to remain, to be sustained."

What are the benefits of quiescence? What is the value of being able to attain and remain in a state in which the mental afflictions are subdued? Throughout the course of our lives, from a very early age, we have continually vacillated between pleasure and sorrow within this cycle of existence. This instability of our emotions indicates that we have not been able to remain in a quiescent state in which the mental afflictions have been calmed. That is why we undergo swings in mood, for example, between feeling lonely and feeling that we need more space. –

The Sūtra on the Meeting of the Father and Son states:

> With respect to all of the Dharmas of the Buddha, I see no other way. If you achieve quiescence and great primordial wisdom, you will certainly become spontaneous.

– The Buddhas of the past attained enlightenment because they subdued their own minds, whereas we have failed to attain enlightenment because we have not subdued our minds. Without first achieving quiescence, great primordial wisdom cannot arise. Cultivation of quiescence is often likened to tilling a field: if you fail to prepare the ground, even though you plant the crop, it will not bear a good harvest. Similarly, the cultivation of quiescence must precede the cultivation of insight and wisdom. Such cultivation is indispensable, and as a result of this training, you will certainly become spontaneous, or literally "self-arisen," which is a mark of realization. –

The Sūtra on Possessing the Roots of Virtue states:

> Even though you guard ethical discipline for an eon and cultivate patience for a long period, if you do not become acquainted with reality, you are an extremist in relation to my teachings.

– In this passage, "becoming acquainted with reality" means cultivating quiescence. Thus, if you don't develop quiescence and subsequently insight, you are not really following the Buddha's path, even though you are attempting to practice the Dharma. You remain an "outsider" with respect to the teachings. –

The Sūtra of Ānanda's Instruction on Entering the Womb states:

> Whoever lacks the mind of meditative equipoise lacks pure primordial wisdom. The contaminations will not be eliminated, so by all means accomplish it!

– Here, "the mind of meditative equipoise" means quiescence, without which pure primordial wisdom does not arise; without such wisdom, the mental afflictions cannot be eliminated.

In these teachings, we must distinguish between two terms: wisdom (Tib. *shes rab*, Skt. *prajñā*) and primordial wisdom (Tib. *ye shes*, Skt. *jñāna*). The first term has the connotation of "supreme knowledge," and it refers to a kind of insight, intelligence, and wisdom that is acquired through hearing, thinking, and meditating. In contrast, primordial wisdom is innate insight, particularly into the nature of emptiness. –

A Lamp on the Path of Enlightenment comments:

> With inadequate preparation for quiescence, even if you practice meditation with great effort, *samādhi* will not be achieved even in a thousand years.

– Quiescence is an indispensable foundation for other types of meditation, such as insight. However, the practice of quiescence itself requires preparation, without which success will be impossible, despite great effort. –

A Guide to the Bodhisattva Way of Life states:

> Recognizing that the mental afflictions are eradicated by insight imbued with quiescence, one should first seek quiescence. That [quiescence] is achieved with detachment towards the world and with joy.[9]

And:

> ...a person whose mind is distracted lives between the fangs of mental afflictions.[10]

And:

> The Omniscient One stated that if recitations and all austerities are performed for a long time with a mind obsessed with something else, they are actually useless.[11]

And:

> One who wishes to protect the practice should zealously guard the mind. One who neglects to guard the mind cannot protect the practice.[12]

And:

> By subduing the mind alone, they all become subdued.[13]

And:

> Once I have forsaken the vow of guarding the mind, of what use are many vows to me?[14]

– In the Vajrayāna tradition, there are vast numbers of teachings, vows, and techniques that we can practice. All are intended to protect the mind. There are many ritual implements and wonderful ornaments that we can wear, but we can become so preoccupied by such outer paraphernalia that we look as if we were costumed for a Halloween party. We can get so caught up in these external things that we miss the primary point, which is to subdue our own minds. –

And:

> Once the elephant of the mind has been let loose, it inflicts the harm of Avīci Hell.[15]

And:

> But if the elephant of the mind is firmly restrained by the rope of mindfulness, then all fears vanish and all virtues are obtained.[16]

And:

> Let my possessions, honor, body, and livelihood vanish; let even other virtues decline, but may my mind never degenerate.[17]

> To you who wish to guard your minds, guard mindfulness and introspection, even at the cost of your life! This I ask with folded hands.[18]

And:

> In brief, this alone is the characteristic of introspection: the repeated investigation of the state of the body and mind.[19]

The root of quiescence is meditative stabilization, so the meaning of the scriptural collection of the *sūtras* is that the discipline is training the mind. Here there are four, as stated in *The Jewel Ornament of Liberation*:

> There are the first, second, third, and fourth meditative stabilizations. The first stabilization is endowed with investigation and analysis. The second stabilization is endowed with pleasure. The third stabilization is endowed with mental joy. The fourth stabilization is endowed with equanimity.

The way to cultivate those four stabilizations and the characteristics and benefits of them are stated by the Lord in *The Perfection of Wisdom Sūtra in Twenty-five Thousand Stanzas*:

> Subhūti, Bodhisattvas, the great beings, dwell in the perfection of meditative stabilization, isolated from desires and isolated from evil nonvirtuous things.[20] Endowed with investigation and analysis, and imbued with the pleasure and joy born of isolation, they accomplish the first stabilization and dwell therein.
>
> Having calmed investigation and analysis, [their minds become] completely limpid, and due to the unification of their mindstream, they are imbued with the pleasure and joy that arises from *samādhi* that is free of investigation and analysis. They accomplish the second stabilization and dwell therein.
>
> Freeing themselves from attachment to pleasure, endowed with mindfulness, and dwelling in introspection and equanimity, they experience physical joy and possess the mindfulness of the Āryas.[21] Living in joy and a state called equanimity,[22] they accomplish the third stabilization, free of pleasure, and dwell therein.
>
> Abandoning joy as well as suffering, mental pleasure and displeasure are overcome even more than before. Due to the absence of both joy and suffering, they accomplish the fourth stabilization, in which equanimity and mindfulness are fully purified, and they dwell therein.

> Moreover, they do not grasp at the characteristics of stabilization and its attributes. Due to being endowed with minds of such meditative equipoise, they experience numerous types of paranormal abilities: they cause even the earth to quake; they transform from one to many; they transform from many to one; they experience becoming visible and invisible; they pass through walls; they pass through fences; they pass unimpededly through mountains like birds in the sky; they also move through space like birds; they rise up and penetrate down through the earth as if they were moving in water; and they walk on water without sinking.

Such characteristics and benefits are extensively discussed. The glorious Tsuglak Trengwa says:

> Due to the nine methods for sustaining attention [presented] generally in the *sūtras*, one first accomplishes single-pointed quiescence of the desire realm. Upon accomplishing the fourth [stabilization], one achieves the five extrasensory perceptions resulting from the path of extrasensory perception. These are common to non-Buddhist adepts and to the Buddhist *sūtras* and *tantras*. In contrast, this quiescence, which is accomplished by means of the sequence of instructions of Mahāmudrā and so on, arises from the essential points of practical teachings. In the very nature of single-pointed attention of the desire realm there are qualities comparable to the four stabilizations, and upon that basis the stabilizations of divine abodes[23] are achieved. Then even without difficulty one first achieves just a portion of quiescence as the basis of insight. But one does not practice as if the mundane stabilizations alone were the most important.

– "Single-pointed quiescence of the desire realm" refers to single-pointed attention of a mind-state that remains in the desire realm, as opposed to the form or formless realms. While extrasensory perceptions are not unique to Buddhist practice, the technique for developing quiescence in this context is unique to Mahāmudrā and this lineage. The single-pointed attention of the desire realm is a more basic or coarse degree of *samādhi* than those of the four stabilizations, and yet its attributes and benefits are said to be comparable to these more subtle states of *samādhi*. Upon the basis of this quiescence, higher states of rebirth may be achieved: the abodes of the gods of the desire realm, form realm, and formless realm. We do not practice meditative stabilization simply because it gives rise to paranormal abilities and extrasensory perception; the cultivation of meditative stabilization is significant because it acts as a basis of insight. –

THE PHYSICAL POSTURE

Having abandoned distractions, the physical posture must be maintained. *The Great Instructions*[24] states:

> The body should possess the seven attributes of Vairocana. These seven attributes are: [1] the legs are in [the *vajra*] position, [2] the hands are placed in [the *mudrā* of] meditative equipoise, four finger-widths beneath the level of the navel, [3] the forearms are held upright, without moving, and the shoulders are extended like the wings of a vulture, [4] the neck should be curved like a hook, pressing on the Adam's apple, [5] the spine is straight like an arrow, [6] the eyes are directed into space four finger-widths in front of the tip of the nose, without fluttering the eyelashes, and without straying to either side, and [7] the lips are slightly joined, as are the teeth a little bit, and the tongue is pressed up against the palate. Sit upon a comfortable cushion.

– The torso should not sway from side to side, and the gaze should be directed in front of you without wavering. The teeth are together but not clenched. –

The Tantra of the Garland of Vajras states:

> The practitioner should sit upon a comfortable cushion and direct the eyes over the tip of the nose. Position the nose in line with the navel. Let the shoulders be even, and press the tongue against the palate. Let the teeth and lips be comfortable. Relaxing the respiration, slightly release effort. By so doing, remain properly in the *vajra* position, with such *mudrās*.

– These last few instructions indicate that you must find the right balance between being too tight and too loose, while placing your hands in the proper position. –

Thus, be free of three flaws. The condition of the body, [composed] of four elements, is joyful, light, and relaxed. The purpose of having such [qualities] is stated in *The Hevajra Tantra*:

> Great primordial wisdom dwells in the body, it perfectly eliminates all conceptualization, and it pervades all phenomena. The posture does not arise in the body.[25]

The Perfection of Wisdom Sūtra in Seven Hundred Stanzas states:

> Sons and daughters of good breeding, sit firmly on a solitary cushion, take pleasure in the absence of amusements, do not bring signs to mind, and sit properly in the *vajra* position.

The Tantra of the Lotus Net states:

> Upon a very soft cushion sit upright in the *vajra* position, with the eyes gazing down over the tip of the nose. With slow respiration, slightly press the tongue against the palate. Slightly tuck in the navel, and by so doing let the mind remain conscientious.

Je Düsum Kyenpa also says:

> To look at the mountain over there, look over here. If you desire emptiness, establish appearances. If you wish to sustain attention, subdue the body with *adhisāras*.

– *Adhisāra* is the Sanskrit term for the Tibetan *trulkor* (*khrul 'khor*), or a class of physical exercises practiced in the Buddhist tradition. If you need to accomplish something difficult, you sometimes need to take an indirect approach. For example, if you want light in your living room, you may want first to take advantage of the light outside by opening the shades at the window, rather than creating light inside. Similarly, if you wish to look at a distant mountain, you may want to start by focusing on something that is closer. If you wish to understand emptiness, instead of looking for emptiness itself, you may first establish the nature of appearances. And finally, if you wish to stabilize the mind, first subdue the body with the *adhisāras*. By training the body through the practice of the *adhisāras*—in this case, sitting in the proper posture, with the proper *mudrās*—although you are ostensibly working with the body, you are indirectly subduing and stabilizing your mind. –

The Great Instructions states:

> Furthermore, these are the purposes of having an appropriate posture: By having the legs in the [*vajra*] position, the descending wind is directed into the central channel, the mental affliction of jealousy is calmed, and one is not struck by interferences. By having the hands in the *mudrā* of meditative equipoise four finger-widths beneath the navel, the vital energy of water is directed into the central channel, and the affliction of hatred is calmed. Due to the spine being straight like an arrow and the shoulders being raised like the wings of a vulture, the vital energy of earth is directed into the central channel, and delusion is calmed. By tucking the chin slightly down towards the chest, the

> vital energy of fire is directed into the central channel, and attachment is calmed. By not squinting the eyes, but directing the gaze four finger-widths beyond the tip of the nose, and by pressing the tongue up against the palate, the vital energy of air is directed into the central channel, pride is calmed, and awareness is made clear.
>
> Moreover, the critical factor for the mind is the vital energy; the critical factor for the vital energy is the channels; the critical factor for the channels is in the eyes, so it is important that the manner of gazing not be faulty.

Thus, due to the body having the five attributes or the seven attributes of meditative stabilization, the five poisons naturally subside, and the vital energy and mind are naturally directed into the central channel. Then all conceptualizations naturally cease, you feel comfortable, at ease, and bright; and realizations swiftly arise. Therefore, the physical posture is important.

– The normal function of the descending wind is expelling the urine and feces. In this posture, a great deal of emphasis is placed on the way to direct the gaze. Mastering this point is good preparation for the more advanced phase of Atiyoga practice called the "Leap-over," in which the gaze is of critical importance.

The "Space Dharma" lineage of the Nyingma Order strongly emphasizes the central channel. Other lineages may have more elaborate practices and visualizations involving many different channels, but in the Space Dharma lineage you concentrate only on the central channel, because that contains the gist of the practice: to draw the vital energies into the central channel, and thus to pacify the mental afflictions. In more elaborate practices, with more complex visualizations, there is the danger that some of the vital energies may be directed into the other visualized channels. –

If the body is in disorder or crooked, conceptualization becomes agitated and the attention is not sustained. If the posture tilts to the right, first a sense of clarity arises, then hatred occurs in the mindstream, and there is the danger of being harmed by *grahas* and *pārthivas* and the like. If you lean to the left, first there is a sense of joy, and then strong attachment occurs, and *grahas*, *nāgas*, and *mātṛkās*, and so forth inflict harm. If you lean forward, at first nonconceptuality arises effortlessly, but afterwards it turns into delusion, and *kṣamāpatis* and so on inflict harm.[26]

In particular, if you were to see two or more people in conversation, you might think, "These two are slandering me a lot," [leading to] unhappiness and so on. There are also many problems of the life-sustaining vital energy being misdirected. If the posture leans backwards, at first there effortlessly arises a sense of vacuity, then such afflictions as pride occur, and thoughts of the previous harmful spirits arise. In particular, attention cannot be sustained, conceptualization proliferates, the body becomes bluish and thin, and there occur problems of the vital fluids seeping out.

Therefore, the critical factor to prevent all problems and obtain all benefits is the physical posture, so it is important that the *adhisāra* not be in error.

The five attributes of meditative stabilization are explained by Lama Zhang:

> There are five [aspects of] the physical posture: [1] straight like an arrow, [2] curved like a hook, [3] arranged together like the squares on a chessboard, [4] fastened like shackles, and [5] held fast like a razor.[27]

Straight like an arrow: The spine is straight like an arrow. This does not mean straight like an arrow drawn horizontally. Rather, you lift your neck vertically so that the lines on your throat disappear, and you arch your lower back. The purpose of doing that is that the three channels remain in their own places, the central channel becomes straight, the channel-knots are released, and the vital energy is easily directed into the central channel.

Curved like a hook: The neck is slightly, naturally curved. The purpose of that is it stops the dispersion of the vital energy and ideation from the two channels on the left and right, which are like the open mouth of a fish, and, thus, realization arises.

Arranged together like the squares on a chessboard: The ankles are arranged together. The purpose of this is that this is a characteristic of the *vajra* position, and so one is not troubled by interferences.

Fastened like shackles: With a *vajra*-knot meditation belt and so on, one is firmly wrapped in from the knees. The purpose of this is to prevent the posture from being wrong.

Held fast like razor: Placing a ball of cloth under the anus, the lower orifice is tightly closed. The purpose of this is that the channels and vital energy meet inside, causing the warmth of joy to swiftly and superbly arise.

About these five critical aspects of the posture the venerable Marpa Lhodrak says:

> My practical instructions on the five critical aspects of the posture are greater than all the practical instructions of Tibet put

together. Why? Simply due to possessing these five critical factors of the posture, the vital energies are directed into the central channel. Due to that, the inner heat naturally blazes up from the navel. Due to that, the drop of *bodhicitta* naturally descends from the crown of the head. As a result, joy spontaneously arises. Thus, without needing to stop conceptualization intentionally, nonconceptuality effortlessly arises. As a result, the primordial wisdom of realization arises as a side-effect.

Therefore, at the outset the way of positioning the body is important, and by familiarizing yourself with just this for a long time, the inner elements become balanced; you will have a long life; pre-existent illnesses will be healed, and they will not occur later on; the channels, vital energy, and nutritive essence are strengthened; weight from above does not inflict injury below; due to the unified assembly of the channels, vital energy, and essential fluids, there is no discomfort even if you remain [in meditation] for months or years; and due to the excellent ripening of the nutritive essence of the nutritive essence, awareness is naturally clarified and realization effortlessly arises.

– As a result of familiarizing yourself with the body posture over a period of time, you gain mastery over the channels, the vital energy, and the essential fluids. –

THE CULTIVATION OF ATTENTION

Possessing those critical factors of the posture, practice cultivating the attention. In the great Indian treatise *The Nine Collections of Concentration* composed by the Indian master Bodhibhadra, it is said there are two types of quiescence: that which is achieved by looking inwards, and that which is focused looking outwards. In terms of looking inwards, there is focusing on the body, and focusing on things dependent upon the body.

In terms of focusing on the body, there are three types: [1] focusing on the body in its divine aspect, [2] focusing on its unattractive aspects, such as the skeleton, and [3] focusing on special signs such as a *khaṭvāṅga*.

– One way of developing quiescence is to imagine yourself in the form of a deity, that is, an emanation of the Buddha. This is an aspect of the practice known as the stage of generation. As you visualize yourself in the form of the deity, you avoid any dispersion of the attention. During this practice, it is very important that you do not visualize the deity's form as something tangible or substantial, like a table or cup. Instead, visualize it as appearing and yet devoid of any inherent nature. This is a crucial factor of this practice.

In this approach, visualize yourself as either a male or female deity, attractive and glorious in appearance. You may begin thinking, "Oh, I'm very special." But what is saying, "I'm very special"? It is the mind, grasping onto this mere mental appearance as being special. Note that attitude of grasping.

Then visualize your body in its unattractive aspect. For example, imagine yourself as a skeleton, a pile of bones, or even in the form of a *preta*, that is, a repulsive-looking spirit living in a continual state of frustration and unfulfilled desires. In this practice, you may feel a sense of revulsion from this self-image.

This compulsive attitude of grasping onto one appearance as if it could be of benefit to you, and grasping onto the other as if it could harm you, is deluded. This point is highlighted in some Atiyoga initiations, in which both attractive and repulsive objects are brought into the ceremony to elicit the responses of desire in the one case and disgust in the other. We should recognize the bondage to which we subject ourselves by responding to appearances with such grasping.

Then focus on a special symbol, such as a *khaṭvāṅga*, which is a staff held by tantric deities such as Padmasambhava and Vajrayoginī, and is an element of tantric iconography. –

In terms of focusing on things dependent upon the body there are five types: [1] focusing on the breath, [2] focusing on subtle signs, [3] focusing on a *bindu*, [4] focusing on the attributes of light rays, and [5] focusing on pleasure and joy.

In terms of looking outwards there are two types: special and ordinary. In terms of the special there are two types: focusing on [the Buddha's] body, and focusing on [the Buddha's] speech. These are ancillary to entering into quiescence.

– These techniques aid the practice of quiescence. Analogously, the great Indian Bodhisattva and poet Śāntideva points out in his *A Guide to Bodhisattva Way of Life* that the first five of the perfections—namely, generosity, ethical discipline, patience, zeal, and meditative stabilization—support the cultivation of the sixth, the perfection of wisdom. –

Maintaining the attention on impure things [such as] a pebble and a stick is discussed by the venerable Dönden Zhap: "As the basis, focus on a pebble, a stick, an oil lamp, or on spiritual mentors."

– There is nothing special about the specific objects mentioned here; they are simply ordinary objects that can be used as the focus of meditation. You could also use, for example, a wristwatch, a diamond ring, or even a picture of your boyfriend or girlfriend, though the use of such objects might be detrimental if they arouse desire and attachment. Focusing on your spiritual mentor, one in whom you have faith and confidence, can be especially beneficial. You can begin by offering prayers of supplication, and then focus on the visualized image, without excessive attachment. This may be practiced within the broader context of the *guruyoga*, as taught in the preliminary practices. This can be a very meaningful and beneficial approach.

The distinction made above between pure and impure objects of meditation accords with the distinctions made by a dualistic mind. You may focus on a statue, a stick, a pebble, a lotus, the body of the Buddha, or an image of Vajrasattva or Śākyamuni. You may also focus on the Nirmāṇakāya, the Sambhogakāya, or the Dharmakāya, or on no appearing object at all.

Focusing on the Nirmāṇakāya means focusing, for example, on the Buddha Śākyamuni visualized as an object about four finger-widths tall. You start by focusing first on his forehead, then on his heart, and then on the space right in front of him (he may be encircled by a ring of *vajras*). The fourth phase is to focus on the entire body. So, you proceed point by point, and work up to the whole body at once.

In focusing on this image of the Buddha, bring to mind the specific qualities of the Buddha's body, notably its thirty-two signs and eighty symbols, and the aura of golden light around about the Buddha's body. Bringing to mind these specific characteristics is very beneficial in dispelling obstacles to your practice.

Americans tend to ask a lot of questions in order to learn all the details of a practice. One such question is: what kind of image is suitable as the basis for meditation? A wide variety of Buddha images may be used, including ones made out of clay, stone, gold, or precious jewels. It could be a two-dimensional representation like a *tanka*, or a statue made out of wood. Any of these is suitable.

However you bring this image to the mind's eye, learn to view it as being purely of the nature of light. This perception will develop gradually. Bring the object to mind in a nondualistic fashion, as a mere appearance, empty of an intrinsic or substantial nature. Doing the practice in this way will prepare you for the practice of the stage of generation and eventually for the stage of completion as well. In both these stages of tantric practice you do not regard your body as a substantial object.

In the practice of quiescence, if at times you feel a bit lethargic and your mind becomes heavy, temporarily set aside the major object of meditation, and spend a bit of time pondering the excellent qualities of the Buddha. This will inspire and enliven your mind. You may also bring to mind the fine qualities of the Dharma and inspiring Dharma practitioners. All of this should help to uplift your mind. Another antidote for mental dullness is to focus on the crown of the Buddha's head. You may also elevate your visualization of the image.

On other occasions in practice, you may find that your mind becomes quite excited and agitated. In that case, lower the focus of your attention. You may focus on the Buddha's navel, or feet, or even on the throne upon which he is sitting. Also imagine the visualized image as lower in position. As a rule of thumb, when the mind is agitated, bring the visualized image down. When the mind starts to "sink" and feel lethargic, bring it up.

Finally, another remedy for an agitated and excited mind is to reflect on any of the Four Thoughts that Turn the Mind, namely, the preciousness of human life with leisure and endowment, impermanence, the suffering of the cycle of existence, and the nature of *karma*.

In the practice of focusing on the Sambhogakāya, the suggested object of the meditation is Vajrasattva. Visualize Vajrasattva fully adorned with the jewels appropriate to the Sambhogakāya. Aside from that, the procedure is exactly the same as in the case of the Nirmāṇakāya. You scan from the top down, then from the bottom up. You may also inspire the mind simply by thinking of the qualities of Vajrasattva.

It is very important that you look upon the visualized object as appearing, but devoid of an intrinsic nature. Look upon this as a mere appearance that is devoid of any tangible, concrete, or inherent existence.

The practice of quiescence should not be regarded as a final practice, but it is pertinent to all different kinds of practice, including Hīnayāna and Mahāyāna, and within Vajrayāna, the Mahāyoga and Anuyoga. This is a critical point that can really empower these tantric practices.

The preceding practices, focusing on the Nirmāṇakāya and the Sambhogakāya, entail directing the attention outwards. Another type of practice involves directing the attention inwards. In this case, visualize the Buddha Vajradhara at your heart. He is blue in color, the size of your first thumb-joint. Imagine him sitting in the *vajra* position upon a lotus on a moon disc, holding a *vajra* and bell, and adorned with silks and jewels. Maintain your attention steadily upon this object as well as you can.

In the practice of quiescence, you calm all transient thoughts, memories, and mental images, and you stabilize the mind so that the attention becomes like a lamp in a room where there is not even the slightest breeze.

The techniques discussed above are said to be with sign, which means with a conceptual construct, because you focus on a specific object, such as the Nirmāṇakāya or the Sambhogakāya. But now we move on to a different technique that is said to be signless, meaning without a conceptual construct: focusing on Samantabhadra, the Dharmakāya of the Buddha. The Dharmakāya is without form, without shape, without color; it is emptiness itself. In this kind of practice, there is nothing to bring to mind as an object. As memories and thoughts of the past arise, do not follow after or examine them. Do not anticipate or indulge in any anxiety about the future. Neither affirm nor negate anything in the present. Instead, without distraction, remain in a relaxed state and keep your gaze steady. If your gaze slips up or down, to one side or the other, this will naturally stimulate a corresponding distraction of the mind. So keep your gaze steady. By the time you have entered into this type of practice, you are actually very close to Atiyoga practice, although it is not yet genuine Atiyoga.

The nature of emptiness is primordially free of grasping. No one, not even a Buddha, can create emptiness. It is a primordial reality. This must be the way you approach the state of nongrasping. If you should grasp onto it, thinking, "This is empty," that is simply one more form of grasping, one more form of attachment. That would be missing the point of this practice. It would be fabricating a kind of contrived emptiness, whereas genuine emptiness is not something created. Any thought, "This is empty," or "This is emptiness," is already part of the problem, not part of the solution.

According to the Geluk Order of Tibetan Buddhism, all sentient beings have the capacity to become enlightened. According to the Kagyü and Nyingma Orders, every sentient being is in reality already enlightened; each of us is pervaded by the Dharmakāya, which is of the same nature as the Buddha-nature, or *tathāgatagarbha*. These are different interpretations, but each is valid in its own way. We should not think that approaching the issue from the former viewpoint of conventional reality is useless. That approach is very important as a basis for gaining insight into the nature of emptiness.

In the Kagyü and Nyingma Orders, there is great emphasis on recognizing the nature of dream appearances. To understand this, let's begin with an analogy: to teach a child to recognize his own face, you could hold up a mirror and say, "Look, that is a reflection of you." Then as he gazes into the mirror, making faces, he would see that just as he scrunches his face up, the same thing happens in the mirror. So he indirectly comes to recognize that as an image of himself. The reflection is not himself, but this is a way to recognize his own nature.

Likewise, in the Kagyü and Nyingma view of dream appearances, you look into the nature of these experiences, whether they are experiences of your environment, your body, or the events going on about you. Recognize that these appearances are the same sort of phenomena as the appearances in the waking state. Neither one is any more substantial than the other; both are simply appearances, devoid of any inherent existence. This is not to say that conventional reality is insignificant; indeed, it is a very important reality, and it is the basis for gaining deeper realization. –

COUNTING THE BREATH

The Primary Tantra of Mañjuśrī states:

> By resorting to mindfulness of the respiration, ideation is calmed. Since the mind is completely inflamed, fasten it firmly to one meditative object.

– In cultivating quiescence focused on the breath, first recognize the breath. Then attend to the inhalation, the brief retention, and then the exhalation. As expounded below, you can attend simply to the breath itself in these three phases, or you can conjoin these three phases with the three-syllable *vajra* recitation. –

The Perfection of Wisdom Sūtra in Ten Thousand Stanzas states:

> Śāriputra, take the analogy of a potter or a potter's apprentice spinning a potter's wheel: if he makes a long revolution, he knows it is long; if he makes a short revolution, he knows it is short. Śāriputra, similarly, a Bodhisattva, a great being, mindfully breathes in and mindfully breathes out. If the inhalation is long, he knows the inhalation is long; if the exhalation is long, he knows the exhalation is long. If the inhalation is short, he knows the inhalation is short; if the exhalation is short, he knows the exhalation is short. Śāriputra, thus, a Bodhisattva, a great being, by dwelling with introspection and with mindfulness, eliminates avarice and disappointment towards the world by means of nonobjectification, and he lives observing the body in the body internally.

A *sūtra* states:

> When the breath is going out, he correctly knows, "The breath is going out." When the breath is going in, he correctly knows, "The breath is going in."

Here is the meaning: Without distraction, direct mindfulness to the going and coming of the air, and when the air moves out, do not be distracted from that; when it comes back in, do not be distracted from that. Thus, the basis of mindfulness is the two movements of the *prāṇāyāma* of the air. While so doing, do not forsake the guard of mindfulness. *The Sūtra of the Ten Wheels of Kṣitigarbha* states:

> How do you correctly note, with the power of mindfulness, the in-and-out movement of the breath? You count them correctly....

THE THREE-SYLLABLE *VAJRA* RECITATION

The Nyingma teachings called *The Manifestation of Vairocana* state:

> With the simultaneous arising of the vital energy and the mind, the aspect of *Oṃ* with the inhalation, *Āḥ* with the pause, and *Hūṃ* with the exhalation transforms the obscurations of the body, speech, and mind, and the entire three realms into the three *vajras*. The *vajras* of the [Buddha's] body, speech, and mind are achieved, and great, inborn joy arises.

This is the meaning: When [the breath] moves inside the nostrils coming inside, recall the sound of *Oṃ*. When it pauses slightly inside, recall *Āḥ*. When it goes outside, recall *Hūṃ*. The shape of the syllables and [their colors] such as white do not need to be considered. Do this some fifty times without interruption by other thoughts; then increase up to five hundred and so on. Be at ease and avoid exerting effort at alternately restraining and releasing the *prāṇa* vital energy on the left and the *āyāma* vital energy on the right.

– Start by counting these rounds of mental recitation up to fifty, without interruption; then gradually build up to five hundred rounds. Don't be irregular or sporadic, but simply attend to the breathing evenly. –

The Essential Instructions of the Mahāsiddha Maitrīpa states:

> First there are three types of quiescence: [1] quiescence that depends on signs, [2] quiescence focused on conceptualization, and [3] quiescence that is settled in nonconceptualization.
>
> [1] In the first there are two types: [a] maintaining the attention outwards, and [b] maintaining the attention inwards.
>
> [a] Outwardly there are two types: [i] impure and [ii] pure.
>
> [i] With the posture endowed with the seven attributes of Vairocana, adopt the gaze. Maintain your attention without distraction upon a pillar, a pot, a stick, or a pebble, etc., together with the posture and the gaze. Do this without indulging in distraction elsewhere and without the dispersion of conceptualization. While so doing, settle in relaxation. Moreover, if laxity or excitation arises, recognize whether the attention is being maintained above, below, to the right or to the left.
>
> [ii] In the pure type, maintain the attention upon the Jina's body. In front of you place an image of Lord Amitābha, or if you do not have one, imagine it. Do not let thoughts proliferate away from it or indulge in distractions. While so doing, settle [the mind] while relaxing in simple nondistraction. This is maintaining the attention upon the pure body of the Jina.

– In the practice of focusing on the Buddha's body, place before you a statue or some other representation of the Buddha's body. It may be large or small; it may be any manifestation of the Buddha, such as Śākyamuni, Amitābha, or any other embodiment. Gaze upon this image for awhile.

Then, without looking at it, create a mental image of it. Scan this mental image from top to bottom, examining the details from the top of the head, to the face, and so on to the bottom of the body. Then scan again upwards. There are great benefits in attending to the Buddha's body in this meditative context: by doing so, you store karmic seeds for attaining a Buddha's body yourself.

There are various ways in which you might practice visualizing the Buddha. You could visualize the Buddha stupendously large like a galaxy, or you could imagine it being microscopic in size. You could imagine it being single or multiple. The point of the training is to master this untamed mind, which is rigid and inflexible, so that it can become flexible and pliant, and can be applied to whatever you wish. At the end of the session, whatever the size of the image, you can gradually shrink it down to a single point; then allow that point itself to vanish into nothing. Finally, dwell in that nothingness for awhile.

The real point of all this is to bring about the inner balance and serenity of your mind. That is the crux of the matter. It's important not to get into a great deal of conceptualization as to whether this is a Mahāyāna or Hīnayāna practice, or what sect it might be from—none of this is necessary. Don't be too clever. Just keep it simple and train the mind in this way, knowing that the real point is inner serenity, maintaining quiescence in the mind. If you make it too complicated, you simply create unnecessary obstacles for yourself in the practice of Dharma.

One way to focus on the Buddha's speech in the cultivation of quiescence is to focus on the syllable *Āḥ* or *Hūṃ*. You can imagine the syllable as large or small, as one or many; and you can imagine them dissolving into emptiness. There are various valid approaches. The direct benefits of this practice are that you sow the karmic seeds for your own accomplishment of a Buddha's speech, and you purify unwholesome influences and imprints due to your own nonvirtuous speech in the past. –

> [b] In terms of maintaining the attention inwardly there are two types: [i] impure and [ii] pure.
>
> [i] Maintaining the attention upon an impure *bindu*: Maintain your attention on a white *bindu*, about the size of a pea, emitting rays of light, upon a lotus and moon-disk at your heart. Do not let thoughts proliferate away from it, or indulge in distractions. These are practical instructions on transforming ideation into the path without abandoning it. Quiescence that is of the [nature of the] spiritual path transforms ideation into the path, and attention is maintained by focusing on the ideation of the path. These are the practical instructions.

– Instead of trying to stifle your thoughts, in this practice you transform them into the very path itself. The thought that is being transformed into the path is the visualization of the white *bindu*. –

> [ii] Maintaining the attention on the pure body of the Jina: maintain your attention on Avalokiteśvara upon a lotus and moon-disk at your heart, his body the size of the outer thumb

> joint, and radiant with light. Do not let thoughts disperse away from it, or indulge in distractions. If laxity or excitation arises, for both the impure and pure methods maintain the attention by meditating on the forehead or the navel.
>
> That is quiescence that is dependent upon signs.
>
> [2] Quiescence in which the attention is focused on conceptualization: In relation to the excessive proliferation of conceptualization, including such afflictions as the five poisons or the three poisons, thoughts that revolve in duality, thoughts such as those of the ten virtues, the Six Perfections or the Ten Perfections—whatever virtuous and nonvirtuous thoughts arise—steadily and nonconceptually observe their nature. By so doing, they are calmed in nongrasping; awareness vividly arises clear and empty, with no object of grasping; and it is sustained in the nature of self-liberation, in which it recognizes itself. Again, direct the mind to whatever thoughts arise, and without acceptance or rejection, you will recognize your own nature. Thus implement the practical instructions on transforming ideation into the path.
>
> [3] The ultimate quiescence of maintaining the attention upon nonconceptualization: With the body possessing the seven attributes of Vairocana, sit upon a soft cushion in a solitary, darkened room. Vacantly direct the eyes into the intervening vacuity. See that the three conceptualizations of the past, future, and present, as well as virtuous, nonvirtuous, and ethically neutral thoughts, together with all the causes, assembly, and dispersal of thoughts of the three times are completely cut off. Bring no thoughts to mind. Let the mind, like a cloudless sky, be clear, empty, and evenly devoid of grasping, and settle it in utter vacuity. By so doing you will experience the quiescence of joy, clarity, and nonconceptuality. Examine whether or not attachment, hatred, clinging, grasping, laxity, or excitation enter into that, and recognize the difference between virtues and vices.

Everything is synthesized in that passage.

The nine methods for sustaining attention as taught in the *sūtras* are: [1] placement, [2] certain placement, [3] thorough placement, [4] close placement, [5] subduing, [6] pacifying, [7] fully pacifying, [8] unification of the mind-stream, and [9] meditative equipoise. Here is the meaning: [1] focusing on a single meditative object, [2] maintaining it continually, [3] restraining the attention with mindfulness when it becomes scattered, [4] settling it in that, [5] bearing in mind its virtues, [6] countering scattering when it occurs, [7] recognizing the conditions for scattering, [8] sustaining the attention there without effort, and [9] flowing into that state.

– The nine stages leading to the accomplishment of quiescence are not actual Atiyoga practice. Their style and content are quite different, yet they are not incompatible with Atiyoga, because the practice of quiescence, followed in terms of relative truth, provides a basis for Atiyoga. The practice of Atiyoga is said to be free of conceptual elaboration, and it does not proceed in a step-by-step manner. If you are able to sit right down and engage in genuine Atiyoga practice, that's great! However, it is very helpful to have a foundation for it, and this is the purpose of quiescence; it is not just another way of doing the same thing. Quiescence provides a basis for the practice of Atiyoga, just as relative truth is a basis for ultimate truth.

The first stage is called placement, referring to the placement of the attention. This is accomplished when you can find the object and focus on it single-pointedly, if only for a moment.

The second is called certain placement. This is attained when you can bring a little continuity to your attention.

At the third stage, thorough placement, your mind is still prone to distraction from the object, but you quickly recognize this, and draw it back again. So, although the attention is not completely continuous, lapses are very brief.

By the fourth stage, close placement, you have sustained continuity of attention, so that your mind never completely forgets the object. This continuity can be maintained for a considerable period of time.

The fifth stage is called subduing, referring to subduing the mind. In this stage, you are aware of the benefits of having this degree of stability of mind, and you take delight in it.

In the sixth stage, pacifying, whatever mental imagery or ideation arises, good or bad, virtuous or nonvirtuous, you don't follow after it or respond to it with either attachment or aversion.

In fully pacifying, the seventh stage, you recognize the causes of the occurrence of avarice, attachment, and the like, as well as the causes of aversion, hostility, and the like. As you recognize the causes and sources of these afflictions, they are released automatically. They are naturally liberated.

This is the very nature of ideation: thoughts, mental imagery, and other mental events arise naturally, and naturally pass away, like waves on the ocean. Like clouds forming in the sky, they naturally arise, come into formation, and naturally disperse, just as a snake looped into a knot unravels itself. All these mental events naturally arise and naturally vanish. There is no one who creates them, no one who invites them in the first place, nor anyone who destroys them or banishes them. Having come without invitation or creation, they vanish of their own accord.

Even if all the thousand Buddhas of this fortunate eon worked together, they would not be able to create a thought for you, or destroy your thoughts. Likewise, all the sentient beings of the three realms working together would be unable to create or destroy your thoughts. It is simply in the nature of these mental processes that they naturally arise, and they naturally disappear.

Does this mean that there is no hope of finding any degree of mental stability? No, it is not hopeless, but it is necessary to shift to another level, beyond hope and hopelessness. The problem in attaining stability of mind is not in the nature of the mental events, which are naturally arising and vanishing, but in grasping onto these thoughts. This is true throughout the entire path. Within all the paths in Buddhism, from Atiyoga, the very apex of the teachings, to the Hīnayāna, the most basic, the fundamental problem is mental grasping.

In the Hīnayāna practices, you seek to realize personal identitylessness. Grasping obstructs that realization. Grasping occurs when you think, "This is this," and mentally latch onto it and reify it. This process of conceptual grasping obstructs realization, be it the Hīnayāna realization of personal identitylessness, or the supreme Atiyoga realization of the single essence that is the unity of *saṃsāra* and *nirvāṇa*. At all levels, the culprit that obstructs realization is grasping.

The eighth stage is unification of the mind-stream. At this stage, having become thoroughly familiar with this meditative process, the mind effortlessly engages with its object. You simply direct the mind to its object and, with no effort or difficulty, it engages with that object single-pointedly.

By contrast, the untrained mind is like a softball thrown against a wall: we bring the mind to the object and it bounces right off in a different direction. This instability of the mind is reduced in the earlier stages of this meditative process; those are difficult to attain because you need to train the mind to develop new habits. However, the result of gradually training the mind in this way is that at the eighth stage effortless mental engagement takes place. Wherever you wish to focus your attention, whether on the crown of the Buddha's head or the entire body of the Buddha, you can do so single-pointedly and effortlessly.

The ninth and final stage is called meditative equipoise. When you attain this, your mind becomes stable and unwavering at all times, both during and between sessions. –

Once the scattering of ideation is calmed, sustaining the attention single-pointedly wherever it is directed is quiescence. This is common to non-Buddhists, Bönpos, Śrāvakas, Vaibhāṣikas, and Sautrāntikas. By the power of stopping ideation, and familiarizing oneself with that, one remains in a state of brilliant clarity without scattering. Quiescence must occur first, but quiescence is not the point of Mahāmudrā and Atiyoga, for this is common to the view of the Chinese Hvashang, the four meditative stabilizations of non-Buddhist traditions, and the cessation of Śrāvakas. Why is it not Mahāmudrā or Atiyoga? Because it is not a [conceptually] unstructured state, but a structured one; and because there is grasping in which one reflects, "attention is being sustained." *The Great Tantra of Sampuṭa* states:

> Ideation is the great ignorance that casts one into the ocean of cyclic existence. Abiding in nonconceptual *samādhi*, there is stainless clarity like space.

The Tantra of the Garland of Vajras states:

> In the extinction of all conceptualization, great bliss perfectly arises.

There are two avenues to this, and in this context quiescence is sustaining the attention in brilliant clarity once ideation has been calmed. *The Jewel Ornament of Liberation* states:

> Quiescence is dwelling in perfect *samādhi*, with the attention fixed upon itself, remaining in its own state, and sustained in serene, still balance.

Those are the complete ordinary meditative objects of quiescence. Since the great vase meditation[28] is not included with the ordinary ones, it is not explained here.

The King of Samādhi Sūtra says that there are incalculable benefits in maintaining the attention upon the body of the Buddha. Similarly, *The Sūtra of the Samādhi Which is Established in the Presence of the Contemporary Buddha* says there are incalculable benefits in imagining the body of Amitābha in front of you. As there is a strong connection with this teaching, imagine the Buddha Amitābha in front of you, and focus your awareness single-pointedly on his form. Do your best to sustain your attention there without wavering. If you do not apprehend that meditative object, at the sphere of your heart focus your awareness on a radiant white *bindu*, about the size of a pea, and sustain it there as well as you can. If your attention does not remain there, rest your attention in a relaxed state without bringing any thoughts to mind. Sever the dispersion of ideation of the three times, and drawing the attention in upon itself, rest it in relaxation without conceptual proliferation.

– The Buddha Amitābha is often depicted above the crown of Avalokiteśvara, because he is the Lord of the Padma Buddha Family, of which Avalokiteśvara is a member. Alternatively, instead of focusing the attention outward, direct it towards itself. Allow your awareness to rest in its own nature. –

Not thinking about events of the past is the *emptiness* door of liberation. Resting without reaching out in advance to the future is *nonanticipation*. Relaxing without grasping at whatever appears in the present is *signlessness*. This accomplishes the quiescence of the three doors of liberation. The *Bhadrakarātri Sūtra* states:

> Ānanda, one who does not follow after the past, does not cherish hopes for the future, and does not conceptualize about the present is said to dwell in the collection of the *Bhadrakarātrisūtra*.

The Primary Words states:

> Look at your own mind.

The Primary Words of the Great Instructions states:

> The critical factor for the body is to possess the flawless seven attributes[29] for meditative stabilization. The critical factor for the mind is to sever the conceptual proliferations of the three times. Whatever appears, do not get distracted, but rest in effortlessness.

Accordingly, do your best to let the mind remain in its own nature. By so doing, the three stages of inferior, middling, and superior sustained attention will arise. This completes the chapter on quiescence.

– The three degrees of inferior, middling, and superior sustained attention arise as you progress through the stages of practice.

The foregoing discussion covers simple quiescence practice not combined with anything else. The point of this is to maintain attentional stability, without scattering or wavering. Likewise, try to maintain the best posture possible. As a result of this practice, the compulsive ideation that continually stirs up the mind will gradually subside. For example, when water that has been stirred up with silt is let stand, it becomes clear as the silt gradually settles down. Similarly, when ideation is gradually subdued, a limpidity of awareness arises, and this is quiescence.

In this practice you may make the mistake of withdrawing your mind so much that you enter into a stupor in which you don't hear any external sounds, and instead feel as though you are asleep. This is not the proper state of quiescence, but an obscured state of mind. The mind has indeed been calmed, but it has been drawn too much inside, without clarity. This is not genuine quiescence.

If you persist in this incorrect state of meditation for a long time, the result will be rebirth as an animal. There are a number of accounts of Lamas taking just such a rebirth as a result of their efforts in meditation. So if such a state of nonconceptual stupor should arise, it is not a hopeless situation, but you should not be attached to it. Instead, you must arouse yourself.

As long as you are alive, conceptualization will continue to arise, and the correct response to that is nongrasping: whatever thoughts arise, virtuous or nonvirtuous, look at them and recognize their nature, but don't grasp onto them. Recognize that they are incapable of either harming or benefiting you. Just observe them arise and pass away, naturally. –

CHAPTER FOUR

The Cultivation of Insight

Homage to Avalokiteśvara!

These are the profound practical instructions of Avalokiteśvara, the method for escaping from the cycle of existence and reaching the path of the Āryas. Develop the wisdom of insight!

Due to what fault do we wander around in the cycle of existence? It is the fault of apprehending that which is without a self as being a self.

– Even before asking that question, we must first recognize the nature of *saṃsāra* and carefully evaluate its qualities. Then we must determine if this cycle of existence is somebody else's problem or our own. Although there is a great temptation to focus on other people's problems, they are not our concern. Instead we must recognize that we are samsaric beings. The reason for this is that we have failed to fathom the depth and breadth of the truth of suffering, the first Noble Truth. Furthermore, we have also failed to penetrate the second Noble Truth, which is the cause of the suffering that manifests in our lives. All sentient beings desire happiness and wish to be free of suffering, and yet by and large, we're not very successful because we fail to recognize the sources of the happiness we desire and of the suffering we wish to avoid. Do we suffer due to other people's malice? Are we being punished by other people? Is some external agent the root cause of our suffering? On the contrary, we sow the seeds of our own grief by grasping onto our own personal identity. Specifically, due to our own delusion, we fail to recognize what behavior is beneficial and what is detrimental.

Moreover, by the force of our attachment, we continue to sow the causes for perpetuating our own cyclic existence. All Buddhists, not only those engaging in the practices of quiescence and insight, must recognize the Four Noble Truths: the truth of suffering, its source, the nature of liberation, and the path to liberation.

Meditations on the Four Thoughts that Turn the Mind, which were taught by Padmasambhava, invert our attitudes by turning our minds away from the causes of suffering and directing us towards Dharma. With such a shift in attitude, we engage in the practices of quiescence and insight. We must bear in mind that since we are the ones experiencing suffering and happiness, it is for us to fulfill our aspirations by engaging in the discursive meditations on the Four Noble Truths and the Four Thoughts that Turn the Mind.

We wander in cyclic existence because we confuse that which is without a personal identity for that which has a personal identity. Similarly, we grasp onto phenomena other than self as having true inherent existence whereas, in fact, there is none. –

The Sūtra of the Questions of Guṇaratnasaṅkusumita states:

> Those with minds attached to the cycle of existence revolve forever. They are not empty of the two real phenomena of "I" and "mine," and these childish people themselves tie knots in the sky. This is like taking poison with the sense that you need it, and fainting even though the poison does not enter inside you. Childish people take on actions as "I" and "mine." Their attitude towards the self is to see it as real, impermanent, as being born and dying. Mental fabrications appear in accordance with grasping. It is taught: act without the objectification of "I" and "mine."

– In fact, there are no real phenomena of "I" and "mine," and those who continue to revolve in *saṃsāra* have not realized this. We construct ourselves as if we were truly existent, and we fabricate a tangible, truly existent environment around us. We engage in activities with the sense that there is an "I" doing the actions and there is truly a "mine" in the things that we possess. To act without objectifying the "I" and "mine" is simply to act in accord with reality.

Similarly, during the dream state we appear to have a personal identity and to interact with other people. The environment seems to be filled with real phenomena. The same seems to be true during waking experience. Although we and our environment seem to be real while we are dreaming, when we wake up, we recognize that it was simply a dream. So on what grounds can we uncritically assume that was just a dream, whereas in this waking state we *do* exist as some real entity and we *are* surrounded by other real phenomena? If we investigate carefully, we may find that our daily life is, in fact, no more tangible than a dream. –

A Commentary on Verifying Cognition states:

> For one who objectifies the self there will be always be the obsession of "I." Due to this obsession, there is craving for joy; due to craving, one is obscured with faults. Due to seeing excellent qualities, there is more craving, and this is taken as proof of "I." Therefore, as long as there is the obsession with the self, one will revolve in the cycle of existence.

And:

> When there is the self, there is the discernment of others. Grasping and hatred occur towards the factions of self and other, and in relation to those all mental afflictions occur.

– The moment that there is grasping onto one's own personal identity, "I am," there is a discernment of others, which creates the division of self and others. By grasping onto our own side and having aversion towards others, anyone can appear as an adversary. –

The King of Samādhi Sūtra states:

> Due to the concept of the self, mental distraction arises, and it blazes like a wheel of weapons. Following after objects defeats the mind, and this causes the ripening of unbearable suffering.

The Perfection of Wisdom Sūtra in One Hundred Thousand Stanzas states:

> Form is empty of "I" and "mine."

And:

> And due to grasping onto "I" and onto "mine," sentient beings revolve in the cycle of existence.

A Guide to the Bodhisattva Way of Life states:

> If all the harm, fear, and suffering in the world occur due to grasping onto the self, what use is that great demon to me?
>
> Without forsaking one's own self, one cannot avoid suffering, just as one cannot stop being burned without avoiding fire.[30]

The root of "I" and "mine" must be cut, and since the root of "I" and "mine" arises from the aggregate of form, you must examine in this aggregate where the "I" and self exist and how the "I" and self exist. Nāgārjuna says:

> As long as there is grasping onto the aggregates, together with that there is grasping onto the "I." If there is grasping onto the "I," there is also *karma*, and due to that there is birth.

The Sūtra of Basket Weaving states:

> Those who are attached to ideation concerning form and so on always regard the self as a static entity. The continuum of their births does not end, and they descend drastically to the miserable destinations.

It is more important to subdue your own mind than it is to subdue elephants, wild horses, and wild mules, and it is better to conquer self-grasping than to conquer an army of a hundred thousand soldiers. *The Set of Aphorisms* states:

> It is better to subdue yourself than to subdue the mightiest of elephants, the superb horses of Sindhu, and young mules. You who well subdue yourselves cut your fetters and are liberated, whereas with those mounts it is impossible to achieve that state.[31]
>
> You who engage in the discipline should subdue only yourselves as you would a fine horse. By well subduing yourself you go beyond suffering.[32]
>
> You alone are your master. You are your own refuge, so subdue yourself.[33]
>
> Upon one seat and with one teacher of the path, live alone without lassitude. Dwelling alone in the forest, subdue yourself in solitude.[34]
>
> Those who gain victory over themselves are more victorious in the battle of men than those who conquer a host of thousands.[35]

– When you subdue yourself by realizing the absence of a personal identity and the absence of an inherent identity of other phenomena, your own mind becomes subdued and liberated from suffering and its sources. You are your own master, your own source of refuge, in the sense that you receive the teachings and put them into practice. By taking on the responsibility for your own liberation through your own practice you will gain liberation, not by expecting someone else to do it for you.

The true victory is subduing yourself. Then you are truly a warrior. As a result of engaging in genuine Dharma practice, your mental afflictions, such as anger and jealousy, will decline, which allows serenity and equanimity to manifest in your outer behavior. –

Now you must examine whether the "I" and self are the body or the mind: My name is given adventitiously. If my name is changed, do I change? If I am given a good name, do I become good, and if I am given a bad name, does this make me bad?

Well, is this body "I" and the self? Dissect this form into its components, and look for the self among the individual parts of the body from the head to the feet. Also look for it carefully among each of the areas inside the body. Moreover, come to a firm conviction as to where it might exist among the external elements of earth, water, fire, and air.

– We tenaciously hold onto our sense of personal identity, which brings about various obstacles to Dharma practice in general and to the accomplishment of quiescence in particular. Therefore, well investigate the nature of the self. Do you exist, and if you do, how do you exist? Begin by scrutinizing your physical form from the top of your head to the soles of your feet to ascertain where you might be found among any of the individual parts of your body or in its totality. Additionally, examine how you might exist in relation to the elements of solidity, fluidity, heat, and motility. –

A Guide to the Bodhisattva Way of Life states:

> First, with your own intellect peel off this sheath of skin and with the knife of wisdom extract the flesh from the skeleton.
>
> Having severed the bones, look inside at the marrow and examine for yourself, "Where is the essence here?"[36]

Stanzas on the Madhyamaka Root of Wisdom states:

> If the aggregates were the self, it would be subject to creation and destruction. If it were other than the aggregates, it would lack the characteristics of the aggregates.

– If the aggregates of the mind and body were the self, the self would be just like the aggregates. If the self were other than the body and mind, it would lack their characteristics. Therefore, true statements describing the body and mind would not pertain to the self because it would be totally separate from them. Neither of those alternatives stands up to analysis. –

As this is explained at great length, there is no self in this body; for, by dissecting the body into its components, nowhere is there even a trace of an essence that is called "I" or "self."

Well then, since "I" and the self must be the mind, seek out the mind. *The Great Tantra of Sampuṭa* states:

> You who wish to be freed from the bondage of types of suffering, and who desire the joy of perfect Buddhahood, carefully and diligently investigate whether the mind does or does not have a self-nature.

The Tantra of the Full Enlightenment of Vairocana states:

> The Bodhisattva Vajrapāṇi asked of the Lord Vairocana, "Lord, where does one seek enlightenment and omniscience? Whose enlightenment is it?"
>
> The Lord replied, "Master of Secrets, omniscience and enlightenment are to be sought in your own mind."

The Sūtra of the Cloud of Jewels states:

> The mind precedes all phenomena, and if the mind is comprehended, all phenomena will be comprehended.

The Sūtra of Instructions on the Indivisibility of the Absolute Nature of Reality states:

> Precisely examine whether this mind is blue, or yellow, or red, or white, or vermilion, or like the color of crystal, whether it is real or unreal, permanent or impermanent, and whether or not it has form.

The Sūtra of the Questions of Kāśyapa states:

> Thus seek out the mind: What is the mind that becomes lustful or angry or deluded? Is it something that arises in the past or the future or the present?

And it continues in a lengthy discussion. *The Sūtra of Thirty-Three Questions* states:

> All the three worlds come into being from the mind. The mind never reveals itself. It is without form, ethically neutral, and like an apparition. The wise seek the nature of the mind. Whoever seeks out the mind does not see the nature of the mind.

– The "three worlds" may refer either to the desire, form, and formless realms or to the realms below, upon, and above the earth's surface. If the mind were existent, the Buddhas must have seen it; but since they have not, it cannot be posited as existent. Conversely, you can't say that the mind is nonexistent, because it is the basis for both *saṃsāra* and *nirvāṇa*. By seeking out the nature of the mind, you discover wisdom. –

The Tantra of the Blazing Clear Expanse of the Great Perfection states:

> In order to analyze the mind into its components, focus on this idea alone: awareness without conceptual elaboration is the Dharmakāya. In this there is no arising, remaining, or going. Whence did this fluttering, churning, shifting, fleeting phenomenon called the mind initially arise, where is it located in the

> meantime, and where does it go in the end? What are its shape and color? See if you can break it down in terms of its being external, internal, or in between.

– Awareness free of conceptual elaboration or modification is the Dharmakāya. Analyzing the mind into its components and scrutinizing its mode of existence addresses the issue of whether the mind even exists. If you accept the hypothesis that it does indeed exist, then probe further to determine its origins, its location, and the manner of its departure. Continue to ask: Does the mind have a form? Does it have a shape or color? Is it hot or cold? Answer these questions in terms of your own introspective experience. –

The Primary Tantra on the Penetration of Sound states:

> Investigate with certainty the initial origin of the mind, its subsequent location, and its final departure. Such mental training is of benefit to the mind.

The meaning of this is stated in *The Pith Instructions on the Clear Expanse*:

> The initial investigation of the origin, location, and departure is as follows: Engage in discursive meditation and stabilizing meditation on each point. And regarding the initial arising of the mind, perform discursive meditation on externally appearing objects: the external environment, its inhabitants, earth, stone, rocky precipices, grass, trees, forests, mountains, and hills. In short, whence did it arise? How did it arise? What was the manner of its origination? Investigate this with your intelligence, analyze it well, and meditate.

– By engaging in discursive meditation involving conceptual elaboration, you come to some insight. Then, engage in stabilizing meditation in which you simply rest your awareness in the insight gleaned from your analysis. Don't stop with discursive meditation, but as soon as a certainty arises, stabilize your mind in that so it saturates your mind. Otherwise the investigation by itself is pointless. –

> Then investigate well where it arises and how it is present throughout your own body, in the upper and lower areas, in the limbs, the vital organs, the heart, and in the outer and inner regions. Then practice stabilizing meditation, examining well the mind in your own being.
>
> Investigate well your own nature, asking, "This so-called *mind*, which recalls so many things and knows so much, whence did you arise? What are your characteristics?" Similarly, investigate

> its location and all the places its goes. In particular, for articulate people and beginners this is to be investigated meticulously.

– First we must hear the teachings, and then we must apply what we have heard in meditation. It is not enough to say complacently, "Oh, I've heard that before." We must investigate for ourselves and actually penetrate the subject matter by means of our own experience. As we acquaint ourselves with insight through stabilizing meditation, we may come to the point at which we know with utter certainty whether the mind has color or shape. It then can be said that we have gained confidence in the training. Until then we are still on the way. –

> Furthermore, examine the reason why the mind-itself, this Dharmakāya, this authentic reality, wanders around and is deluded in the six types of sentient existence. What is its nature, its color, its shape, or its characteristics? And how did this dynamic conceptualization occur? Whence did it arise? Does it or does it not exist as a real entity? If it does, how did it come into being? If it does not—if it is emptiness—how is that so...?
>
> Then again, once it has come into being, what are its characteristics, its form, color, and so on? If it is empty, how is it empty? Is it empty like space? Examine well how it could be empty.
>
> Then again, are the mind and thoughts the same or different? If they are the same, how do appearances and emptiness, stability and movement become distinct? When do they become distinct, and where do you draw the demarcation between them? Whence arises the root of delusion? Who created the duality of self and others? Examine those issues well. In that way investigate until you have a clean, decisive question.

– To use an analogy, miners, who by great effort sift through the earth to uncover and separate gold, do not make the gold or transform something impure into gold. They simply recognize that which was pure from the beginning as pure. It is through great efforts of refinement and examination that they are able to recognize that which was primordially pure. Similarly, the nature of the mind is primordially real, but it is necessary to engage in this method of analysis to gain realization of the actual nature of awareness. If expending effort to mine gold is worthwhile, then it should be all the more worthwhile to exert great effort in the analysis to recognize the nature of awareness itself. –

The Dharma master Rangjung Dorje says:

> In general, there is no set time when death occurs, so do not think about a lot of things. Look to one decisive instruction.

And:

> If great joy is not realized in the mind, there is no point in words being spoken in the mouth. If there is no critical certainty in the mind, there is no point in being skilled in words and conventions. If you do not see with contemplative perception, there is no point in meditating with inference.

And:

> Observe and examine your own mind and awareness, for it is the crucial root of everything.

Geshe Jayülpa says:

> If the fire in the stove is extinguished, the smoke seeping out the cracks in the walls naturally disappears. Cut off conceptual elaboration from within.

Gyalwang Je says:

> Unlike the discursive meditation of *paṇḍits*, this is contemplative, introspective, discursive meditation. Cut off conceptual superimpositions from within.

– The discursive meditations of *paṇḍits* are broad-ranging and they are not the contemplative, introspective, discursive meditation taught in this text. *Paṇḍits'* meditations require years of studying Madhyamaka, Prajñāpāramitā, epistemology, and logic. That is not bad, but due to the uncertain duration of our lives, we may not wish to spend our lives in that way. If one follows that scholarly training over the course of years without subduing one's own mind, that learning may simply give rise to greater pride. And, as self-importance arises, the door to liberation closes. –

The venerable Kachö Wangpo says:

> O fortunate ones, place your present mind vividly in single-pointedness. Observe the nature of that which is placed: how does it exist? If you think it does not exist at all, who is it that apprehends its absence? Is that a realization of your own mind or not? And if you think, "When I look for it, it does not appear," observe that thinker, and also observe that observer. Moreover, as in the case of a treasure hidden underground, something is not nonexistent simply because it is not seen. So carefully examine: What is the color of this mind? What is its shape? What is its nature? Is it existent or nonexistent? Is it something that is both or something that is neither? Is it male, female, or neuter?
>
> If you do not recognize it when it is still, intentionally make it move, and accurately observe the nature of that very movement.

> If you do not see the mode of existence of just that mind, once again observe the basis of the mind. Does it internally arise in the body, or does it arise from other external phenomena? Within the body, from where does it arise—the upper, lower, or middle region, its exterior or interior? Specifically, does it arise solely from the channels, or from the vital energies or essential fluids? Look well! Does it arise from the external earth, water, fire, or air? Carefully observe whether the mind arises from the physical environment that comes into being from those great elements, or from men and women, or from animate and inanimate objects.
>
> Likewise, truly seek out the basis of its sustenance and cessation, looking for this again and again. What is this so-called "repeated arising" of the mind? From what does it arise? What arises? Into what does it arise? Likewise, decisively seek out how it is sustained and ceases.

Orgyen Rinpoche says:

> Steadily place your mind in the space in front of you, and let it be present there. Look well to see what kind of a thing of yours is this that is being placed today. Look to see if the one who is placing and the mind that is being placed are one or two. If they were two, there would have to be two minds, so one must be in Buddhahood, while the other roams about in the cycle of existence. So carefully, decisively observe whether they exist as two. If there is not more than one, is that one the mind? Observe: what is the reality of the so-called "mind?" It is impossible to find it by searching among external objects.[37]

– Place your mind vividly and quietly in the space in front of you. Investigate what is doing the placing, where it is being placed, and what is being placed. Observe that which places the mind, which has directed the mind to the space in front of you. The nature of the mind is to be investigated in this phase of the practice. It is impossible to find the mind by searching for it in the external elements of earth, water, fire, and air, so we must examine the mind in its own mode of existence.

When the mind is involved in a myriad of activities, it churns out thoughts, plans, memories, feelings, and so forth. But when we turn the attention to the agent who seems to be performing these actions, the nature of the mind itself, it is difficult to say what it is. It neither disappears nor does not disappear, because it is primordially unestablished in reality. –

> Let the one who is pondering what the mind is like observe that very consciousness, and search for it. Steadily observe the consciousness of the meditator, and search for it. Observe: in reality is the so-called *mind* something that exists [tangibly]? If it

> does, it should have a shape. What sort of a shape does it have? Look nakedly and seek it out. Decisively look to see what sort of a shape it has, whether it is a sphere, a rectangle, a semi-circle, or a triangle, and so on. If you say it has one at all, show me that shape! If you say there is nothing to show, tell me whether it is possible for there to be a real shape that cannot be shown. Identify the emptiness of shape.
>
> Likewise, see whether it has any color, size, or dimension. If you say it has none of those, then observe whether it is an emptiness that is nothing. If you say it is an emptiness that is nothing, then how could an emptiness that is nothing know how to meditate? What good is it to say you cannot find it? If it is nothing at all, what is it that brings forth hatred? Is there not someone who thinks the mind has not been found? Look steadily right at that. If you do not discover what it is like, carefully check whether the consciousness that wonders where it is is itself the mind. If it is, what is it like? If it exists, there must be a substance and a color, but are they forthcoming? If it were not to exist, you would be like an unconscious corpse; but isn't there someone who thinks? Thus, within the parameters of existence and nonexistence, decisively observe how it is.[38]

– We who are engaged in the practice must observe our own awareness with precision. If it is a real tangible object, it must have shape, color, and a discernible location. It is inconsistent to assert that the mind is tangible but has no form. Investigate its tangible qualities, and if you think none exist, you may conclude that you cannot find it. But what is it that engages in this mental activity of inquiry? Investigate by circling around and around, seeking out the mind, and determine if it can be found anywhere. Do not simply draw a quick conclusion, but carefully analyze whether the mind is existent or nonexistent, and determine the boundary between these two states. This is a clear route for gaining realization of the essence of the Dharma. –

Pointing Out the Dharmakāya states:

> This is the view of the body and mind being the same or different: are they the same or different? If they were the same, the body, which is subject to birth and destruction, and the mind, which is without birth and destruction, would be identical.
>
> Not only that, the body, which is matter, and the mind, which is consciousness, are two, not one. If they were one, when the body dies, the mind would also die. If the body were pricked with a thorn, the mind would also be pricked. If they were different, would the body or the mind feel the body being pricked

with a thorn? If the body alone were to feel it, a corpse would also feel it. Assuming the mind feels it, since the body and mind are different, when the mind feels the body being pricked, pain should arise in the mind even when soil and rocks are harmed. But this does not happen. So look carefully. Know that all events and feelings are like ripples in the water, and observe them.

– In the dream state we have a wide variety of experiences. We may experience being tortured or subjected to other types of physical pain. But during a nightmare or a pleasant dream, we still have a body and a mind. For example, in a dream, if you are pricked with a thorn, is it your body or your mind that actually experiences being pricked? Investigate carefully what experiences this, and then, with that recognition come back to your physical body and understand its relationship to the body in the dream. Then examine whether the implement that injured you in your dream is created out of matter. Likewise examine the nature of the person who harms or benefits you in the dream. Are the subject and the object the same entity? Are they different phenomena or are they neither the same nor different? It is unacceptable to think that they don't exist at all. Why is that unacceptable? Because there *is* the experience of being harmed, so it's not possible to say that it doesn't happen.

During the waking state and the dream state, investigate whether your body and mind exist and how they exist. Can you say decisively that your body doesn't exist and justify that position? It is not just a question of the existence or nonexistence of the character of the mind. Again follow the parallel modes of experience: the dream and waking state. What is the relationship between the body and the mind? What is the relationship in the dream state? Try to gain some insight. Ask this question in terms of the waking state, then go back to the dream state. Follow these two modes of analysis in conjunction with each other. This will lead to insight for other modes of experience, specifically in the intermediate state. If in the future you go to a Buddha realm, what will be the nature of your body and mind there? Or if you go to a hell realm, the same question can be asked. In all cases determine the nature of your own body and mind. Have you or have you not recognized the nature of your own mind?

If the body and mind are truly separate, and if the body alone feels a thorn prick, a corpse should also feel it. In Tibetan society, corpses are cut into pieces and given to the vultures. If the corpse still has sensation, this would be a very unpleasant experience. Similarly, in the West it is common to bury or cremate corpses. If a corpse still feels, these experiences would be catastrophic. This is true not only for humans. Every day millions of animals are killed for their meat. We are eating their corpses. So if these corpses have feelings, it would be all the more grotesque.

If the mind existed independently from the body, would it feel the body being pricked? If so, why wouldn't it feel the earth when it is stepped on? If you kill someone, the mind doesn't die, so is there nothing wrong with killing or injuring only someone's body? –

The teachings of Drungchen Kün-ga Namgyal state:

> When you investigate a little into the nature of the mind while it is meditating with a suitable degree of firmness, relaxation, and so on, ascertain: What is the nature of the mind as it is present? Does it have color, form, and shape, or not? Where do those scattered, instantaneously arising thoughts come from? Where are they located? How do they finally depart? When the thoughts disappear, do they proceed into nonexistence? Or do they depart just as they were present? Or do they depart as a vacuity? Ascertain just how they disappear.
>
> Ascertain how the appearing forms of mental imprints arise, such as the forms of people, horses, and cattle. How do they remain? And recognize the manner in which they finally depart, and so on.
>
> While the mind is stable, ascertain whether there is just that stillness, joy, and peaceful presence. Is there a clarity, freshness, and unimpededness, or not? What kind of a vacuity is this?
>
> In your own experience, is there a difference between the nature of relaxation and that of investigation? Ascertain these points, and report to me!
>
> Secondly, this is severing the primary root: Examine whether all those specific phenomena are the same or different, and afterwards also chiefly look for the observer. Speak to me in private about whatever you have to say about the degree of precision in your investigation of these things, and also describe all the different pleasant and unpleasant aspects of your practice, the obstacles and breakthroughs, the uncomfortable doubts and skepticism in your mind that come solely from the practice, as well as the events in the earlier and later parts of the training, and so on.
>
> The purpose of having a spiritual mentor who knows the path to liberation is to have someone who knows how to remove the obstacles on the path and remove the veils of ignorance. There are those who fail to speak to their mentor even though they have many things to ask. Due to both the conceit of having fine realizations or a sense of hopelessness, some conceal what is happening, thinking, "There's little reason to speak, for you don't tell the mentor about such things." Due to the mind being carried away as if by a hallucination, some think, "There is nothing even the spiritual mentor can do to help me in such things." Others think, "I must present an amazing report of realizations, not these specific questions that I have." All such attitudes are utterly useless.

Get answers to the questions you put to your mentor; then after coming outside, it is you, the student, who maintains the training at the level of your own present practice. So keep that firmly in mind, and get ready to report.

Moreover, it is said, "If realization does not arise, you may be closed in with dishonesty, you may conceal your previous dishonest, harmful speech, and the meditator burns with self-importance and degradation of others." Thus, some people take quotes from the *sūtras* and *tantras* and from the songs of experience of earlier masters and the like, and substitute these instead of reporting their own realizations. Some mimic the reports of others who have done well. Others tell accounts of the fine events that occurred when they were meditating at some earlier time, even though they lack any experience now. Still others arrogantly want to impress some ordinary spiritual mentor, and say they have already reported their realizations to some other mentor. Having no answers to the mentor's questions from the time they were in their mother's womb—when there were no questions—they trick the jewel of the spiritual mentor with many truths and lies. There is not even the slightest point in accumulating problems for yourself in these ways.

If the people who have encountered realizations get to the point where there is no owner of that which arises in meditation, they have gained access to the path of liberation, so they can rejoice. If you make fine speeches about your experiences even though you have no realization, later on there will be those who want to disparage you on the basis of your view, meditation, and behavior. Then you will have to worry about others' opinions as they judge you by the standards of other meditators' words and deeds. So think about that. As long as you bear that in mind, you should report your realizations; so without fail, gradually come to me.

After awhile, some people think, "I'll take it easy since I've reported my realizations," and, like untying something that was wrapped up, they do whatever they like and leave their retreat. Do not do such things, but just as you found benefit yesterday morning, maintain strong enthusiasm without distraction. Whatever mental experiences and realizations you have, you must gradually apply the introductory teachings, the follow-up instructions, and the personal advice for your practice. So diligence is important. Unlike before, when you were letting time slip by, maintain firm, undistracted mindfulness, and each day will bring great progress. So meditate like that!

– By investigating your own identity, you determine whether or not the mind exists, how it arises, where it is located, and how it departs. The point is to gain genuine depth in your realization of personal identitylessness. A sign of such a realization is that fear does not arise even if someone throws a bomb directly at you. When you have reached that degree of realization, it is said that you have gained confidence.

After you have realized personal identitylessness, cultivate further insight by investigating the identity of phenomena. We have names for everything. For example, within the body we have something we call a "head." When we touch our head we come into contact with what we call "hair." It's not called a head, so the hair can't be called the "head." When we press harder we feel the skin, but it has its own name, "skin," and not "head." If we were to penetrate more deeply, we would come to what is called "brain." But it is still not the "head." Search throughout the entire body for what we call "body." You find components, but not the body. There is no way to point to something and say, "This is really it." Nothing stands up to such analysis, and realizing this leads to insight into phenomenal identitylessness.

There is no intrinsic identity or nature to other phenomena, let alone the self. This is the basis for Mahāmudrā and Atiyoga. This view is indispensable, and if we fail to cultivate it, we will have no success. There is one root to all of our experience, both in the fortunate and miserable states of existence, and that is the mind. Therefore, it is most important to seek out the nature of this one root. –

Drung Gampopa says:

> Mere intellectual understanding of all virtues is not of benefit. Just dabbling in various meditations and making fine speeches is empty. That accomplishes nothing, and it is nothing. That is nothing but the truth. Why do those people not ask questions? Now whatever is asked, you want to report, "The mind is like this," so come to this certainty. Nothing worthwhile comes from an inability to come to any conclusion whatsoever.[39] Therefore, since it is unsuitable not to want even a word of Dharma, only words of foolishness, I want you to say, "As a result of meditating in such a way, this is it. It is like this, and this happened." Meditate diligently. Do not ask your neighbors or relatives about their realizations. If you do not maintain introspection and your meditation progresses anyway, I would conclude that the counsel of the Kagyü elders is untrue. You think about this, too.

Between sessions, come to the certainty of great conviction about these points, then settle your mind again in meditative equipoise. Continually engage in seeking, investigation, and analysis, and do not drift off into daydreams. The great master Maitrīpa says:

> All great, all-encompassing realities are primordial, and their nature is not fabricated. If you do not seek, but settle your mind in the inconceivable absolute nature of reality, that is meditation. Meditating while seeking entails a deluded state of mind.

– Through analytical meditation, you come to a point of clarity and decisive insight, and at this point it is beneficial to abide in that revelation. Your insight will grow gradually like a sprout. Simply be present and settle your mind in the absolute nature of reality. Remain in a state of meditative equipoise, and do not think of this as a waste of your time. If you think you should rather be actively engaged in such practices as circumambulations or the stage of generation, it is the time for you to be simply present in meditative equipoise. But do not just sit and space out. –

In some scholarly discursive meditations in the *sūtra* tradition, one continually seeks out the mind, and there is a tradition in which investigation is needed. Here, in the tradition of Mahāmudrā and Atiyoga, it is enough to seek and investigate during this phase of Dharma practice, but afterwards it is not necessary to continue the search. In the Katok[40] tradition, the investigation of the mind is said to takes months, for one examines for three days each of the points of the mind's color and shape as well as the exterior and the interior of the body. Our tradition does not take so long, so until tomorrow's phase of practice, it is important for you to seek out the mind without even a moment's distraction.

– Westerners often comment that they wish they could study in a situation like the one we once had in Tibet. But here in the West we have freedom of speech and freedom to lead our lives as we wish. We are free to turn the television off and free not to answer the telephone. If we lack the simplicity of traditional Tibet, it's only because we have chosen not to have that simplicity. We are free to do as we like, and there are no excuses. –

Geshés[41] dwell in monastic colleges for many years and study both Madhyamaka and the Prajñāpāramitā. They memorize many volumes, and, devoting their lives to explanations and discussions, they cut through conceptual elaboration from the outside. That way is difficult to learn, difficult to understand, difficult to know, and difficult to realize; among those who study and acquire knowledge in that way, there are many who fail to realize the meaning. The entire meaning of all that education is included in this examination of the mind. This cuts through conceptual elaboration from within, so it is easy to learn, easy to understand, easy to know, and easy to realize. Cutting through conceptual elaboration from the outside is like wanting dried pine wood, and drying it by cutting off the pine needles and branches one by one. So that is difficult. In contrast, cutting through conceptual elaboration from within is easy, for it is like cutting the root of the pine tree so that the branches dry up naturally. Tilopa says:

> For example, if you cut the root of a tree having a trunk, branches and leaves, its many thousands of leaves dry up. Similarly, by cutting the root of the mind, the leaves of the cycle of existence dry up.

– The root of *saṃsāra* is the mind. It is not enough simply to be introduced to the nature of your own mind; rather you must maintain that insight by engaging in the practice. If you fail to deepen through practice, the initial insight will vanish; whereas if you practice, deeper and deeper insights will open up naturally as you proceed. –

Therefore, since the examination of the mind is crucially important, until tomorrow examine it without distraction or sleep. Tomorrow morning you should report to your mentor. If you do not come to certainty here, later, more advanced teachings will have little impact. If you do not find it, tell how you did not find it. Your realizing or not realizing the nature of the mind depends on this. You who have received these instructions should also seek out [the mind]. The Druk tradition says that after you have realized great single-pointedness, by seeking the mind again, you realize freedom from conceptual elaboration.

CHAPTER FIVE

Identification

Homage to Avalokiteśvara!

These are the profound practical instructions of Avalokiteśvara, identifying your own mind-itself as Mahāmudrā, as Atiyoga, and as the fundamental Breakthrough.

The Sūtra of Cultivating Faith in the Mahāyāna states:

> Child of good breeding, a Bodhisattva who has achieved *samādhi* does not regard mere quiescence and the mere taste of *samādhi* as being enough. Rather, while remaining in *samādhi*, one calculates and evaluates, analyzes and investigates the Mahāyāna Dharmas, and by calculating and evaluating, analyzing and investigating them, insight arises.

– Śrāvakas gain realization of personal identitylessness, but they retain some degree of conceptual grasping. However, they feel that their level of realization is sufficient and they become complacent. Similarly, the Pratyekabuddhas gain realization of both personal and phenomenal identitylessness, but again traces of grasping remain, and they, too, feel that their level of realization is enough. The point of this training is to engage in the cultivation of insight to its culmination—to the point where grasping is discarded and insight is utterly free of doubt—just as gold is refined until it is pure.

We who are intent upon eradicating the source of our own suffering and gaining perfect enlightenment must avoid a false sense of complacency. As long as we remain within *saṃsāra*, we are subject to suffering. As long as we are vulnerable to domination by the poisons of the mind—delusion, attachment, hatred, jealousy, and pride—on what grounds can we be complacent? Similarly, as long as we are enmeshed in the eight worldly concerns—profit, loss, pleasure, pain, praise and abuse, and fame and defamation— how can we be satisfied? When we haven't gained even a glimpse of liberation and are still subject to suffering, this false sense of complacency is an exercise in self-deception. On the other hand, if our confidence in Dharma and faith in practice does not wane, in future lives these qualities will grow and give rise to good results. Just as we don't let a single day pass without eating food, similarly, we shouldn't let a single day pass without the practice and study of Dharma. When we have leisure time, let it be meaningfully spent by developing our inner qualities. At the same time, we must always be cautious, because one outburst of anger has the power to undermine much of our good progress. –

The Great Mound of Jewels Sūtra states:

> Kāśyapa, the mind is not found by seeking it. Whatever is unfindable is unobservable. Whatever is unobservable does not occur in the past, nor in the future, nor in the present.

– If from the beginning of your practice, you investigate inwards to discover the nature of your own mind rather than devoting yourself to external activities, you'll be on the right track. Some practitioners engage in the practice of quiescence and then progress to the stages of generation and completion without ever discovering the nature of their own mind. Liberation is nowhere other than the nature of your own mind. Enlightenment is nothing other than the nature of your own mind. Do not look elsewhere. –

The Tantra of the Full Enlightenment of Vairocana extensively explains:

> Lord of Secrets, how is one's own mind to be known? Whether one seeks out the mind as an image, a color, a shape, an object, a form, a feeling, a recognition, a mental formation, as consciousness, as "I," as "mine," as something apprehended, as an apprehender, as pure, impure, as an element, as a sense-base, or in any other way, it is nonobjectifiable.

Nāgārjuna states in *A Commentary on the Spirit of Awakening*:

> The mind is a mere label, and it is nothing other than a label. Recognize awareness as a mere label. Moreover, a label has no intrinsic nature. The Jinas do not find it inside, nor outside, nor in-between those two. Thus, the mind is of the nature of an apparition, and the nature of the mind does not exist as any type of color or shape, as something apprehended or as an apprehender, as a man, a woman, or a neuter, and so forth. In short, the Buddhas have not seen it and they will not see it; they accurately see it as having the nature of being without an intrinsic nature.

Pagmo Drüpa says:

> When the mind is active, there is the cycle of existence, and when it is devoid of activity there is liberation. Without severing the root of the mind, the root of delusion is not cut; so first sever the root of the mind.

– A mind imbued with conceptual elaboration is a mind of *saṃsāra*. A mind free of conceptual elaboration is liberated. The very nature of the mind-itself is primordially, intrinsically free from conceptual elaboration. Consequently, when we abide in that state, we are abiding in the essential nature of the mind. That is *nirvāṇa*. The central challenge, whether you are a scholar or a practitioner, is to sever the root of the mind. People go awry in their practice because they fail to recognize this point and pursue it. Great scholars or practitioners who fail to sever the root miss this central point. For example, Devadatta, the nephew of the Buddha, acquired knowledge and engaged in practice during the years he spent with the Buddha, but arrogance arose in the meantime. Externally, he became very competitive and aggressive towards the Buddha, thinking he was equal to the Buddha. Why did his practice and whole life go awry? Because he failed to sever the root of his mind. He grasped onto the mind as if it existed. Our untrained minds are no different from an elephant in rut, which causes much damage. That wild elephant must be trained and subdued. So too, our mind must be subdued in order to sever the root. –

The Great Brahmin [Saraha] says:

> My son, look! Observe your own mind! The mind is not verified by observation. How amazing that this unestablished mind-itself appears in manifold ways!
>
> Your own unborn mind is the Dharmakāya, and the Dharmakāya is without birth or destruction. How amazing that this embodiment of unborn, great bliss is present within you!
>
> In the Dharmakāya mirror of your own mind, nondual primordial wisdom arises as luminosity. From the moment it arises, it is unestablished, and it is inborn great bliss.

Tilopa says:

> Hey! This is self-knowing primordial wisdom. It is beyond articulation and is not an experienced object of the mind. It is nothing that can be demonstrated by me, Tilopa. Know it by letting your own self-awareness indicate itself.

– It is amazing that we look externally for happiness and for the nature of the mind when it is already present within us. Its nature is beyond description and cannot be pointed to, but it can be known by allowing self-awareness to reveal itself. –

The Sūtra of Thirty-three Questions states:

> All the three worlds have arisen from the mind, but that very mind is not something demonstrable as *this*. Without form, and ethically neutral, it is like an apparition. The wise seek the reality-itself of the mind, and when they seek the reality-itself of the mind, the mind and the reality-itself of the mind are not to be seen. With whatever mind the mind is sought, the intrinsic nature of the mind is not seen.

– In this exploration of the ultimate nature of the mind, the mind that is doing the seeking and the nature of the mind that is sought are ultimately one. Both are nonexistent, but not like water that has evaporated. If you really understand the nonexistence of the seeking and the sought mind, you will see it is not simply empty. You will see it is simultaneously empty and luminous, and it is of the nature of the three embodiments of the Buddhas—the Dharmakāya, Sambhogakāya, and Nirmāṇakāya. That is the insight that arises when you truly recognize the nature of the mind. –

The Tantra of the Full Enlightenment of Vairocana states:

> Even the Tathāgatas have not seen, do not see, and will not see the mind. It is not a color, it does not appear as shapes, and it is not male, female, or neuter.

A Commentary on the Spirit of Awakening states:

> The Jinas do not find the mind inside or outside or between the two.

And:

> The mind is just a label, so look upon it as a mere label. Moreover, a label has no intrinsic nature, so the mind is of the nature of an apparition.

The Sūtra of the Questions of Kāśyapa states:

> Kāśyapa, the mind does not exist inside, nor outside, nor is it observed between the two. Kāśyapa, the mind is unanalyzable, undemonstrable, nonappearing, unknowable, and without location. Kāśyapa, even the Buddhas have not seen, do not see, and will not see the mind. Kāśyapa, even if the mind is sought, it is unfindable. Whatever is unfindable is unobservable. Whatever is unobservable does not arise in the past, in the future, or in the present.

The Sūtra of the Questions of Maitreya states:

> Maitreya asked, "How shall one observe the inner mind?"
> [The Buddha] replied, "The mind is without shape, without color, without location, and is like space."

Śāntideva says:

> The Protector of the World stated that the mind does not perceive the mind. Just as the sword does not cut itself, so it is with the mind.[42]

The Condensed Perfection of Wisdom states:

> Not seeing form, not seeing feelings, not seeing recognition, not seeing mental formations, and not seeing consciousness, the mind, or cognition anywhere—the Tathāgata indicates that such a person sees reality.

– One who recognizes that there is no intrinsic nature to be found sees reality. By grasping onto form, feelings, and so forth, we obscure the nature of reality-itself; whereas the Tathāgatas, who do not grasp onto these psychophysical aggregates, recognize reality-itself. –

Orgyen Rinpoche says:

> Astonishing! The ongoing awareness and clarity called *the mind* exists, but does not exist even as a single thing. It arises, for it manifests as *saṃsāra* and *nirvāṇa*, and as a myriad of joys and sorrows. It is asserted, for it is asserted according to the twelve vehicles. It is a label, for it is named in unimaginable ways. Some people call it *the mind-itself*. Some non-Buddhists call it *the self*. The Śrāvakas call it *personal identitylessness*. The Cittamātrins call it *the mind*. Some people call it *the middle way*. Some call it *the perfection of wisdom*. Some give it the name *tathāgatagarbha*. Some give it the name *Mahāmudrā*. Some give it the name *ordinary consciousness*. Some call it *the sole bindu*. Some give it the name *the absolute nature of reality*. Some give it the name *the total ground*.

– This mind can be said to exist in the sense that it is the basis from which arises the whole of *saṃsāra*. Moreover, it is the basis from which the experience of *nirvāṇa* arises, and it is the basis from which the pure lands arise. All of these experiences have the mind as their foundation. It is amazing that this one phenomenon, the mind, has so many exalted names. –

To introduce this by pointing it out directly, past consciousness has disappeared without a trace. Moreover, future realization is unarisen, and in the freshness of its own present, unfabricated way of being, there is the ordinary consciousness of the present. When it stares at itself, with this observation there is a vividness in which nothing is seen. This awareness is direct, naked, vivid, unestablished, empty, limpid luminosity, unique, nondual clarity and emptiness. It is not permanent, but unestablished. It is not nihilistic, but radiantly vivid. It is not one, but is manifoldly aware and clear. It is not manifold, but is indivisibly of one taste. It is none other than this very self-awareness. This is a real introduction to the primordial nature of being.

– During the waking state, a thought arises and passes in a single moment. In the interim prior to the arising of the next thought, there is a glimmer of the reality of emptiness. As you fall asleep at night, before dream appearances arise, but after the appearances of waking consciousness have vanished, there is the same facet of clarity and luminosity of awareness. However, do not mistake this quality of awareness with consciousness in the deep sleep state. As you emerge from the dream state, when all dream appearances have vanished and before waking consciousness arises, again this facet of clarity can be recognized. These in-between states are the actual nature of awareness that is being introduced in this practice. –

In this the three embodiments are indivisibly complete. As utterly unestablished emptiness, it is the Dharmakāya. As the clear radiance of emptiness, it is the Sambhogakāya. Appearing everywhere without impediment, it is the Nirmāṇakāya. Simple, singularly complete, it is the Svabhāvakāya.

To introduce this by pointing it out forcefully: it is your very own present consciousness. When it is this very unstructured, self-luminous consciousness, what do you mean, "I do not realize the mind-itself"?

There is nothing here on which to meditate, so what do you mean, "It does not arise due to meditation"?

When it is just this direct awareness, what do you mean, "I do not find my own mind"?

When it is just this uninterrupted clear awareness, what do you mean, "The nature of the mind is not seen"?

When it is the very thinker of the mind, what do you mean, "It is not found by seeking it"?

When there is nothing at all to do, what do you mean, "It does not arise due to activity"?

When it is enough to leave it in its own unstructured state, what do you mean, "It does not remain"?

When it is enough to let it be without doing anything, what do you mean, "I cannot do it"?

When it is unified, indivisible clarity, awareness, and emptiness, what do you mean, "It is affirmed and unaffirmed"?

When it is spontaneously self-arisen without causes or conditions, what do you mean, "I can't do it?"

When the arising and release of thoughts are simultaneous, what do you mean, "They do not occur together"?

When it is this very consciousness of the present, what do you mean, "I do not recognize it"?

The mind-itself is certainly empty and unestablished. Your mind is intangible like empty space. Is it like that or not? Observe your own mind!

Empty and void, but without a nihilistic view, self-arisen, primordial wisdom is original, clear consciousness. Self-arisen and self-illuminating, it is like the essence of the sun. Is it like that or not? Observe your own mind!

The primordial wisdom of awareness is certainly unceasing. Uninterrupted awareness is like the current of a river. Is it like that or not? Observe your own mind!

The dispersing discursive thoughts are certainly not being grasped. This intangible dispersion is like a hazy sky. Is it like that or not? Observe your own mind!

Recognize all appearances as self-appearing. Self-appearing phenomena are like reflections in a mirror. Is it like that or not? Observe your own mind!

All signs are certainly released in their own state. Self-arising and self-releasing, they are like clouds in the sky. Is it like that or not? Observe your own mind!

– The nature of the mind-itself is empty, but not like an empty cave, for it is the very nature of *saṃsāra* and *nirvāṇa*. The statement, "It is not found by seeking it," implies that the seeking mind and that which is sought are the same. Since there is nothing on which to meditate and nothing to see, why search externally for the nature of the mind? This unstructured, self-luminous consciousness is already present; there is nothing to do.

People complain, "Oh, I can't get my mind to become still; I can't remain in meditative stabilization." In reality, it is enough to leave the mind in its own unstructured state. Why have so many complaints and questions? Why complicate the issue? The arising of thoughts is like the arising of the waves in the ocean. They are of the same nature as the ocean, just as thoughts are of the same nature as the mind. The nature of the mind is empty and intangible—without substance and with nothing to grasp onto.

Buddha Śākyamuni did not see the mind in the past, he does not in the present, nor will he in the future. Although we may think we can see the mind, how can we see something that the Buddha himself could not see? However, test this challenge with your own empirical observation. Liquid by nature is fluid; fire by nature is hot. Likewise awareness by nature has the indelible qualities of emptiness and luminosity, which are not adventitious or fabricated. Just as the current of a great river continues without interruption, as long as we are sentient beings, the unceasing flow of conceptual elaboration of the mind occurs. On the other hand, once enlightenment has been attained, there is the endless presence of the two types of wisdom—the ontological wisdom of the actual nature of reality-itself and the phenomenological wisdom of the nature of the phenomenal world. Thoughts are primordially unestablished, they have no basis in reality, and therefore it is inappropriate to grasp onto them. All appearances of *saṃsāra* and *nirvāṇa* and all appearances of impure and pure realms are self-appearing. All signs naturally appear and naturally vanish of their own accord, like the clouds in the sky. –

The Tantra of the Blazing Clear Expanse of the Great Perfection states:

> Because the inner apprehending mind is empty, the nature of all phenomena is inner emptiness.
>
> Because the apprehension of outer objects is empty, their nature is outer emptiness.
>
> The five outer, inner, and intermediate sense-faculties, free of grasping, are nondual emptiness. This is emptiness devoid of "outer" and "inner."
>
> In the emptiness of all that, even the apprehender itself is empty, so this is nondual emptiness.
>
> Because one has abandoned the grasping of craving for anything, including the four continents made up of the great elements and Mount Meru, this is great emptiness.
>
> Realization, including [that derived from] present hearing, thinking, and meditating, is ultimate emptiness.
>
> Due to the conceit of the roots of virtue and good thoughts, there is compounded emptiness.
>
> Due to uncompounded virtue, and because the conceited mind is naturally empty, there is uncompounded emptiness.
>
> Empty apprehension that transcends extremes is emptiness that transcends extremes.
>
> Because apprehensions fulfill the needs of sentient beings at the beginning, the middle, and the end, and since apprehensions are empty, there is emptiness at the beginning and the end.
>
> Because the needs of all sentient beings are not neglected at the time of great liberation, there is unneglecting emptiness.

> The nature of all appearances is empty, and this is the emptiness of intrinsic nature.
>
> Because the nature of the entire phenomenal world of *saṃsāra* and *nirvāṇa* is empty of substantiality, there is the emptiness of phenomena.
>
> Although the Buddha is adorned with the signs and symbols of enlightenment, because there is no self-grasping onto them, there is emptiness of self-characteristics.
>
> In the nonobjectifiability of phenomena, because of the emptiness of even a trace of grasping, there is the emptiness of nonobjectifiability.
>
> Because intangible apprehensions grasp extremes, they are without substance, and this is the emptiness of an intrinsic essence.

– In this passage "apprehension" refers to conceptual grasping onto objects. While apprehending outer and inner emptiness, we must remember the emptiness of the very apprehender who apprehends these. Great emptiness is the rejection of craving for anything, including the entire phenomenal world. When we engage in virtuous deeds, we may do so with the sense that we are "doing something good." That is only conceit, and that is compounded emptiness. Uncompounded emptiness is doing a virtuous deed without thinking, "I did something." The gist of this quote is freedom from grasping. –

Tilopa says:

> Even if a name is given to empty space, space cannot be described. Similarly, even though the luminous mind is discussed, there is no basis of designation that can be established with speech.

And:

> Like the state of space, the mind transcends thought. Set it at ease in its own nature, without rejecting it or maintaining it. When the mind is without objective content, it is Mahāmudrā. Through familiarization with that, supreme enlightenment is achieved.

– Even though we have designations for the mind, we cannot actually point out what we are talking about. Like space, the mind has no demonstrable borders or center, and it is beyond the intellect. When you seek to rest the mind in its own nature, there is nothing to reject or to endorse.

"Objective content" refers to the "targets" on which the mind is focused. Whenever there is such a target, there is grasping. However, when we cease grasping and drop the target, the mind is without "objective content." That is Mahāmudrā. Again remember not to let your mind simply space out, but let it rest in its own nature. –

Saraha says:

> The root of the whole of *saṃsāra* and *nirvāṇa* is the nature of the mind. To realize this, rest in unstructured ease without meditating on anything. When all that needs to be done is to rest in yourself, it is amazing that you are deluded by seeking elsewhere! Everything is of the primordial nature, without its being this and not that.

– Unlike the sun and moon that can be studied with a telescope, the primordial nature of the mind cannot be objectified or grasped conceptually. In the cultivation of quiescence and of insight, the mind has "targets," or objects on which to focus. In this more advanced stage of practice, which is based upon the prior two stages, the mind has no target. Until perfect enlightenment is achieved, we are still subject to the network of actions and their consequences. Padmasambhava remarked that while his view was as vast as space, his care with respect to actions and their consequences was as fine as flour. The karmic relationships between actions and their consequences are not present in the nature of the mind-itself, in ultimate reality, or in the Buddha-nature. Nevertheless, as long as we are on the path, the relationships of actions and their consequences are a pertinent part of our existence. Some practitioners may think that they have progressed to an advanced stage of practice that is beyond karma. But as soon as they think, "I'm beyond that," this indicates they have not transcended.

In reference to this point, a famous story is told from the life of Dudjom Lingpa. While he was teaching Atiyoga, a shepherd was listening in. In the context of this teaching, Dudjom Lingpa pointed out that there are no causes and effects in the nature of awareness, nor are there any other divisions of "this" and "that." As a result, the shepherd left the teaching thinking, "Oh good, in that case there are no consequences from my actions." Thinking he would not experience any consequences from his actions, he butchered a sheep. Dudjom Lingpa heard how this man had totally misconstrued and distorted his profound teachings on the Great Perfection. Disheartened, he refused to teach for many months. –

The Mahāsiddha Nyima Tsal says:

> Amidst the various apparitional displays of the mind, there is no way to point out, "This is the mind." Thus, that very freedom from the root of the cycle of existence and of liberation is to be known as the Dharmakāya.

Nyima Beypa says:

> Observing the mind, it is without birth; observing objects, they are without conceptual elaboration. This nondual reality transcends the intellect. I know nothing at all.

Jñānaśrī says:

> Like a tree trunk separated from its root, my mind-itself is free like space. Whatever delusive appearances occur, welcome them! I am a contemplative of space.

– Whether white or black clouds appear in the sky, the nature of space is not altered. The clouds do not influence space, either by harming or benefiting it. They simply appear in space and then vanish. Similarly, all thoughts, whether good or bad, are purely displays of awareness. They, too, do not have the power either to injure or aid awareness. –

Cherbupa says:

> In self-release that transcends the intellect set your unstructured body, speech, and mind at rest. Settle without distraction and without rejection or affirmation. Settle in great unwavering equality.

Padmaśrī says:

> As this inborn consort is not intellectually structured by means of thinking and meditation, there is no need to seek the Dharmakāya elsewhere. As it is self-arisen, set yourself at ease.

The venerable Naropa says:

> This consciousness of self-awareness, bliss, and clarity is the Dharmakāya of nothingness. If it were established, this would be a structured awareness, but as it is unestablished, there is no structuring.

Śavaripa says:

> Although one says "space, space," the nature of space is utterly unestablished. It transcends existence, nonexistence, no existence, and no nonexistence, and any other object that can be posited.

Virupa says:

> Mahāmudrā—the equality of cyclic existence and peace, intrinsically unborn, pristine in nature, defying articulation due to having no mode of being that can be indicated, ineffable in nature, its essence free of all relativity, unanalyzable, incomparable, not even existing as something incomparable—it transcends the intellect.

Stanzas on the Madhyamaka Root of Wisdom states:

> Do not say, "It is empty," and do not refer to it as "not empty," nor as dual or nondual.

A Refutation of Objections states:

> If I were to have any theoretical position, then I would have this problem, but since I have no theoretical position, I have no problem at all.

A Treatise in Four Hundred Stanzas states:

> Since no position is taken anywhere as to "existence, nonexistence, or existence and nonexistence," however long you wait, you cannot find grounds for an argument.

The Mahāsiddha Maitrīpa says:

> The mind-itself is free of the three extremes of birth, cessation, and abiding. It is released from dualistic grasping onto "I" and "mine," its essence is empty, its nature is luminous, and its character is unceasing awareness that is without an object, yet it appears in numerous ways. This luminosity transcends objects that are grasped as the seen and the seer. It is released from the objects that are objectified as the topic of meditation and the meditator. Without bringing anything to mind, that very freedom from mental engagement is inactivity free of all action, set at ease and unstructured. There is no grasping, for whatever appears is not apprehended. One is mentally vacant, for one is free of the structured contamination of the consciousness of meditative equipoise. There is pristine emptiness, for there is no grasping onto signs. It is luminous, for it is by nature clear light. It is unmediated, for it is not contaminated by the dualistic grasping of ideation. It is vivid, for it knows its own nature. Appearances and the mind are indivisibly, unimpededly homogenous, for the grasping onto subjects and objects has dissolved. It is ordinary consciousness, for awareness is settled in its own unstructured nature. It is "fresh awareness," for the stream of ideation does not enter the heart, and this is the real essence of the practice of insight.

– The mind-itself is released from the objectification of "him," "her," "them," and so forth. Its essence is empty; its nature is luminous; its character is unceasing awareness that is without an object. The essential nature of this mind cannot be found. Although the mind-itself is not an object, it is the basis for both *saṃsāra and nirvāṇa*. It transcends the duality of subject and object and is released from the distinction of meditation and meditator. There is no grasping and no conceptual apprehension in the mind-itself. There is not even the slightest identification of anything as being anything. There is nothing structured or contrived in this state of awareness. It is by nature clear light. It is naked, unmediated awareness. The mind-itself doesn't need an external agent to introduce it to itself, because when it manifests, it knows its own nature. The mind and appearances are an indivisible continuum. They are unimpededly homogeneous, so grasping onto subject and object has simply collapsed. This mind-itself is called "ordinary consciousness," for it is not an exalted, highly developed state of consciousness to which you must progress. Rather, it is the primordial nature of the mind. Nevertheless, don't confuse that with your ordinary consciousness that is fabricated and structured. It is simply the nature of the mind-itself without modifications that either exalt or debase it. As thoughts arise, they are instantaneously released. In this sense, the mind-itself is utterly fresh, moment by moment, without the stream of ideation entering into the heart. This is the real essence of the practice of insight. This is the direct introduction to the nature of awareness, to the nature of the mind-itself. –

> Moreover, the mind-itself is also Avalokiteśvara, for Avalokiteśvara unobstructedly looks over all beings with the eyes of great compassion. It is Avalokiteśvara, for, with the eyes of omniscience, beyond the intellect, free of a center and extremes, it sees all phenomena as unmixed and self-luminous, like reflections. It is Avalokiteśvara, for, with the eyes of self-knowing, primordial wisdom, it sees the meaning of unborn reality-itself. It is Avalokiteśvara, for, with eyes purified from the state of the apprehender and apprehended, it sees the mind of clear light free of conceptual elaboration.

– When you realize the nature of the mind-itself, you realize that it is none other than Avalokiteśvara, the embodiment of the Buddhas' compassion. With the eyes of compassion he unobstructedly, unceasingly looks over all beings. This is the effortless, unimpeded, unceasing, omniscient mind of a Buddha. This compassionate vision of all sentient beings is comprised of ontological knowledge and phenomenological knowledge. A Buddha's awareness of phenomena is like a mirror that clearly reflects all images. Phenomena are not fused together; rather everything is seen distinctly, unmixed, and self-luminous. A Buddha sees distinctly and vividly the causes, natures, and effects of every sentient being. Moreover, a Buddha simultaneously sees *saṃsāra* and *nirvāṇa* without confusing them. Reality-itself is the ultimate nature of reality, and it is synonymous with emptiness. It transcends the state of an apprehender and an apprehended object. This mind-itself does not see itself as an object, for it is awareness of nondual clear light free from conceptual elaboration. –

Avalokiteśvara said to Songtsen Gampo:

> The essence of the mind is empty and totally unestablished. As its displays from emptiness are unimpeded, it arises as the body and primordial wisdom of a Buddha. In sentient beings the five poisons and so on arise. In those in whom the essence of the mind is empty, the Dharmakāya is present. Even though the displays

> of the five poisons and ideation are unimpeded, since the root is empty, they are not blocked but are self-appearing and do not remain; and since they are self-releasing, they arise as primordial wisdom. Regard the essence of the mind-itself as the empty Dharmakāya. As it is unceasingly clear, regard it as the Sambhogakāya. Regard self-arising, self-releasing, manifold appearances as the Nirmāṇakāya.

– The emptiness of the mind is not a mere vacuity, or nothingness. Rather, while it is empty, it manifests as the embodiments and primordial wisdoms of a Buddha. It isn't empty for some people and not for others. In fact, the essence of the mind is primordially empty, and for those individuals who realize the empty nature of their own mind, the Dharmakāya manifests within them. There is no need to look for it elsewhere. Check this out for yourself. Once you have realized the nature of the mind, all mental activities appear as manifestations of primordial wisdom. Moreover, if you have gained this genuine realization of the Dharmakāya nature of your mind, no other practice is necessary to bring forth the luminous manifestation of the mind-itself as the Sambhogakāya, because it is implicitly present and naturally arising. –

The Pith Instructions of the Ḍākinīs states:

> Its initial non-arising is the Dharmakāya. Its intermediate non-remaining is the Sambhogakāya. Its final non-departure is the Nirmāṇakāya.

– This relates back to the investigation of the origin, location, and departure discussed earlier. The three *kāyas* are all implicitly and primordially in the nature of the Dharmakāya itself. It is not as if the Dharmakāya does something extra to display itself as the Sambhogakāya, and then does something more to display itself as the Nirmāṇakāya. All of these are inherent in the nature of the Dharmakāya itself. –

And:

> The mind-itself is self-liberating in the nature of the three embodiments.

This self-manifestation as the nature of the three embodiments is primordial reality. It is not contrived or structured in any way. This reality is simply to be accepted, but that is not so easy to do.

The Pith Instructions on the Clear Expanse states:

> The essence of whatever arises is such that it is released as soon as it arises. However it may change or disperse, in reality it is unestablished, and its dispersion, its remaining, and its clarity are empty. Without an object and unmediated, apart from being

> a display of the nature of emptiness, it is unestablished. In this ineffable reality free of elaboration, by simply not impeding its radiance, everything appears. Know that the essence of appearances is empty, without an object, and free of the intellect. Not being separated from that reality is called vividness.

– Whatever arises—whether good or bad, attractive or ugly—is released as soon as it arises. It is simply an appearance and has no basis in reality. The mind-itself is beyond conventional reality, and it while it is characterized by luminosity and clarity, it has no inherent existence whatsoever. All appearances are no different from dream phenomena, and from the beginning they are unestablished, for they have no reality in and of themselves. They simply appear and then vanish. In fact, this instantaneous arising and vanishing is simply a conceptual construct. –

The Primary Words states:

> Look at the essence of your own mind. No essence whatever is established.

– You don't need to draw on a vast body of scholarship or on external phenomena to see the essence of your own mind—just watch your own mind. Anyone can do this, and if you look for the essence of your mind, you will discover that nothing is to be found. –

The venerable [Karmapa] Rangjung Dorje says:

> The point that all the Buddhas of the three times have in mind, that which is sought by holy beings, the great sound and renown of the Dharmakāya Mahāmudrā, is called your own mind. If you do not know the essence of your own mind, it is just conceptual nonsense to think "my mind" or "this mind." All the phenomena of *saṃsāra* and *nirvāṇa* are nothing more than this awareness, and this is also the essence of the collection of the *sūtras* and *tantras*. There is nothing at all to practice or on which to meditate. Just leave this awareness in its own radiant state. There is no need to wonder whether or not this is Mahāmudrā. Have no hope of getting better and no fears of getting worse. Do not follow after many miscellaneous thoughts. Vividly leave awareness to itself. Set it at ease. There is nothing on which to meditate. From the time that you meditate like that again and again, thoughts recognize their own face, and in an instant the darkness of habitual propensities is utterly dispelled. That is Buddhahood. The difference occurs in an instant. Know there is nothing greater than a single word of essential speech on Mahāmudrā, the ultimate practical instruction of the holy *gurus* and *siddhas*.

– There are no grounds for saying, "I don't know the nature of my own mind." It is your own mind that is coming up with all thoughts about the past, present, and future. It is this mind that is to be known. All the 84,000 teachings of the Buddha are essentially concerned with the nature of the mind. Americans tend to have a lot of questions, but here there is nothing to wonder about. Simply go right into the essence of the mind-itself. Leave the spider's web of miscellaneous thoughts alone. Do not follow after them. Do not try to place awareness someplace else, but leave it in its own place. Indeed, just let awareness rest in its own nature. Perhaps this is not so easy. When you set your awareness at ease, with nothing on which to meditate, it is imperative that grasping not be present.

It would be a great mistake to adopt this alone as your Dharma practice right now, thinking, "I don't need to practice or meditate." As long as we are on the path, we are still bound up in conventional reality. Therefore, there is still a meditator, and there is something on which to meditate. It is imperative that we lay a foundation for this practice by contemplating the Four Noble Truths, the Four Thoughts that Turn the Mind, and the nature of actions and their consequences. In that way, we create a foundation for engaging in these subtle practices. If we omit the foundation and simply try to be at ease with nothing on which to meditate, we will just end up "hanging out." That is a big mistake!

In the West, many of us look forward to the time when we can set our work aside and retire. Then, we imagine, we can simply be at ease, having nothing on which to meditate. Nevertheless, when many people do finally retire, they are even busier than when they were working. When they finally do have the opportunity to be at ease, they compulsively engage in further activity. Similarly, although we may want to go directly into this practice and to try to be simply present, we may find ourselves engaged in activity due to our powerful habituation of compulsive thinking and grasping onto ideation. In that case, our attempt to be at ease and to have nothing on which to meditate won't work. These habitual propensities give rise to our habits and compulsive thinking. However, the moment all habitual propensities are dispelled, Buddhahood is achieved. –

The teachings of the venerable Kachö Wangpo state:

> O child of good breeding, if your present mind were something existent, it would have to be outside, inside, or in between. Is it truly there? Colors and shapes may not appear, but if you think you are simply aware of appearances, what awareness knows that awareness? If you think it is aware of any object, is that object other than that awareness or is it the same? When it indivisibly appears to the mind, what is known and observed in the mind? If it were the mind-itself, it would be like the blade of a sword cutting itself. How could that be so? Everything—including enemies, friends, attractive and unattractive things—is like that.

Therefore, calling awareness "consciousness" is just a designation. If it is explored and analyzed, it is like that. However, you may think it is evidently empty when you cognize, know, and realize, "It is like this." At the time of realizing, knowing, and cognizing, it is certainly unestablished. Thus, until now you have been distracted by grasping the absence of awareness as awareness, the absence of consciousness as consciousness, the absence of mind as mind, the absence of cognition as cognition, and the absence of realization as realization. But do you understand?

O child of good breeding, this mind is like space. Can space be established as being "this"? Likewise, the mind is like the color of space. Like the horn of a hare, it is unestablished, rootless, without basis, undemonstrable, without intrinsic nature, signless, lacking characteristics or marks, colorless, shapeless, devoid of an essence of its own, not arising, not departing, and not remaining. It is by its very nature uncompounded, so even the Omniscient One has not seen it, does not see it, and will not see it. If it were even slightly established, the Omniscient One would see it, but since it is not the slightest bit established, it is not seen. Have you taken to heart this ascertainment of reality?

Until now you have succumbed to negating and affirming by grasping onto the mind, cognition, consciousness, likes, dislikes, joys, sorrows, delusion and liberation, the pure and impure, the best and the worst, good and bad, and the like. But the mind is not observed. How can it be observed? Leave that in the state of your nonexistent mind. Leave it in the state of no thinking. Leave it in the state of no negation or affirmation. Leave it in the state of no rejection or acceptance. Leave it in the state of no hopes or fears. Leave it in the state of no "is" or "is not." Leave it in the state of no good or bad. Leave it in the state of no delusion or liberation.

– Just when you think you have realized the empty nature of awareness, grasping lingers on. You may think, "Ah, this is the nature of the mind—now I've got it." But it is precisely at this point that you lose it, because this is when conceptual grasping comes in and derails you again. In this way, the mind is carried away and distracted. Until now, because of grasping, we have regarded that which is not the mind as being the mind. We have regarded that which is not consciousness as being consciousness. Space is primordially unestablished in reality, so it's impossible for it to have any color. Likewise, the mind is beyond the past, present, and future. It is also beyond all kinds of objectification. If it were to have even a slight basis in reality and the Omniscient One could not see it, that would contradict the entire meaning of "Omniscient One." Therefore, if it had any existence at all, the Omniscient One would see it. Until now, we have been involved in rejecting and accepting due to grasping onto our emotions, joys, suffering, and delusion. Why do we fall into these states when none of them has any true existence? Remember the reality of last night's dream appearances. All of these are unestablished. None of them has objective existence. However, don't ignore actions and their consequences. –

Orgyen Rinpoche says:

> Oh, once you have calmed the compulsive thoughts in your mind right where they are, and the mind is unmodified, isn't there a motionless stability? Oh, this is called *quiescence*, but it is not the nature of the mind.
>
> Now, steadily observe the very nature of your own mind that is being still. Is there a resplendent emptiness that is nothing, that is unestablished in the nature of any substance, shape, or color? That is called the *empty essence*.
>
> Isn't there a luster of that emptiness that is unceasing, clear, immaculate, soothing, and luminous, as it were? That is called the *luminous nature*. Its essential nature is the indivisibility of sheer emptiness, not established as anything, and its unceasing, vivid luster—such awareness is resplendent and brilliant as it were.
>
> This present, unmoving consciousness, which cannot be directly expressed in words, is given the name *awareness*. That which thinks is this alone, so it is given the name *mind*. It is this that is mindful of all kinds of things, so it is given the name *mindfulness*. While it is not seen, it is a special seeing that is clear, steady, unmediated, and steadfast, so it is given the name *insight*. It is that that makes distinctions among all specific phenomena, like separating the layers of a mushroom, so it is given the name *discerning wisdom*. All terms such as *the sugatagarbha, the sole bindu,*[43] *the absolute nature, primordial wisdom, the middle way, ultimate truth,* Mahāmudrā, Atiyoga, and *emptiness* are names of this alone.[44]

Pointing Out the Dharmakāya says:

> Now all objective appearances are like water and waves, all are apparitions of the mind and in reality are unestablished. By realizing this, one recognizes all appearances as the mind. By analyzing the essence of the mind in terms of going, staying, and arising, it turns out not to be established as anything. So, like horses and elephants in a dream, it is unestablished in reality. By

realizing this, one recognizes that the mind is empty. From the state of emptiness, clarity, and limpidity in unceasing great joy, it spontaneously arises as manifold appearances, like the moon's reflections in water. By realizing this, one recognizes emptiness as spontaneous presence. Thus, from simple spontaneous presence arising and release occur spontaneously, without wavering from immutable great bliss that is clear, empty, spontaneous, and free of elaboration, like a snake that unravels its own knots. By ascertaining this, one recognizes spontaneous presence as self-liberating.

– In certain meditative disciplines the following sequence of realizations occurs: one recognizes all appearances as the mind; one recognizes the mind as being empty; and one recognizes emptiness as spontaneous arising. Previously, we looked at the three phases of arising, remaining, and disappearing. By analyzing the nature of the mind, one can recognize that the mind is empty, and from that emptiness all appearances spontaneously arise. The reflections of the moon in the water are dependent upon the water, yet they are not indivisible from the water. The water is dependent upon neither the moon nor the waves. Likewise, the mind is not dependent upon appearances, but appearances are dependent upon the mind.

Once you recognize that all appearances are of the mind, there is a tendency to reify the mind. To counteract that, you must further investigate the nature of the mind, and by so doing, you will find that this mind that seems so real is, in fact, empty. It is empty of any essence; it is empty of any intrinsic nature. However, it is not merely a void. As you continue to investigate, you will find that the emptiness of the mind-itself is naturally spontaneous. What exactly is meant by this natural spontaneity? Investigate and you will find that the very meaning of spontaneity is self-liberation. Here is the sequence: from mind to emptiness, to spontaneous presence, to self-liberation. Where is all of this taking place? In our own ordinary consciousness. This is Mahāmudrā, the union of quiescence and insight. –

The mind that is recognized is ordinary consciousness that disperses in various ways, vividly knows all kinds of things, that is clarity and emptiness united, great bliss, "emptiness bearing all supreme aspects," and Mahāmudrā. Knowing its essence is called realization of Mahāmudrā. So, without having anything on which to meditate, without being distracted even for an instant, settle your awareness in clarity. Without fostering any hope for a good outcome or fear about a bad outcome, be at ease. By sustaining the essence of ordinary consciousness, in that moment

> the Mahāmudrā union of bliss and emptiness is seen, like the state of pure space, free of clouds. Now quiescence and insight are integrated, extraordinary experiential realization arises, and you succeed in entering the path of liberation.

– Calling this ordinary consciousness emptiness, clarity, limpidity, spontaneity, and immutable great bliss implies that it is sublime. Where can we acquire something that is so wonderful? It can't be purchased or obtained, because we already have it. It is our ordinary consciousness. Moreover, it is our ordinary consciousness that produces all of our ideation, imagery, and thoughts, while its nature is primordially free of distraction. The mind-itself can't be distracted. Just as the ocean doesn't have to do something to be the ocean, the mind-itself has nothing on which to meditate. Therefore, settle in that mind, which by nature is never distracted. The occurrences of hope and fear are only expressions of grasping. Grasping is the contamination, the obscuration. Dispense with grasping. When the union of bliss and emptiness is seen, you realize your own nature. –

The Questions and Answers Between Lord [Atīśa] and Drom Tönpa states:

> Venerable One, I repeatedly seek it but I do not find it.
> Drom, you repeatedly see your own nature.
> Venerable One, should I rest in not finding?
> Drom, it is best to set yourself at ease.

Jigten Sumgön says:

> When you look at your ongoing, clear awareness, you see nothing.
> That is seeing thatness.

The point is that the continuous stability of the mind without scattering is quiescence. By looking at its essence there is insight into emptiness, such that upon the basis of stability, insight arises. If the mind is not the slightest bit stable, it is not seen, so the observation of the various scatterings of the mind is quiescence. By looking at its essence, one sees it as empty. Thus, insight arises on the basis of dispersion. In the Dharmakāya space of the nonconceptual mind, if the mass of clouds of ideation is not cleared away, the sun and moon of the two kinds of knowledge will not shine forth. So assiduously apply yourself to this primordial meditation!

– Continuous attentional stability, when the mind is not carried away by ideation, is quiescence. Beyond that, it is possible to have a stable awareness of the movement of ideation. This is characteristic of entering into the practice of quiescence. Before you enter into the practice, you may feel that your mind is more or less stable and that you have some continuity of attention. However, when you actually begin to cultivate quiescence, you find that you are overwhelmed by the sheer quantity of the ideation that arises. The more closely you look, the more thoroughly you are inundated by the dense onslaught of thoughts. As you continue to practice, you will detect a more and more subtle degree of ideation, although it requires an extremely subtle degree of awareness to realize the most subtle level of thoughts. Insight arises by analyzing the nature of the thoughts that disperse and flow out. The Dharmakāya is likened to space and ideation to clouds. The clouds of our thoughts obscure the two types of knowledge—phenomenological knowledge of reality in its diversity and ontological knowledge of reality as it is. –

This completes the identification [of awareness]. May there be virtue!

CHAPTER SIX

Practice

Homage to Avalokiteśvara!

These are the profound practical instructions of Avalokiteśvara, the method for actualizing the reality that has been introduced. *The Tantra of the Blazing Clear Expanse of the Ḍākinīs* states:

> All adventitious arising of ideation is the display of awareness, so there is no need to block it. While conceptualization arises, nonconceptuality grows.
>
> The Dharmakāya transcends the mind; the Sambhogakāya transcends cognition (i.e., the luminous, empty clarity of cognition); and the Nirmāṇakāya is free of grasping (i.e., without individual grasping onto "this").[45]
>
> While suffering arises, bliss increases. The greater the mental afflictions, the mightier the primordial wisdom. The larger the pile of wood, the greater the fire blazes. The larger the mass of ice, the more the river rises. The denser the mass of clouds, the stronger the torrent descends.
>
> Rest as the knots of the snake suddenly release. Rest as if you were casting off a human corpse. Rest as if you were discarding a foul odor. If it is restrained, this will be a cause of its dispersing again. If it is rejected, this will be a cause of its returning again. If you clamp down on it, this will be a cause of its rebounding. If you subdue it, this will be a cause of its getting tough again. If

> you burn it, this will be a cause of its icing over. Stop blocking and affirming, and rest in equality.

– Ideation arises instantaneously and adventitiously, and then it vanishes. It is not intrinsically in the nature of the mind. This implies that all mental events are impermanent and fleeting. The displays of awareness include not only attachment, but ignorance, anger, pride, and jealousy. As paradoxical as it may seem, nonconceptual realization of emptiness can be sustained in the midst of conceptualization, but only if the nature of the mind-itself has been realized. Even in the midst of the arising of suffering, joy can arise, but only if you do not grasp onto the suffering. Normally when joy arises, we grasp onto it, thinking, "Oh, this is so blissful." The bliss that arises even as suffering increases is without even a trace of mental or conceptual grasping.

For example, if you were to take rebirth in one of the miserable states of existence, such as a hell realm, beings there would inflict great harm on you. If you were able to recognize these apparent inflicters of harm as emanations of the Buddha, that hell realm would be instantaneously transmuted into a pure realm. That is one way to transmute suffering into joy. Another possibility is to realize the various beings who appear in your field of experience as the natural appearances of your own pure awareness. This realization leads directly to Buddhahood, bypassing the need to go to a pure land. Whether you gain this realization in a miserable state of existence, in the intermediate state, in the dream state, or right now, the end result is the same.

Some sentient beings can be subdued through peaceful, enriching, or powerful methods. Others whose minds cannot be tamed by these means must be subdued by ferocity. If you transmute the mental afflictions without being overwhelmed by them, each one arises as a display of primordial wisdom. For instance, the mental affliction of delusion arises as the primordial wisdom of the absolute nature of reality.

Be present and allow the knots of the snake of your mind to release. When mental afflictions arise, simply be present and rest in that state. If the mental afflictions are restrained, as if caught by the throat, this will cause them to flow out again. If you try to suppress conceptualization, this will reactivate it. The reason for this resurgence is that the root of the mind has not been severed, and there has been no fundamental transformation. You have not yet transmuted the poison into medicine. If you suppress ideation, it comes bounding right back like a yo-yo. If you try to soften it up, it just gets tough again. So, without blocking it, affirming it, or grasping onto it, just rest in equality.

This point can be understood in terms of a common Buddhist metaphor. If you have to walk over a very large area with many thorns on the ground, there are two approaches you might take to protect your feet. You could buy thousands of square miles of leather to cover the ground, or you could wear a pair of leather shoes which would serve the same function.

In the course of spiritual practice, many situations cause suffering as if they were thorns. Instead of manipulating these many aggravations one by one, like trying to cover the earth with leather, cultivate mindfulness, introspection, and conscientiousness in your mind-stream. By so doing, you will protect yourself from your own mental afflictions. In this way your mental afflictions cannot be easily stimulated by external aggravations.

This text deals explicitly with practice. When mental afflictions and thoughts arise, do not counteract them with specific antidotes. Do not block them, do not follow after them, do not affirm them, but simply rest in equality. By resting in equality and simply recognizing the instantaneous arising and passing of the ideation, you will be protected from coming under the sway of your mental afflictions. That is like putting on leather shoes. –

The Chapter on Breakthrough: The Mode of Being in Which the Mind and Awareness Are Integrated states:

> The indivisibility of the mind and awareness is great bliss. Thinking, "The mind is present in the cycle of existence," examine all that is pure in its own state.
>
> Encounter the three embodiments indivisible from great bliss as Samantrabhadrī. Realize ideation as your own spiritual mentor. Recognize the indivisibility of the spiritual mentor and self-awareness. Ideation itself dissolves into the center. Awareness is self-empowered and capable of supporting itself.
>
> Determine for yourself the freedom from the barriers of guarding the various pledges.
>
> Thoughtfully investigate the body with ideation, and recognize your own nature as the body of the Tathāgata.
>
> Thoughtfully investigate speech with ideation, and recognize your own nature as the speech of empty sound.
>
> Thoughtfully investigate primordial wisdom with ideation, and recognize your own nature as unmediated, empty awareness.
>
> Whole, clear, and pervasive; primordially liberated, devoid of activity and fresh; implicitly liberated, innately pure and fresh; effortless, totally present, and inactive—so-called "awareness awareness" is awareness due to knowing and clarity.
>
> Earlier ideation is released in its own state, grasping onto future ideation has not yet arisen, and the interim is free of the contamination of remedial modification. Recognize this enactment of stainless, luminous transparency as awareness. Its essence is empty, its nature, luminous. Its compassion can illuminate everything. This is the mode of being of awareness.

> In the empty six collections [of consciousness] its many expressive powers are exercised. In the emptiness of form the expressive power of awareness operates. Experience great empty luminosity.

– To realize that the mind-itself is the three embodiments [Dharmakāya, Sambhogakāya, and Nirmāṇakāya] is to encounter Samantrabhadri.[46] This does not mean, however, that you will have a vision of a blue female deity. Moreover, to realize the indivisibility of your awareness with your spiritual mentor is not to recognize two separate things mixing together and becoming indivisibly merged, as when water is poured into milk. To realize the nature of your awareness is to realize that your own awareness is your spiritual mentor. This has always been the case, but now you recognize that primordial reality. If you want to learn about two things merging, study science. To understand primordial indivisibility, study the nature of the mind-itself.

No one can do anything to you to make you understand the nature of awareness. Awareness is self-empowered and capable of supporting itself. This phrase, "capable of supporting itself," is important. As long as we have not attained perfect enlightenment, we are not capable of supporting ourselves. As long as we are confined to conventional reality, we are not independent or genuinely free. No relative truth is self-supporting, because it is impermanent. Only in ultimate reality is genuine freedom self-supporting and autonomous.

Don't we all want freedom? If so, we must not simply talk about it; we must actually accomplish it. To accomplish freedom we must put these teachings into practice. It's not enough to hear them; they must be put into practice. It is the practice that empowers us and grants us the autonomy we seek. If we truly want to attain freedom and establish our own human rights, we must, through practice, bring about our own inner transformation.

By being empowered through a tantric initiation, you have the freedom to engage in tantric practices. Along with the freedom to practice, there are various precepts and pledges that must be guarded in order to progress in the tantric practice. In this context, when you have gained an experiential realization of the basis of *saṃsāra* and *nirvāṇa*, all pledges are spontaneously and naturally kept. You will not have to exert special effort. As a monk you won't have to remember to maintain your vows, because you will primordially keep your monastic precepts. In the same way, as a tantric practitioner, from the power of your realization, you will naturally and spontaneously keep the tantric precepts.

Another method for gaining deeper realization is to conceptually designate your body, speech, and mind as those of your chosen deity in the stage of generation practice. The practice taught in this chapter is complementary to the stage of generation practice. In this training, simply disengage from conceptual designation altogether and realize the truth that is primordially present. This method entails pure recognition, rather than the structured, contrived practice of conceptual designation.

Ideation of the past doesn't need anything else to release it, for it is released in its own place and is self-liberating. There is an interval following past ideation and future ideation. Do not try to modify or contaminate this interim by altering it or structuring it in any way. In this moment of awareness there is no conventional reality. It is utterly free of conceptual elaboration or structuring.

As mentioned earlier, these moments provide you with the opportunity to realize the nature of awareness: the interval after you have fallen asleep and before you begin dreaming; the interval after you have stopped dreaming and before you wake up; and the interval following the passing of one conceptualization and before the next. Each of these instances provides an opportunity to realize the nature of awareness. This gap, or interval, is like the space seen in a gap between two cloud banks. The space you see is not a narrow sliver of space. In fact, this space is infinite, but you see it through a very narrow sliver. Don't mistake the borders for the reality that lies between the borders.

The empty essence of awareness is not a mere vacuity. The very nature of that emptiness is luminosity, or clarity, and pervasive, illuminating compassion. This emptiness displays itself in the five sensory consciousnesses and in mental consciousness. –

The Hevajra Tantra states:

> Because one is not meditating with the mind, one meditates on the whole world. Meditating even with knowledge of all phenomena is not meditation.

The Guhyasamāja Tantra states:

> In the absence of real phenomena there is no meditation. The act of meditating is not meditation. Thus, since phenomena are unreal, meditation is without an objective referent.

The Great Brahmin [Saraha] says:

> If you release this mind-itself, which is tied up in knots, no doubt it will be freed. Due to what phenomenon is it bound in stupidity? The wise are completely liberated from that.

And:

> All appearances that present themselves to you are like flames spreading in a forest. Behave in accordance with the root of the mind, which is emptiness.

The Hevajra Tantra states:

> By not knowing that which entraps the world and that which liberates us from bondage, the world is unfree, and by disregarding that, *siddhis* are not attained.

And:

> The world is entrapped due to attachment, and it is liberated due to attachment itself. This inverted meditation is unknown by non-Buddhists.

– Normally, attachment gives rise to bondage, but if you have realized the nature of awareness, attachment can lead to freedom from bondage. This entails an inverted meditation because there is no grasping onto the attachment. Although many types of meditation do entail grasping, quintessential meditation is without grasping. The emphasis in this meditation on the nature of the mind is nongrasping and nonconceptual proliferation. This is one mode of practice. Indeed, within Buddhism other legitimate forms of practice do entail conceptual grasping in which you work with and modify your mind. But that is not done in this practice. In the stage of generation practice, you use your conceptual mind to generate your body as your chosen deity. Thus, experience is transmuted by the use of conceptual grasping. Similarly, practices in which the vital energies are directed through the channels (*rtsa rlung*) entail grasping. Even the Leap-over stage of Atiyoga practice entails specific postures and gazes, which carry a vestige of conceptual grasping. However, in this practice dispense with all conceptual elaboration and rest in the unmediated nature of awareness itself. The quintessence of this is to recognize the nature of awareness of the moment. –

Avalokiteśvara's Teachings to Maitrīpa states:

> Whatever arises is primordial being, so if appearances are not disengaged from mindfulness, when all appearances arise as emptiness, you will certainly become a king of contemplatives.
>
> All that appears is that, and that appears nowhere. So whatever arises is unarisen, and that is the way of its arising.[47]

The Great Brahmin [Saraha] says:

> The dispersion out from the mind and its recovery are the nature of the Protector. Are water and waves separate? Cyclic existence and equality are of the nature of space.

Dadak Metri says:

> Being unborn, ideation is adventitious, and ideation is the absolute nature of reality itself. Who knows that they are different? I say they are unified.

The Jewel Radiance of the Ḍākinīs states:

> Now when there is no realization, all the dispersions of consciousness are ideation. When there is realization, ideation itself is none other than freedom from conceptual elaboration.

> This is a problem of Mahāmudrā: just as the nature of ice is water, the wise comprehend that conceptualization and nonconceptualization are nondual.

The Tantra of Inborn Inconceivability states:

> Since that which is inborn is free of conceptual elaboration, there is nothing on which to meditate. Do not interrupt the flow of the objectless nature.

The Perfection of Wisdom Sūtra in One Hundred Thousand Stanzas states:

> Non-mental-engagement is going for refuge in the Buddha.

The Great Brahmin [Saraha] says:

> Once you have seen your own mind free of conceptual elaboration, contemplation in which you ceaselessly produce elaborations is like searching for a glass trinket after having found a precious gem.

And:

> As there is nothing on which to meditate, bring nothing to mind. Do not contaminate the primordial, natural state of ordinary consciousness with structured objects, for the mind that is inherently pure is in no need of modification.

Śavaripa makes a similar comment, and Virupa says:

> Without thinking of existence or nonexistence, rest in nondistraction. Bringing to mind anything at all, even the absence of extremes, is to fail to abide in the reality of the nature of existence, and it is a great distraction.

– In the context of this practice it is misguided to engage in a myriad of conceptual elaborations—identifying this, grasping onto that—thus becoming snared in the web of ideation. Doing this is like losing touch with the trunk of a tree and scrambling around in the branches and leaves. –

Tilopa says:

> You do not see the intellect-transcending reality of that which transcends the intellect, which is the nature of the intellect. You do not realize the reality of inactivity, which is the nature of activity.

Śavaripa says:

> In Mahāmudrā, in which nothing is brought to mind, there is not the slightest thing on which to meditate; so do not meditate! The supreme meditation is inseparable from the reality of no meditation.

– The practice discussed here is the practice of taking refuge; it is the practice of cultivating the Spirit of Awakening, and it includes the stages of generation and completion and propitiatory practice. All those are included in this uncontrived, conceptually non-elaborated practice of the nature of the mind. –

The Synthesized Words states:

> Without modifying its nature, leave it in its natural state. The absence of thought is the Dharmakāya. If you let it be, without seeking, that is meditation, whereas seeking and meditating entails deluded mental activity.

Nagpopa says:

> Whatever is realized with the intellect is a realization that is no realization. That is the arising of an illness, like before. Meditating on the referent of a realization is to be deceived by ideation. Neither an object nor an agent is established. They are impermanent and false, so they are not truly existent. Therefore, that is a path of delusion.

– While meditating, if you maintain the sense of "I" as a meditator and think, "I realize that," this delusion is simply one more symptom of the problem. Such grasping perpetuates the same process that you've been in all along, namely, *saṃsāra*. This is like a person going for plastic surgery to eliminate wrinkles due to age. As time passes, the wrinkles return, and one has to repeat the whole process all over again. In reality, you can't repair that which is in no need of repair. –

And:

> If one cuts through too strongly with the essence of primordial wisdom, this becomes a problem for insight.

– Primordial wisdom is naturally free of conceptual elaboration and grasping, but you must have a very firm basis in quiescence and insight to enter into this advanced stage of practice. Even without a sufficient basis in taking refuge, cultivating the Spirit of Awakening, and cultivating the Four Thoughts that Turn the Mind, one may be fascinated by Atiyoga. But this is like wanting an apple without having any apple trees. The path is sequential. First, we must recognize, through investigation, the nature of our various mental afflictions. Following this investigation, we must recognize what antidotes can counteract these diverse afflictions. Then we must continually apply these remedies in order to subdue our minds. Just as you must prepare the soil before you plant a crop, in order to practice Atiyoga you must have a sufficient foundation, or you will encounter problems. –

Kamalaśīla says:

> Thinking, "All phenomena are ultimately devoid of an inherent nature," and pondering, "No inherent nature exists at all," is to abandon genuine wisdom. With respect to such an object that transcends existence and nonexistence, consciousness also transcends existence and nonexistence. Meditate like that, without an object.

– The moment you think you have realized that all phenomena are ultimately devoid of inherent nature, conceptual grasping arises again. That is, genuine wisdom has been abandoned. –

Norbu Lingpa Déwé Dorje says:

> If you recognize the clear light, there is no need for reasonings concerning unity and multiplicity. In the direct perception of the appearance of great bliss there is no need to seek out textual citations or inferences.
>
> Since experience is of the nature of reality, there is no need for a nihilistic view. Since one does not think "that is" with respect to anything, there is no need for conceptual superimposition.

– Once you have recognized the clear light, there is no need to engage in the Madhyamaka analysis of examining the relationship between phenomena and their components, investigating whether they are a unity or a multiplicity. Experience itself is of the nature of reality. Therefore, don't fall to the one extreme of denying that which does exist or to the other extreme of conceptually superimposing something upon reality, which, in fact, does not exist at all. –

Namké Dorje says:

> If you recognize the clear light, there is no need for meditations on the two types of identitylessness. Likewise, once you have actually found the elephant, why look for its tracks?

A Commentary to the Dohas, which was translated by Vairocana, states:

> Turning away from the intellectual authentic view, I assert the intended meaning of the Buddha to be the view of recollective awareness and ideation. Both appearances and emptiness are adventitious and are therefore fabricated.

Tilopa says:

> Without representing, without thinking, without meditating, and without analyzing, the mind remains in its own nature.

Orgyen Rinpoche says:

> Merely having awareness pointed out as before and knowing your own nature is not enough. As an analogy, due to letting one's wild stallion roam freely for many years, its owner will not recognize it. It is not enough for the owner to recognize the horse once it is pointed out to him by a herdsman. Methods must be used to capture the wild stallion, then subdue it and put it to work. Likewise, it is not enough simply to identify this wild mind. It is said, "Oh, at this time, when the transitional process of meditative stabilization is appearing to me, the delusive multitudes of distractions have been cast off, and without wavering and without grasping, I shall enter into the domain that is free of extremes."
>
> Beginners must practice and meditate with unwavering mindfulness. When the wild stallion is not subdued, it must be trained with unwavering enthusiasm. If you waver, you will lose control of the horse, fall down, and hurt yourself. Likewise, if beginners pursue ordinary thoughts, they will descend to miserable states of existence and will be hurt; so sustain your meditation with unwavering mindfulness.[48]

And:

> Without meditating on anything, simply without wavering, let [your awarness] be steady, luminous and even. First practice in short sessions, and as you become accustomed to it, practice in longer and longer sessions. When you bring the session to an end, do not get up abruptly, but rise slowly without losing the sense of meditating; and proceed without losing the sense of awareness, without wavering, and without grasping. As you eat, drink, speak, and engage in every activity, do so without losing the sentry of unwavering mindfulness. If this happens in meditative equipoise but not afterwards, by integrating this with your spiritual practice and all activities of moving, walking, lying down, and sitting, whatever you do will arise as meditation.[49]

– First, practice in very short sessions, but have as many of them as possible. This approach is like drops coming down one by one through a hole in a leaky roof. As you become more familiar with the practice, gradually increase the duration of each session and decrease the number of sessions per day. If you can maintain this uncontrived awareness in the post-meditative period, this is excellent. However, if you are not able to maintain such undistracted, fresh mindfulness, don't give up. Just try to imbue the post-meditative awareness with mindfulness and introspection. Between sessions many thoughts will arise, so you should enhance your practice by observing their nature. Integrate as much Dharma practice—

including *mantra* recitation, discursive meditation, and so forth—as you can throughout the entire course of the day, so that all your mental states arise as meditation.

For example, after a session of practicing the stage of generation, attend to the fundamental, equal nature of appearances by seeing all forms as the Buddha's body, all sounds as the Buddha's speech, and all thoughts as expressions of primordial wisdom. By so doing, your post-meditative experience will be enhanced by the insight gleaned from your formal sessions.

Being introduced to the nature of awareness is often likened to conception in the mother's womb. Once you recognize that a child has been conceived, you nurture the child in the womb. Similarly, after being introduced to the nature of awareness, you cultivate awareness by sustaining your realization of its nature. The actual birth of the child is likened to engaging in the practice. Once the child is born, parents do all they can to nurture and protect the child, until it is able to take care of itself. Similarly, after our introduction to and initial realization of the nature of awareness—like parents nurturing their child through infancy, youth and adolescence—we must protect our practice, so that our realization is not overwhelmed by the various outer and inner obstacles that arise.

How should we practice Dharma? If you were on death row waiting for your execution, only one thought would constantly occupy your mind day and night: "How can I get out of here?" In the same way, if you recognize the nature of the suffering of cyclic existence, you will naturally want to escape from that suffering and its sources. The way to escape is to enter through the gateway of Dharma.

To enter this gateway, you must first receive Dharma so that you can put it into practice. Receive Dharma like a bee taking nectar, careful not to destroy the flower that is the nectar's source. People learning Dharma often become easily tired and frustrated, indicating that they're not yet tired of *saṃsāra*. This is due to having not gained a deep realization of the Four Noble Truths and the Four Thoughts that Turn the Mind. Thus, they do not have a clear understanding of why they are studying and practicing Dharma. Practitioners with a genuine commitment to Dharma and a sincere aspiration to achieve perfect enlightenment are rare. It is chiefly pride in their own qualities, ideas, and opinions that obstructs their understanding drawn from hearing, thinking, and meditating on Dharma. Once you enter through this gateway of Dharma, you are committed to adhering to ethical discipline. If you fail to maintain ethical discipline, your practice is a mere pretense. Such a person is like a bee that mutilates the flower from which it takes nectar.

If you seek liberation, you must have more than an intellectual understanding of suffering, its causes, and the antidotes; you must practice for this understanding to mature. Just as a deer shot by a hunter retreats into solitude to heal itself, so too, you should withdraw from all superfluous activity. At the very least, occasionally withdraw into solitude in order to practice. As a result, you may realize the one taste of reality and cut through the divisions created by delusion, attachment, and hatred. Once you have gained this realization, you become as fearless and powerful as a snow lion. You have then achieved the state of confidence. At this point, your own self-interest is fulfilled as you observe all phenomena as displays of awareness. Having brought your own inner transformation to perfection with the motivation of being of benefit to others, you are now fully capable of serving others' needs. This is the path of a true Dharma practitioner. –

The Tantra of the Synthesized Mysteries of Avalokiteśvara states:

> With a balanced degree of tension and relaxation, meditate on the empty state free of conceptual elaboration.

– In the course of meditation, the degree of tension may be too strong, in which case we tend to feel tense or stressed out. When the mind is too relaxed, it becomes muddled. Through our own experience, we must find a balance so that we do not fall to either of these extremes. Then, in this state of balance, meditate on the empty state free of conceptual elaboration. There is nothing on which to meditate; rather, allow your mind to rest without a specific focus. –

And:

> First, like placing a looped rope in water, firm up your posture and awareness to a suitable degree, and in that state gently relax. Right after that, rest in fresh, stable, present, lucid openness. That tension gives rise to clarity, and the relaxation gives rise to steadiness and a degree of joy. Resting in a state of freshness gives rise to emptiness and a primordial absence of focus. Entering into this state in a single session and with a single gaze is said to be unmistaken meditation of the kind the Buddha intended.
>
> Meditate like that for a long time. If ideation proliferates, concentrate. If clarity decreases, relax. Most importantly, rest naturally when there is no problem. At that time, in terms of awareness, the essence is empty lucidity, the nature is unmediated luminosity, and the display is undirected openness. Remaining in the single state of luminosity, awareness, and emptiness is flawless Mahāmudrā, so the *tantras* state, "Meditate in a state of emptiness free of conceptual elaboration."

– It is most important that you find a suitable balance for your physical posture as well as for the quality of awareness, so that it is not too tense or too lax. If you find a balance that has the characteristics of freshness, stability, and so forth, then it is said that all excellent qualities are complete. You need to persevere in practice to gain familiarity. This creates habitual patterning, so that progress can be made on the path. If the mind becomes filled with thoughts, bear down a bit. If clarity decreases, relax. If no problems arise, apply no antidote at all. Remaining in a single state of luminosity, awareness, and emptiness is the very quintessence of Mahāmudrā. –

Songtsen Gampo says:

> The reality-itself of Avalokiteśvara accords with Mahāmudrā, and the meditation is presented in terms of analogies together with their referents.
>
> First, nonconceptual luminosity is like a butter lamp unmoved by wind: in a butter lamp unmoved by wind, the base of the wick is aflame, the shaft of the wick is luminous, and the tip is sharp. Likewise, when the mind is left without modification, it is fresh, naturally limpid, and relaxed.
>
> Second, recognizing memories and thoughts as empty is like recognizing a thief: due to recognizing a thief, he cannot steal. Likewise, whatever experiences of laxity and excitation arise, by recognizing their nature as empty, you abide in Mahāmudrā through mindfulness alone.
>
> The lifestyle is presented in terms of analogies together with their referents. The nondual encounter is like the meeting of a mother and son: once a mother and son recognize each other, there is no doubt about the matter. Likewise, whatever appearances arise and whatever is recalled in the mind, one recognizes them as Mahāmudrā.

In the same vein, Songtsen Gampo says:

> This Dharma of Avalokiteśvara is taught in accordance with the Great Perfection. Encountering reality-itself is like meeting someone you have known before. That and nothing else is reality-itself. The condition of remaining without recognizing your own mind-itself is to be understood like this: when you meet a man you have known earlier, you clearly recognize him. Likewise, you recognize your own mind-itself as reality-itself, simply by the spiritual mentor pointing this out.
>
> The reality of ideation arising as primordial wisdom is like fire spreading in a forest. In the unceasing ideation of the present there is nothing to be apprehended. For example, if a fire is lit in a thick forest, all the shrubs and trees assist the fire. Likewise, all the coarse and subtle thoughts of the three times initially have no origination and are empty; in the interim they have no location and are empty; and finally they have no departure and are empty. So they arise solely as empty primordial wisdom.
>
> The meaning of the self-releasing of signs is like water merging into water. All phenomena that appear as real signs are none other than reality-itself. For example, once bubbles have arisen, they dissolve back into the water. Likewise, all phenomena arise from reality-itself, then all phenomena are released in their own state.

– Once you have recognized the actual nature of ideation, then as thoughts arise, they actually enhance the emergence of primordial wisdom. Ideation is like kindling that fuels the blaze of primordial wisdom. The expression, "In the unceasing ideation of the present there is nothing to be apprehended" refers to the specific phase of the practice in which your mind is overwhelmed by layers of ideation. There are so many thoughts that you can't possibly recognize all of them. But step by step, through engaging in the practice, you refine your awareness so that the moment they arise you recognize them and simultaneously see their nature. Moreover, you gain deeper insight into the absence of their origination, location, and departure. In other words, you understand they are thoroughly empty in nature. In order to do that you must first recognize them, but before this is possible you will probably be overwhelmed by them. This whole process transforms ideation into an aid to spiritual maturation. These conceptual constructs are self-liberating, without any external intervention. –

Dagpo Rinpoche taught the meaning intended by Ḍombi Heruka:

> Just as water is limpid if it is not disturbed, rest without modifying the state [of awareness]. Like the sun unobscured by clouds, rest in your own nature, without inhibiting the six fields of experience. At all times and during all activities be without distraction.

– When the sun shines into a pool of limpid water, the pool is transparent and luminous. In this practice, if you do inhibit your thoughts, feelings, and so forth, the exertion itself disturbs the awareness and limpidity is lost. Therefore, relax into your own nature without inhibiting any of the six fields of experience. At all times do your best to maintain the qualities of mindfulness, introspection, and conscientiousness, and do not fall into the other extreme of following after the six fields of experience. –

The venerable Dragpa Gyaltsen says:

> Observe the mind of the mind that is mindless. If you see something, that is not the mind-itself. Seeing without seeing is seeing the mind-itself. Do not be distracted from the unseen mind.

– If you think that the mind does exist, that is fine, but then look at it. Can you identify its essence? If you do see something, what you see is not the mind-itself. Do not be distracted from the unseen mind-itself, because, as soon as you do, you will lose it. –

The venerable Sakya Paṇchen says:

> When self-arisen primordial wisdom arises, all conceptualization turns into the nature of primordial wisdom. There is no difference

> between meditating and not meditating, and ideation dissolves into the absolute nature of reality.

Kyemé Zhang says:

> In Mahāmudrā meditation there is no definite sequence. There is no order or enumeration of preliminaries, main practice, and conclusion. There is no need to calculate the time or date. Whenever you remember, maintain your practice and be at ease. There is no beginning, middle, or end. Your own mind is unborn and unceasing. In the case of water in which silt has been raised up by waves, if you leave it to itself, it will become placid and limpid. In the case of your mind that is obscured with conceptualization, if you leave it in its own nature without modifying it, it becomes limpid. Do not modify it, but be at ease. Do not draw in your consciousness, but let it roam. Do not crave anything, but let it be. Do not fix your attention on an object, but let it be. Do not engage in many activities, but simply be present. Without seeking a place to put the mind, let it be like space with no foundation. Do not think of the past, future, or present, but let your consciousness be fresh. Whether or not ideation flows out, do not intentionally meditate, but be loose. In short, without meditating on anything, let your consciousness be just as it is. There is no need for anxiety about anything, but know that everything moves in the state of the Dharmakāya.

– In this phase of practice, you don't need to contemplate the Four Noble Truths or the Four Thoughts that Turn the Mind. You don't need to take account of particular times of day or auspicious times to practice.

If you leave your mind in its own nature, without modification, structure, or adulteration, it becomes limpid. In that state of awareness, there is no question of either contamination or noncontamination because all kinds of duality have been left behind. Do not have fancy ideas about this or complicate it. Do not pursue further questions at this point. This quality of freshness is not something contrived nor is it brought to consciousness; rather, it is a primordial freshness that you allow to be present in the mind. Be loose by allowing the mind to be relaxed in its own nature. –

The glorious Gö Tsangpa says:

> In a relaxed and loose manner, place your consciousness in its primordial state that is inconceivable and ineffable. "To place" is just words. There is nothing grasped that is to be picked up and attended to, nor anything modified on which to place the attention. Apart from settling in the nature of being, there is nothing mentally created on which to meditate. There is no meditation on indistinct deities. There is no impossible recitation. There is

> no training in unmasterable techniques. Let the mind settle in itself. Let it be, without fabricating or managing anything. Although you are told to be present without structuring anything, you want to fabricate bliss, stillness, limpidity, clarity, nonexistence, and emptiness. Stop that! Leave your mind fresh, relaxed, and naturally limpid.
>
> It is fresh because the newness has not been lost. It is relaxed because it is effortless. It is settled in natural limpidity because it is remedy-free.

– In this stage of practice there are no deities to imagine, so you can't be frustrated because your visualization is unclear. There is nothing to recite, so you don't have to accumulate hundreds of thousands or millions of *mantras*. You don't need to train in unmasterable techniques, so arduous disciplines involving the channels and vital energies and so forth are not needed. Simply let the mind settle in its own nature. –

Yang Gönpa says:

> The essence of thoughts that suddenly arise is without any nature. Do not inhibit their appearance in any way, and without thinking of any essence, let them arise clearly, nakedly, and vividly. Likewise, if one thought arises, observe its nature, and if two arise, observe their nature. Thus, whatever thoughts arise, let them go without holding onto them. Let them remain as fragments. Release them unimpededly. Be naked without an object. Release them without grasping. This is close to becoming a Buddha. This is the self-extinction of *saṃsāra*, *saṃsāra* is overwhelmed, *saṃsāra* is disempowered, and *saṃsāra* is exhausted. Knowledge of the path of method and wisdom, appearances and emptiness, the gradual stages, the common and special paths, and the 84,000 entrances to the Dharma is made perfectly complete and fulfilled in an instant. This is self-arisen, for it is present like that in the very nature [of awareness]. Natural liberation is the essence of all the stainless paths, and it bears the essence of emptiness and compassion.
>
> The basis is the nature of existence that does not dwell in *saṃsāra* or *nirvāṇa*. The path is the union that does not dwell in *saṃsāra* or *nirvāṇa*. The fruition is the transcendence of misery that does not dwell in *saṃsāra* or *nirvāṇa*.
>
> In an instant there is self-liberation of the nature of existence that is not created by anyone. This complete, unmistaken, definite path is called self-arisen, essential self-liberation. Recognize this very stream of ordinary consciousness as an unmediated,

objectless phenomenon. It arises without anyone creating it; it is primordial, for it is originally pure. Because its nature remains like that, it is simply present, and meditation is self-arisen, primordial, and simply present.

In such practice it is important to rest the mind without distraction and without meditating. If you are distracted, you remain an ordinary being. If you meditate, however you do it, it will be misleading. In the state of not meditating, do not be distracted!

– Suddenly arising thoughts have a dreamlike quality. Whatever thoughts occur, let them go to pieces. Then *saṃsāra* loses its glamour and is disempowered. In an instant all the 84,000 entrances to the Dharma are perfectly complete; nothing is added to them, and nothing is left out.

Avoid the two extremes of nihilism and substantialism, in which *saṃsāra* represents the extreme of substantialism and *nirvāṇa* represents the extreme of nihilism.

To illustrate the self-arisen, essential nature of self-liberation, if we regard the Buddhas or the pure realms as existent and grasp onto them, we fall to the extreme of substantialism. On the other hand, if we regard them or other phenomena as nonexistent, we fall to the extreme of nihilism.

While meditating, if you allow your mind to be carried away by thoughts, you will remain an ordinary person. If you do something other than simply allowing the mind to rest in its natural state, you have gone astray from this practice. –

Siddha Orgyen says:

(1) Rest in unstructured freshness. (2) Let go of memories and thoughts. (3) Transform diversity into an aid. (4) Practice letting go of appearances.

(1) Rest in unstructured freshness: Be at ease, like a brahmin spinning yarn. Be loose, like a sheaf of straw for which the cord has been cut. Be gentle, like stepping on a soft cushion. Otherwise, you will trap yourself as if you were caught in a spider's web. Even if you tighten up your whole body and mind like a woodcutter on the side of a cliff, your mind will not want to be still. In a state free of a meditation object and a meditator, post a sentry simply by undistractedly withdrawing the mind, then evenly let it be. Thus, awareness circles back to its own resting place, like a mother camel who has been sent away from her calf.

Therefore, the critical point of sustaining the attention is just knowing how to relax in a state of nondistraction without meditating. This is profound. Again, it is said that relaxed consciousness is not something easy.

– Brahmins spin yarn skillfully, without frantically trying to finish their job. In fact, they do it as if they don't care if anything gets done. They just methodically, gently, but steadily carry on the task without too much tension or too much looseness. So be at ease like a brahmin spinning yarn.

Perhaps you have traveled to Asia and seen the farmers carrying enormous bundles of straw on their backs. When they arrive at their destination, someone cuts the cord that holds the bundle together, and the straw falls into a loose heap on the ground. Just so, let your awareness be like a fallen sheaf of straw.

Woodcutters in Asia unable to find wood in the valleys search for it on the face of cliffs. Holding onto the cliff face for dear life with one hand, they cut the wood with the other. If you restrain your mind that tightly, it will not be still.

A mother camel who has been separated from her calf circles back until she finds her young. Likewise, even if awareness becomes caught up in thoughts, it will circle back to its own resting place. –

> (2) Let go of memories and thoughts: This mind primordially, originally exists as the Dharmakāya. The very forms of that are the six fields of experience arising as various memories and thoughts, and the mind moves after each of those objects. Once there arises in your mind-stream the experience of all of them recognizing their own nature in their own state, the essence of Mahāmudrā is seen. In such realization there is no expulsion of bad things that are not meditation, and there is nothing to be affirmed. Whatever thoughts arise, do not be distracted from them, but practice like the flow of a stream.

– Memories, thoughts, and fantasies are simply like formations of clouds that arise in the sky and then vanish. To recognize the actual nature of them is not to get in touch with your feelings, but is to recognize the empty nature of these thoughts in their own state. By doing this, you see the essence of Mahāmudrā. Thus, whatever comes up is not identified as being incompatible with your meditation, and so you don't need to get rid of it. –

> (3) Transform diversity into an aid: Whatever appearances of the eight mundane concerns arise, do not regard them as a problem, but relate to them as aids. If you know that point, there is no need make a point of seeking nonconceptuality, and there is no need to regard thoughts as a problem. Your awareness is then bountifully sustained, without the onset of a famine of spiritual practice. So, without seeking mental stillness, clarity, or joy, practice without rejecting or accepting anything that appears. Such ordinary consciousness is without fabrication or structure. This very self-illumination is the encounter with all phenomena.

> (4) Practice letting go of appearances: Then all memories and thoughts, all appearances, and all experiences of activities arise in the nature of Mahāmudrā. Just as no ordinary rocks are found on a golden island, the various phenomena of *saṃsāra* and *nirvāṇa* naturally do not lose their freshness; their countenance does not change; and they arise as self-originated, inborn, primordial wisdom, in the nature of unfabricated, uncreated, primordial Mahāmudrā.

– If you regard the appearances of the eight mundane concerns as aids, there is no need to try to still the mind or get rid of thoughts.

If you arrive on an island composed totally of gold, not even a single ordinary rock will be found on it. Similarly, when you come to this phase of genuine Mahāmudrā practice, all thoughts arise as aids. None will simply be ordinary. In this way, the various phenomena of *saṃsāra* and *nirvāṇa* naturally do not lose their freshness.

When you come to this genuine state of Mahāmudrā, there are no grasped appearances. Even if you search for them, they cannot be found. This is called actual primordial wisdom. The fruition of this practice is the total presence of awareness. Quiescence, insight, identifying the nature of the mind, and subsequent practice all lead to, and culminate in this total presence of awareness. At this point, there is no grasping onto appearances. Appearances do arise, but there is no grasping onto an appearance as being "this" or "that" or as being "good" or "bad." They are present, but without any grasping whatsoever, and awareness is totally present.

Here is a more detailed account of the phases of the practice: first, recognize thoughts as they arise. One thought arises and you recognize it. Another arises and you recognize it. Then upon recognizing the ideation, penetrate further to realize its empty nature. Then by the very recognition of the empty nature of thoughts, they naturally vanish of their own accord. In the next stage, the ideation continues to arise, and whether the thoughts are good or bad, they are viewed as an aid to your practice. Each has the quality of self-illumination, or natural radiance. This self-illumination is in the very nature of the thought itself. It is not something added onto the thought. At this point, actual primordial wisdom becomes manifest. You must progress sequentially in the practice, without expecting immediate results. On the other hand, there are some people who enter instantaneously into the fruition stage, but they are very rare.

You may find in meditation that when thoughts are not arising, you are able to maintain a continuity of mindfulness, but when they do arise, you get distracted and mindfulness is lost. In that case, it is very difficult simply to observe thoughts without their obstructing mindfulness. The problem is that you are still grasping onto thoughts. When you begin meditating, you may have the preconception that the thoughts will be helpful, or that they will be a nuisance. Both preconceptions entail grasping. How can you counteract this? Just focus your awareness on the very nature of the thoughts as soon as they arise. It's a very subtle and demanding task, but it can be done. As soon as the thought arises, look into its nature. By so doing, you will not get carried away by it. This approach will counteract grasping. Then you will not regard thoughts as flaws in your meditation, nor will you look forward to a future state of meditation in which thoughts no longer arise. When you reach the state in which thoughts no longer arise, you will most likely be dead. In the meantime, you actually need thoughts because it is through observation and insight into the nature of the thoughts that you eventually recognize them as displays of primordial wisdom. –

According to the tradition of *The Great Perfection Aro Oral Lineage* by Yagdey Paṇchen:

> In the state of luminous, empty awareness, free of grasping, relax gently, be completely loose and totally present; do not inhibit appearances, do not reject them with antidotes, do not alter them with the intellect, and do not fabricate or modify them. Whatever appears, and however it appears, turn inwards upon that alone, and without modifying, negating, or affirming anything, be at ease in your own nature. Settle in luminosity without grasping. That is called "the great total presence of Aro." Amazing! And yet it is so.

– This state of Mahāmudrā, in which you abide in luminous, empty awareness, free of grasping, is beyond any distinction of relaxation and nonrelaxation because it is free of conceptual grasping. It is beyond differentiation and free of extremes. This state of awareness is characterized by two qualities—luminosity and emptiness. The quality of emptiness counteracts the extreme of substantialism; luminosity counteracts nihilism. –

Dong Kachöpa Saraha says:

> Hey, son, listen! Observe your own mind. Unstructured consciousness of the present is what the Jinas of the three times have in mind. This direct perception, devoid of obscurations, and free from all substantialist and nihilistic extremes, is without rejection or acceptance, hope or fear. So do not modify the mind-itself, just as it appears.
>
> The body and mind are unestablished: like a rainbow in the sky, they appear but are empty. Whoever realizes this dissolves like space into space, and when that happens, what a sight it is!

– The first moment that you experience the mind-itself, or your Buddha-nature, it comes as an unprecedented experience, even though it has primordially been present in you. Since beginningless time, you have been touring the six states of existence, searching everywhere. You have spent all this time roaming in *saṃsāra*, never having known the actual nature of your own mind. For that reason when you recognize it for the first time, it is utterly astonishing and unprecedented, even though it has been there all along. Within Buddhism, there are many meditative techniques and systems. There is also much striving. In the Hīnayāna system much effort is given to realizing personal identitylessness. In the Mahāyāna there are various philosophical systems. Even within the Madhyamaka school there are different interpretations that can be differentiated and studied. You can study to be a Svātantrika Mādhyamika as opposed to a Prāsaṅgika Mādhyamika. Similarly, within the practice of the stage of generation, there are three types of *samādhi*, and even in Atiyoga there are the three categories of the Mind Division, the Expanse Division, and the Practical Instructions Division. What is the aim of all of these methods? They are all aimed at this one stunning, unprecedented realization of the nature of the mind. –

Gyatön Chökyi Zangpo says:

> Observe the nature of whatever appears and whatever occurs. If there is an observer, observe that, too.
>
> If there is joy, observe the nature of the joy. If there is an observer, observe that, too.
>
> If there is pain, observe the nature of the pain. If there is an observer, observe that, too.
>
> If you find nothing to observe by looking, leave that, too, in equality, without grasping.
>
> If you do not even find yourself as the observer, leave that, too, in equality, without grasping.

– Whatever mental events arise, observe their nature once they have arisen, and recognize that they are unestablished. You may recognize that simply by investigating their nature, or you may apply the three-fold method of investigating their origin, location, and departure to establish that ideation is unestablished and empty in nature. The gist of the above citation is that whatever you attend to, even if it is identitylessness itself, it is imperative that you redirect your awareness back inward and observe that which is doing the meditation. In other words, seek to observe the observer.

A horse may have a bridle with a rope tied to a stake planted in the ground, which allows the horse some leeway to roam around. But if the stake is pulled up, the horse is completely free. The stake that impedes our freedom is grasping. To have freedom, genuine realization, it is necessary to dispense with grasping. In the course of all of this meditating, we are really searching for ourselves and the nature of our own being, our own Buddha-nature. Samantabhadra is a Buddha because of recognizing this Buddha-nature, whereas we samsaric beings are not Buddhas because we fail to recognize our own nature. We insist upon the duality between our own nature and that of our Buddha-nature, and as a result we continue to revolve in *saṃsāra*. –

Avalokiteśvara's Collected Essential Instructions states:

> In the stage of completion, the posture is characterized by the seven qualities of Vairocana, the breath is left alone, and without intentionally bringing anything to mind, the mind is placed steadily in single-pointedness. That is the initial placement without distraction.
>
> Once you are accustomed to that, then whatever thoughts arise, recognize them and focus just on their nature. That is intermediate placement without structure.
>
> Wherever dependent consciousness goes, to all objects and subjects, leave it in equality, and rest in that. That is the final letting go.
>
> In case of laxity, stay in a cool place and elevate your gaze. In case of excitation, stay in a warm place and lower your gaze.

– These are the phases of the practice. For those of you who are interested in practice, attend to these instructions. Now is the time for practice, even for you who are of a scholarly bent. When we engage in the eight mundane concerns, we are simply perpetuating *saṃsāra* and sowing seeds for the six types of existence. That is not the task here. This is the time for practice.

While you are meditating, if you experience drowsiness or lethargy, stay in a cool place. On the other hand, if you are succumbing to boredom, temporarily suspend the meditation and reflect on the benefits of the practice. Inspire yourself. Arouse your mind. You may want to read and reflect upon the life stories of some of the great adepts of the past. Also, review the Four Thoughts that Turn the Mind. –

The glorious Tsuglak Trengwa says:

> Therefore, whatever happiness and sorrow, mental afflictions including the three poisons, and good and bad thoughts arise, do not follow after them, but turn inwards and steadily observe them. By so doing, the essence of all states of consciousness will vividly appear only as empty, luminous, and pure of a self-nature, just as there is no difference in the fluidity of all water. Thus, you will intuitively know that there is nothing to reject or affirm in anything and that there is no need to do so, and you will spontaneously transcend the intellect.
>
> Whatever virtue you perform, such as generosity, that is imbued with this authentic vision gains the name *the perfection of generosity* and so forth, and it becomes a true cause of supreme enlightenment and the unification of the two collections. This is meditation on the true meaning of all the *yānas* simultaneously, and this is the foremost of all unions of quiescence and insight.

Drungchen Kün-ga Namgyal says:

> The critical point for *samādhi* is to place the mind at ease in its own nature. Nakedly, in a relaxed way, observe the nature of the mind at ease. Rely upon the continuous mindfulness of simple nondistraction. Whatever thoughts arise, observe their nature, without intentionally rejecting or accepting them, and without any kind of modification.

Bring forth the reliable shepherd of mindfulness of simple nondistraction, without meditating on anything, and without indulging in even the slightest trace of hopes for the meditative state to arise or fears that it will not, or hopes for expansiveness and excellent experiential realizations or fears of the occurrence of hindrances or errors.

– Remember that in this practice there is nothing on which to meditate. Remain simply without distraction and without bringing anything to mind as an intentional object of meditation. You may practice the meditation described in this chapter minute by minute, for hours, days, years, or lifetimes. This is something to which you can devote yourself, and this perseverance will eventually lead to genuine realization. –

CHAPTER SEVEN

Mahāmudrā

Homage to Avalokiteśvara!

These are the profound practical instructions of Avalokiteśvara. Here is the manner in which experiential realizations arise. If you engage in the preliminary and main spiritual practices with great perseverance, signs of those two phases of practice will occur. One in whom those signs appear swiftly and simultaneously is called a "simultaneous individual," who bears karmic dividends from past lives. Such people are rare. Those in whom the indeterminate signs appear to a high degree are middling individuals of the Leap-over class. So if they meditate, it will be very effective, but there is the danger of their sliding back to an ordinary state due to succumbing to pitfalls. In "gradually guided individuals" it is hard for the signs to come, but they do gradually appear as a result of continual, sustained meditation.

– The critical point is to practice with zeal. Zeal does not entail mere diligence, but enthusiasm and an enduring quality of delighting in practice. If you practice with zeal, then signs of success in both the preliminary and main phases of practice will occur.

A simultaneous individual hears the teachings and immediately has signs of genuine realization. Such people have purified their obscurations and accumulated merit in previous lives, so they are primed to gain realization. They are like a light sleeper, who, when tapped lightly on the cheek, is immediately and fully awake. Likewise, with the slightest catalyst this type of individual is wide awake. Obviously, such individuals are very rare.

Middling people of the Leap-over class have indeterminate signs, which is to say that when they practice, signs of progress sometimes appear and sometimes don't. At times, one type of sign will appear and at other times another type will appear. There is no definite order or regularity with which the signs appear, but they do nevertheless appear to a high degree. By engaging in rigorous practice, the middling person can progress quite rapidly. It is said that if you squeeze a snake, its limbs will appear. Similarly, if you squeeze a middling individual, good qualities appear. However, such practitioners must be very careful not to fall back into a mundane state of consciousness in which they are swept away by their faults. This precarious situation can be avoided by making frequent prayers for protection to one's spiritual mentor. Although it is difficult for signs to arise for those who are "deep sleepers," by applying discipline and perseverance to their practice, the signs will appear. –

Moreover, there is no certainty as to when the signs of meditating on the preliminaries will occur. They may come gradually or as side-effects, so recognize whether or not the signs have appeared. In the event of good signs, do not be excessively elated. The non-appearance of signs is an indication of thick obscurations, so develop enthusiasm. If bad signs occur, recognize these as indications of the purification of obscurations, and do not speculate about them.

– You need to examine in terms of your own experience whether or not signs of progress have arisen. If good signs do appear, don't get excited or you will fall right back into the cycle of the eight mundane concerns. Whether you are wearing gold or steel handcuffs, the effect is the same. On the other hand, if you don't have signs, don't become disturbed either. Just recognize that there are too many obscurations and respond by arousing your enthusiasm and perseverance.

This advice is valid not only for spiritual practice but for life in general. Commonly, when something good happens in our lives, we respond with elation. Underlying this response is a sense of self-centeredness. If we respond to good fortune with exaggerated elation, then in the face of adversity we will probably respond with exaggerated depression. In either situation, even if the Buddha were to come to us, he would not be able to calm us down. With no sense of equanimity we continue to cycle in *saṃsāra*, which indicates our impatience and weakness.

If bad signs appear, don't wonder and worry. Simply recognize this is an indication of purification and respond with even greater enthusiasm and diligence in your practice. –

First, these are the signs of the preliminary practices. Gö Tsangpa says:

> If you meditate on death and impermanence, [1] the cord that connects you to your homeland will be cut, [2] the glue of your

relatives will crumble, [3] and attachment to food and wealth will be severed.

If you meditate on the difficulty of obtaining a human life of leisure and endowment, [1] you will not engage in pointless activities, [2] you will apply yourself enthusiastically day and night to Dharma activities, and [3] you will avoid evil companions.

If you meditate on the faults of the cycle of existence, [1] you will see sensual attractions as a cause of misfortune, [2] you will entrust yourself to the Three Jewels, and [3] your obsession with mundane concerns will cease.

– The cord that connects you to your homeland is precisely your attachment to and identification with your homeland. People can identify so strongly with their country that they take on the qualities of the nation as a whole—its history, its culture, its government, its wealth, and its influence. It is as if they embody it all. Americans don't have a monopoly on such identification, for other nationalities do this as well. Don't think that it is enough just to leave your homeland and move to another place. The abandonment of grasping is one of the signs of successful meditation on death and impermanence. In truth, you are just severing attachment to rocks, dirt, trees, and so forth.

Just as one can identify strongly with one's homeland, it is also possible to identify strongly with one's relatives. Again, meditation on death and impermanence will crumble the glue of this attachment.

Our obsession with food and wealth can be severed simply by being satisfied with that which is sufficient. If you have enough to eat and your basic needs are met, that is sufficient. Meditation on death and impermanence draws the mind away from the fixation of mundane activities and long-term goals and projects, and it brings the mind to the present.

You must recognize that not only is life short, but we don't even know how short it is, and it is very difficult to achieve this human life of leisure and endowment again in the future. So dispense with the eight mundane concerns and apply yourself to virtuous activity. When you meditate on the difficulty of obtaining this precious human life of leisure and endowment, you will let go of all pointless activities. Moreover, you will apply yourself to spiritual practice that is of genuine benefit to yourself and others in this and future lifetimes. A sign of having such a realization is that you will not flaunt the fact that you have completed a one- or three-day retreat. Rather, you would hide your head in shame because spiritual practice is not a one-day event but a lifetime commitment at the very least.

You will also avoid associating with evil companions, whether they are male or female. Consorting with people who have nonvirtuous tendencies inevitably gives rise to nonvirtue in your life. This is not to say that you never associate with such companions, but that you shouldn't follow their behavior. You may indeed spend time with them, but you do so with the compassionate motivation to be of benefit to them, without following their example.

By meditating on the faults of cyclic existence, you will see the attractions of the desire realm—the realm we live in—as a cause of misfortune, and you will come to venerate and respect the Buddha, Dharma, and Saṅgha. –

Thus, by cultivating the four preliminaries, each of the outer, inner, and secret signs will appear. First, these are the signs of receiving blessings due to making supplications: the outer signs are that due to boundless adoration and reverence, even when your spiritual mentor is present, out of adoration you wish to touch his body; and because your mind has been captivated by the spiritual mentor, you think of nothing else; and prayers of supplication arise unceasingly day and night.

– Thus, by cultivating the four preliminaries, various outer, inner, and secret signs will appear. The essence of the meditation on these Four Thoughts that Turn the Mind is turning your mind away from the attractions of the cycle of existence. If this doesn't happen, you continue to flounder in the ocean of attachment. The blaze of hatred, delusion, attachment, pride, and jealousy continues to arise. Both the teacher and the students may fall under the sway of the eight mundane concerns. Both must recognize that the cycle of existence is without essence and totally turn their minds to Dharma. For Dharma to be of true benefit, the teacher must teach with a pure motivation, and the student must bring forth a pure motivation while listening.

People commonly mix their practice of Dharma with the eight mundane concerns. These people may hear many teachings and study assiduously. They may even think about the teachings and meditate, but basically they have not turned their minds away from the cycle of existence. Rather, they maintain their commitment to *saṃsāra*. The only thing wrong with this approach is that they do not see the essence of the Dharma, because they have failed to see the vacuous nature of cyclic existence.

Due to making prayers to your primary spiritual mentor, by practicing *guruyoga*, great faith and reverence arise for this mentor. Since Buddha Śākyamuni is not present at this time, your spiritual mentor is the only bridge to the Buddha. Therefore, perceive your mentor as the actual Buddha. You may wish to touch his body not out of desire and attachment but because of your pure devotional wish to be close to your mentor. Moreover, this feeling will not come from an attitude of thinking that you are special and holy. If your practice of *guruyoga* is very pure, after some time, you will see all appearances as being the appearance of your mentor, all sounds as the speech of your mentor, and all thoughts as the mind of your own mentor. In other words, all of your experiences will be suffused with the presence of your spiritual mentor.

If you focus on the physical qualities rather than on the transcendent aspect of the Buddha, eventually when your mentor dies, these qualities will vanish, and your practice will collapse. Therefore, the proper way to cultivate a relationship with your mentor is to cultivate deep reverence, faith, and devotion, and with that attitude engage in the practices of hearing, thinking, and meditating, while simultaneously doing your utmost to abandon nonvirtuous activity. By so doing, you will receive blessings from the Buddha himself. When there is such inspiration and blessing, you will find that you will not suffer from fatigue in your practice.

If you have received teachings and initiations from many teachers, that is fine, as long as you purely maintain your relationships with them. Otherwise, even Padmasambhava cannot help you. Students commonly hear teachings, receive empowerments, take precepts, and pose questions to their spiritual mentors. But then they either don't remember the answers or don't apply them to their practice. What benefit is there in that? Traditionally, in Tibet, Lamas posed questions to their students to determine the level of their experience and insight and to see if they were going astray in their practice. In the West, where the Dharma is just beginning to flourish, this situation is reversed, so students often test the Lamas to see how well they answer their questions. –

These are the inner signs: Your realizations are enhanced simply by recalling your spiritual mentor, outer appearances present themselves as if they were apparitions, inner consciousness appears as unmediated, clear, and empty, and the flow of intervening thoughts is cut.

– Outer appearances rise up in an intangible, ethereal fashion. As a result of receiving these blessings, one's cultivation of quiescence increases, as does insight into emptiness. This transforms the way we perceive appearances. Normally, the mind is inundated by ideation, but here that decreases, for thoughts become less dense. –

These are the secret signs: You dream of meeting with your spiritual mentor, being granted empowerment, being taught Dharma, and emitting and retracting rays of light.

– I have heard students talk of having had direct visions of Avalokiteśvara, Buddha Śākyamuni, and so forth, yet their minds are still dominated by mental afflictions. Others claim to have attained Buddhahood in six months, but then say that they lost it later. This suggests that they still haven't scratched the surface of their mental afflictions. Such claims are basically expressions of arrogance, which is itself an expression of delusion and foolishness. The reference here to dreaming about meeting your spiritual mentor comes from deep practice stemming from the Four Thoughts that Turn the Mind. If you ground yourself well in these and then engage in supplications to the spiritual master and so forth, you can receive such inner, outer, and secret signs of blessings. –

These are the signs of having purified evils due to reciting the hundred-syllable *mantra*: Your body becomes light, you need little sleep, you feel well, and heartfelt gladness arises. And the dream signs are bathing, appearing naked, pus and blood oozing from your body, having diarrhea, vomiting, and wearing white clothing.

– As a result of such purificatory practice, your body becomes buoyant, you dream of showering, with the water flowing off you. Pus, blood, vomit, and so forth are signs of the purification of harmful imprints due to negative actions you have performed in the past. Experientially, you will find that the five poisons diminish, faith in the Dharma and Saṅgha increases, and compassion and insight into emptiness may occur. Vajrasattva practice, including recitation of the hundred-syllable *mantra*, brings benefit in this lifetime and in future lifetimes. This practice is especially helpful for those with physical, mental, and karmic illnesses—illnesses that stem from one's previous *karma*. It helps to counteract the causes for taking lower rebirth and to create conditions for higher rebirth. These benefits occur if it is done in conjunction with the four remedial powers.[50] –

These are the signs of having completed the accumulation of merit by offering the *maṇḍala*: You feel well, you have a sense of delight, you are not hungry even when you do not eat, and your intelligence increases. The dream signs are the rising of the sun and moon, ascending to a height, walking in a field of flowers, being given food by a fine woman, gazing into a mirror, and so forth.

– As a result of the Vajrasattva practice, you are purified, but in addition you need to acquire merit, and this can be done by offering the *maṇḍala*. If you progress far in this practice, your intelligence can become like that of Mañjuśri. The essence of offering the *maṇḍala* is to offer to the objects of refuge your body and all the possessions and virtue you accumulate in the past, present, and future. The point is to counteract strong attachment and clinging, and to replace self-centeredness with altruism. The heart of this practice is the cultivation of generosity. –

These are the signs of disengaging from obsessions as a result of meditating on impermanence: You cease craving for sensual attractions. The flow of concerns about this life alone is cut. You live with a gentle sense of mental well-being. The turbulence of the mind becomes vividly distinct. Feeling that there is no point in anything, you set your sights closer and closer to the present. Appearances lose their luster. Your consciousness is not attached to objects, and it becomes contented. In addition, obscurations become more subtle, great zeal arises, a variety of troubles occur in terms of your body, external events, and your mind. Those are portents that the meditative state will arise, so do not regard them as problems. Practitioners of Cutting Through say this is an indication of experience; Zhijé practitioners say it is an indication of virtue; Atiyoga practitioners say this is a sign of receiving blessings; and Mahāmudrā practitioners say this is a sign of the heat of experience. In short, this is a sign that evil imprints are being purified.

– Even some Lamas get the feeling that they are indispensable, thinking, "If I'm not here, what will happen to my students and my monastery?" Parents exhibit this sense of indispensability when they think, "Without me, my children just won't survive." In the meantime, Lamas pass away, parents die, and yet *saṃsāra* still goes on. Children live on. So, in fact, they were dispensable. This feeling of indispensability is by and large simply an expression of the eight mundane concerns, which have no relevance beyond this life. By meditating well on impermanence, concern for this life alone is cut. One sees exactly what is going on in the mind. There is no point to the eight mundane concerns or in any activities that pertain to this life alone. Being aware of the reality of death and the lack of certainty about the time of death, you don't fixate on mundane plans for the future, but focus more and more closely on the present. Appearances lose their sparkle. In the process of purifying imprints from previous harmful actions, temporary troubles may even arise in the course of proper practice. The practitioners of Cutting Through claim this is an indication of experience. The practitioners of Mahāmudrā say it is a sign of the heat of experience—the heat from the purification of evil imprints and the arising of excellent qualities. –

For individuals of superior faculties, the introduction [to the nature of the mind] may be enough. For middling individuals, quiescence will arise, and even inferior people will get a glimpse of stillness.

– With a realized spiritual mentor and a disciple of great spiritual acuity, the direct introduction to the nature of mind may be enough for realization immediately to arise in the disciple. This occurs if the student performed much purification in previous lives and is now ripe for gaining full enlightenment. –

Then these are the characteristics of having cultivated quiescence with and without signs: All ideation is calmed in its own place, and the attention remains wherever it is focused. That is quiescence. Moreover, if you remain in a state of vividness, that is flawless quiescence. If you become blacked-out, as in deep sleep devoid of mindfulness, this is a parody of cessation, and a kind of meditation in which marmots are experts. On the other hand, even if the mind does not become blacked-out, when there are no memories or thoughts in the mind and a person is left with the sense of being unable to move his body, that is quiescence; it is inappropriate to take that person by the hands and make him rise. If that were done, the person would either die, be reborn as an animal, or run the danger of losing consciousness and becoming demented. So sound chimes by his ear, burn incense by his nose, and sprinkle water in his face, and this will arouse him as if waking him from sleep.

Again, the assertion that remaining with no thoughts coursing in the mind and with no mindfulness is Mahāmudrā is the view of the Chinese Hvashang and of non-Buddhists.

– I know of a twenty-year-old nurse who lost her mind for three years as a result of meditating. It was as if she had blacked-out and was in a deep sleep, with no mindfulness. Eventually she regained clarity of mind, but she did herself great harm. This can be one of the drawbacks of meditating incorrectly.

When the mind is not blacked-out, but has lost its clarity, that is a flaw in the practice of quiescence. That is really a state of trance, and if you boisterously disturb such a person, he may take rebirth as an animal or fall into a state of dementia. In this case, sound something very gently and melodiously in the ear or very subtly sprinkle water on the face. Followers of the Chinese Hvashang gaze into a vacuity or allow the mind to become empty without meditating on emptiness. Such practice can lead to such problems. –

Sakya Paṇḍita says:

> Quiescence in which the eight fields of experience have ceased is a parody of Śrāvaka cessation, and it causes rebirth as an animal.

– This causes rebirth as an animal only if one grasps onto it. If one simply experiences it without grasping, then it can be a part of the path, which will develop into a deeper stage of experience. –

Gö Tsangpa says:

> I think such meditation entailing blocking ideation is simply non-Buddhist.

When that first happened to Je Düsum Kyenpa, he consulted Dagpo and was told, "Oh, that is the worst. Be careful of getting into that." When Rāga Asey had been practicing for just five years, he uttered a single line of a song of contemplative experience, which resulted in his slipping for a moment into quiescence devoid of mindfulness. If one takes that to be meditation, it is a false path, for it is simply a portent that meditation will arise.

Once the son of a traveler was out cutting wood and went into a cave to rest. While sitting in the meditative posture, he entered a dazed state of quiescence devoid of mindfulness. His companions looked for him to no avail, and he was given up for lost. The following year some travelers pitched camp there. One of them said that this was the place his nephew had been lost the previous year. They went to cut wood and found the boy sitting in the proper meditation posture. They called to him and gathered in front of him, at which point he came out of his trance and asked, "Are you ready to go?" and he got up. There was not even anything wrong with his body. Later on, he entered the gateway of Dharma and became a *siddha* known as Mé-nyak Gomring.

In this context of practice, if you have a good contemplative background in the experience of clarity of quiescence, there are facsimiles of the ten signs: In the field of your vision there appear [1] smoke, [2] fireflies, [3] a mirage, [4] an oil lamp, [5] the moon, [6] the sun, [7] something like the light of a fire, [8] a sphere, [9] a pod of light, and [10] the colors of a rainbow, etc. Even if you close your eyes, you still see them clearly, and you see and experience many things including sentient beings, forms, sounds, smells, tastes, tactile sensations, and so on.[51]

The Descent into Laṅkā Sūtra states:

> Due to contemplative diligence in the meditative stabilization experienced by children,[52] meditative stabilization that examines reality,[53] meditative stabilization focused on suchness,[54] and likewise virtuous meditative stabilizations, you see things like the shape of the sun and moon, like light and a lotus, like designs, space, and fire. These various signs lead to non-Buddhist paths, and they cast you down to the experience of Śrāvakas and Pratyekabuddhas. When you let go of all those and are left with no appearances, then the divine hand of the Buddha calms them all and strokes you on your head. This is an indication that you are truly following him.

– This citation lists specific states of *samādhi*. "Meditative stabilization experienced by children" entails experiences of the form and formless realms, experienced by spiritually immature beings who have become disenchanted with the gross suffering and mental afflictions of the desire realm, but who have not yet entered any of the paths to liberation or enlightenment. "Meditative stabilization that examines reality" entails meditating on the aggregate of form as being like foam, the aggregate of feeling as being like water bubbles, the aggregate of recognition as being like a mirage, the aggregate of mental formations as being like a plantain tree, and the aggregate of consciousness as being like an apparition. "Meditative stabilization focused on suchness" includes meditative stages experienced by Bodhisattvas on the first through the tenth grounds. The focus of their meditation is on the absolute nature of reality.

The occurrence of any of these signs is not a problem in and of itself, but it is a problem if one grasps onto them and thereby creates hindrances for one's practice. Once again, the key is not to grasp onto any of the events and experiences that arise in the course of meditation. Be aware, however, that this letting go of grasping does not mean entering into a stupor. –

Whatever amazing visions occur, they are minor signs of quiescence, but that is not actual meditation. Then the first mental state arises. *The Sūtra of the Questions of Ratnacūḍa* states:

> Child of good breeding, this—which is ever so swift and moving without pause like a monkey and the wind, like the current of a stream and the flame of an oil lamp, which moves afar without a body, which thinks of objects and has for its fields of experience the six sense-bases; this mind that knows the minds of others, that is single-pointedly stable, without dispersion, which remains single-pointedly in quiescence and without distraction—is mental stability.

Tilopa says:

> The initial task is like a river in a narrow gorge.

Zhang Rinpoche says:

> When the first mental state occurs, there is an unceasing flow of ideation, like boulders rolling down a steep mountain, and you feel you cannot meditate. That sense of the amount of ideation that is occurring is itself a slightly stable consciousness. Before there is any stability, ordinary ideation spills out, and even though it is constantly surging forth, it is not recognized.

– At this stage, not only will you feel that you can't meditate, you won't even want to meditate. When you become aware of the extent to which your mind is inundated by ideation, your consciousness has become slightly calmed. That is a sign of progress. –

Both *The Ocean of Definitive Meaning* and *The Oral Transmission of the Lineage of the Siddhas* state:

> At first it seems as if the mind is firmly stabilized on the meditative object, but that is just the beginning. Then little by little, it

> seems as though there were basically more thoughts than before, but in fact there are not. Until now, due to not meditating, you were unaware of the occurrence of thoughts even when they were arising. Now, with the mind settled in meditative equipoise, they are noticed due to your limpid awareness. Do not block the various thoughts, but let them be, without following after them. Recognize the full extent of the thoughts that arise, without being drawn into their undertow. Without having to alter your practice sessions, if the flow of your meditation is unbroken, and it seems as if your awareness is streaming, that is called the first mental state, which is like a brook flowing down the side of a steep mountain. But that is not like being carried away by a turbulent stream splashing down a steep mountain and entering a narrow crevasse. Rather, it is like observing without obstruction.

– At first, although it seems that the mind is firmly stabilized, there is really only a slight level of stability, for the mind has been strenuously constrained. When you are first aware of the sheer quantity of thoughts arising in your mind, you may think you are going crazy from the chaos, but, in fact, such ideation has been there all along, and you simply failed to recognize it. Again, this is progress. This current of ideation draws you into its undertow, just like a whirlpool. Recognize the full extent of the thoughts without following after them. Gradually, you will begin to recognize the extent of these thoughts as they arise moment by moment. In your meditation, if you note the sheer quantity of thoughts that arise and you are carried away by them, that is faulty practice and not genuine quiescence. On the other hand, if you are like a tourist standing back and observing everything with a camera, you will discover that these thoughts neither harm nor benefit you. They simply arise, then pass. Observe them without obstruction. When you can do that, you have accomplished a small degree of stability. Be careful not to be like the tourist who sees sight after sight and grasps onto each one saying, "Oh, isn't this one pretty. Oh, this one is even prettier." If you approach meditation like that, you will go astray. In contrast, without any preference, simply note the arising and passing of thoughts and look into their empty nature. –

Tilopa says:

> In the middle, it moves slowly like the Ganges River.

Zhang Rinpoche says:

> Then it is like a gently flowing river. Consciousness slows down, and there are few thoughts.

The meaning of this is stated in *The Ocean of Definitive Meaning* and *The Oral Transmission of the Siddhas*:

> By observing and practicing in the previous manner, ideation diminishes, and you enter a nonconceptual state. Even though isolated thoughts occasionally occur for an instant, they do not continue, but vanish like snow that has fallen on a hot rock. Whatever thoughts surge forth, they are discerned and reckoned with, and the flow of your meditation is unruffled. When it happens in that way, that is called the intermediate mental state, which is like the slow descent of a great river. But it is not like being far away and failing to see properly how it is flowing. Rather, it is like seeing it right on the spot.

– This nonconceptual state is not simply devoid of thought; rather, as thoughts arise, you recognize their emptiness. They simultaneously arise and are released. How is it that ideation is naturally released? We have had countless thoughts, and they have already been naturally released. However, in the meantime we have recognized and retained only a very small percentage of the myriad of thoughts that have arisen and been released. Within this enormous quantity of ideation, there are subtle levels of thoughts that we fail to recognize. These arise and self-liberate of their own accord, unbeknownst to us because we lack sufficient discernment to recognize their arising and passing. In the meditative process, as you learn to be aware of the thoughts without any vestige of craving, you begin to see this process. Through your own experience, find out how this occurs. –

The oral tradition of the spiritual mentors says, "At this point, the second sensation is like the descent of a stream in a narrow gorge." Sometimes it stays fairly serene, and sometimes it surges forth turbulently. When there is scattering, relax and observe it. When there is stillness, concentrate a bit and rest in that state. This seems to happen to many people.

The glorious Tsuglak Trengwa says:

> Again, withdraw the mind single-pointedly into thatness, and, most importantly, collapse inside and relax, as if you were resting after becoming exhausted. Without hopes that the meditation will go well or fears that it will not, with a spacious attitude gently rest in the meditative posture and remain with an unwavering gaze. This results in a gentle subsiding of thoughts. With the body and mind imbued with a quiet, gentle, serene, and relaxed sense of well-being, and the physical posture being without discomfort, even when you stop meditating, the mind does not become immersed in external activities, but remains in a stream of bliss and clarity. All of your bodily, verbal, and mental behavior naturally becomes gentle, serene, and relaxed; and at

> this time you are not harmed by even slight problems of mental afflictions. Within the fields of experience of your five senses many unprecedented appearances arise. The best mental state is said to be like the gentle flow of a great river, and that is the intermediate phase of quiescence.

– If you have lived in India, you may have seen men carrying large, heavy loads. When they finally set them down, they lean back, their eyes immediately roll up, and they go to sleep. In this meditative practice, relax in that way, with no grasping, but also without a loss of mindfulness. Without hope or fear, rest in the meditative posture with an unwavering gaze. That results in a gentle subsiding of thoughts. If you are unable to sit in the meditative posture without a lot of pain, perhaps you need a more comfortable posture or a special chair. It is very important to maintain the continuity of the meditative awareness beyond the formal meditative session. Do not rise abruptly and quickly begin doing something else. The signs of this practice are serenity, relaxation, and a state of poise. –

Tilopa says:

> The final state occurs when the rivers meet like a mother and child.

Zhang Rinpoche says:

> Then consciousness remains stable and unwavering, like the depths of the ocean.

– The surface of the ocean may be quite turbulent, but in its depths, there is stillness and serenity. That is like the third meditative state. That state is also likened to the nature of the sun and its rays: the rays of the sun differ in their intensity and strength, but the nature of the sun remains stable. –

Both *The Ocean of Definitive Meaning* and *The Oral Transmission of the Lineage of the Siddhas* state:

> By practicing in the preceding way, the flow of subtle and coarse ideation is cut, and you remain serenely in a nonconceptual state. You have no sense of bodily well-being or of the presence of the body. You do not feel either the exhalation and inhalation of the breath or its cessation. The mind naturally becomes joyful, clear, and nonconceptual. Even in the post-meditative state, you have no sense of the passage of time if you do not pay close attention to it. The mind does not succumb to distraction, and even when you are not meditating, the meditative state arises naturally, so that it seems as if you were absentminded. With the element of limpidity, there is a radiant sense of dimensionlessness, like being in the midst of a transparent, cloudless sky. That is the final

> mental state, which is unwavering like the ocean. It is not like the ocean in darkness, but like the ocean in the daytime.
>
> Those states comprise the main practice of meditative stabilization, so after a sustained period of practice, extrasensory perception and so forth arise, and they support the vision of reality.

– Do not intentionally cut the flow of conceptualization. Rather, allow thoughts to dissolve naturally, like clouds dissolving into the sky. No one destroys them, they simply dissolve by themselves. The ensuing serenity also arises naturally and not as a result of vigorously blocking ideation.

In this meditative state, the mind is disengaged from the respiration, and when the mind naturally becomes joyful, clear, and nonconceptual, this is spontaneous, not something contrived. The karmic result of becoming fixated on this joy is rebirth in the desire realm. If you become fixed on clarity, this leads to rebirth in the form realm. Rebirth in the formless realm results from fixation on nonconceptuality. If you do not cling to them, they simply arise spontaneously. At times one quality may be more predominant than another, but as long as there is no grasping, there is no problem.

In the post-meditative state, you are not really absentminded even though you may appear to be. The term "dimensionlessness"[55] suggests a lack of three-dimensionality. The ocean at night gives one a sense of expansiveness, but no clarity, so this final mental state is like the ocean in the daytime imbued with both expansiveness and limpidity.

Various types of extrasensory perception arise as a result of this meditative state. For example, you may know what is written on a slip of paper without reading it, or you may know in advance that someone is about to come for a visit, and so on. If you think you are special as a result of acquiring any such abilities, this undermines your own practice. On the other hand, if you have even a vision of the Buddha, and you do not grasp onto that experience, your extrasensory perception will become more and more limpid and clear. –

The glorious Tsuglak Trengwa says:

> As a result of single-pointedly practicing just that, without distraction, the body feels well, the mind is clear, there are no thoughts, you feel that no external circumstances can harm you, and you do not sense the passage of the day and night. You feel that manifest mental afflictions are inhibited and do not arise, and numerous apparent qualities arise such as subtle, visionary extrasensory perception. That is called the final mental state, which is unwavering like the ocean, and that is the final phase of quiescence. Everything that arises up to that point is quiescence, so it is common to Buddhism and non-Buddhist religions, to Buddhism and Bön, and it is a path common to the Hīnayāna and Mahāyāna. That meditation is not Mahāmudrā.

– Once you attain this meditative state, you don't register the passage of time unless you attend to it. For example, once when Dzogchen Rinpoche, a highly advanced meditator, came to someone's house for a visit, no one noticed his arrival, so he just stayed outside through the night and into the next day until he was discovered. When people finally noticed him as he sat meditating, they tapped him on the shoulder, and he rose from his *samādhi* and asked, "Oh, is it tea time?" With no sense of the passage of time, he was simply absorbed in his meditative equipoise. In reality, he had gone far beyond the attainment of quiescence alone, and he may have reached the highest state of the Great Perfection, called "the extinction into reality-itself." At the very least, he had arrived at the state called "consummate awareness," which is also an advanced state in the Leap-over stage of Atiyoga practice.

At the above-mentioned stage of quiescence, manifest mental afflictions are inhibited, and they cannot arise. However, if you have reached this point and are congratulating yourself on having realized the state of Mahāmudrā, hold your horses! –

The great being Rangjung Dorje says:

> Virtue that is not imbued with method accomplishes the virtue of gods of the desire realm. Even meditative stabilization with joy and clarity leads nowhere but to [birth as] a god of the form realm. Nonconceptuality in which recognition is blocked leads you astray to [birth as] a long-lived god. Even if you realize all phenomena as being like space, that is the sense-base of infinite space. Even observing the mind-itself as being like space leads you astray to the state of infinite consciousness. The state of no "I" and of nothingness is the pinnacle of mundane existence that is neither existent nor nonexistent. Alas, you who are wise, do not hope that the chaos of the three realms is reality.

– Each of the statements in that citation refers to meditative states accompanied by grasping. If they arise with no grasping, there are no detrimental results. –

The glorious Pagmo Drüpa says:

> If you go to a holy spiritual mentor and practice any of his precepts, your body and mind may be filled with joy. If you practice with craving and attachment, this will lead you astray to rebirth in the desire realm.
>
> There may be space-like clarity and limpidity, like the external and internal appearance of the moon, regardless of whether your eyes are open or closed. If you practice with craving and attachment, this will lead you astray to rebirth in the form realm.

> There may be an absence of even subtle conceptualization, whether you gaze outwards or inwards, and you may regard this as the immaterial Dharmakāya. If you really cultivate that experience involving liking and disliking, this will lead you astray to rebirth in the formless realm.
>
> Even though you meditate without craving for joy, clarity, and nonconceptuality, you may still be a Śrāvaka or a Pratyekabuddha.

– Your Lama may be a holy being; the Dharma which you practice may be pure; your experiences may be very good, but if you grasp onto them with craving and attachment, then you will be led astray. –

The Lord Jigten Gönpo says:

> Joy, clarity, and nonconceptuality are pitfalls of meditation.

Gyalwa Chö Dingwa says:

> If you do not realize that your own mind is unborn, meditating while relaxing the mind is quiescence, and meditating while concentrating is quiescence. By leaving it unstructured, it is still structured.
>
> Meditating on the mind as existent entails substantialism, and meditating on it as nonexistent entails a nihilism. If you meditate on it as the mind, this is idealism. If you meditate on it as the middle way, this is dualism. Even the cultivation of joy, clarity, and nonconceptuality is a pitfall, for it is obscured by conceptualization.
>
> Even the experience of profound skillful means consists of mundane *samādhi*. The various mental afflictions and ideations are causes for rebirth in the cycle of existence of the three realms.

– Wherever there is even the slightest vestige of grasping, the mind becomes structured. If you sit down and consciously think about leaving the mind unstructured, your mind still becomes conceptually modified and adulterated. You may object that Tibetan Lamas do teach specific postures and so on to be performed while meditating. Are these wrong? Such techniques are useful as long as you are on the path. Moreover, while you are still on the path, there is much benefit in practices that focus the attention on the distinctions between *saṃsāra* and *nirvāṇa* and on differences among the body, speech, and mind. But this present practice is concerned with the very essence of the mind-itself in its unmodified state. If you meditate on it as the mind, you have involved yourself in the Yogācāra philosophical view. If you meditate on it in terms of the Madhyamaka view, but you do so with grasping, you have fallen into dualism. –

Then what is to be done? The precious Lord Gampopa says:

> In terms of stillness and realization, do not place a higher emphasis on stillness, for stillness occurs even when you faint, when you are intoxicated, and when you are deep asleep; it is not realization.

Well then, is quiescence something bad that should avoided? Not at all, for it is the basis and foundation for the experience of Mahāmudrā. *The Sūtra of Ānanda's Instruction on Entering the Womb* states:

> One who lacks a mind in meditative equipoise will not eliminate the defilements.

The Bodhisattva Corpus Sūtra states:

> Śāriputra, what does the perfection of meditative stabilization precede? It precedes the realization of the mind.

The Oral Transmission of the Lineage of the Siddhas states:

> When those three mental states have arisen,[56] you will know your own nature by being introduced to it. You will get the taste of it, and you will cut through conceptual superimpositions. If you are introduced to it without their having arisen, your practice will go astray by wanting them to occur. Moreover, the first mental state is incapable of bringing about even a little liberation. There is no way such instruction can be received if at least the intermediate mental state has not arisen.

For any degree of guidance [on the nature of awareness], either the intermediate or final mental state must definitely have arisen. By meditating after being introduced to insight, you set out on the path with single-pointedness. Some members of the Druk tradition, including the Lord Mipam Padma Karpo, say that superior, middling, and inferior single-pointedness consist of quiescence alone. Then by seeking the mind and being introduced to insight, realization free of conceptual elaboration will arise. In that way, there is no way that you can be introduced to insight by receiving just a month-long instruction. Nowadays there are many who meditate for six or seven years without going beyond the middling degree of single-pointedness. If you were to die during that period, you would not have received even the introduction to insight, so you would not have set out on the path. The custom of not being introduced to insight until the superior state of single-pointedness has arisen is the Kadam Lamrim tradition, which follows the *sūtra* tradition.

That is not the tradition of Mahāmudrā and Atiyoga. *The Precepts of the Four Contemplations*, which is a special teaching on meditative practice taught by the incomparable Dagpo, accords with the position of Jigten Sumgön, Zhang Rinpoche, and Gyarey, as well as the experience of Yang Gönpa. Among the four contemplations, following the state in which the dispersion of ideation is uninterrupted, the stability in which one rests in a nonconceptual state is like the unwavering stillness of the ocean. All the Kadampas also regard that as the practice of meditation. If one is skilled in the technique so one experiences no craving for such stable *samādhi*, and if the practice is imbued with the elixir of wisdom, single-pointed meditation arises. *Contemplation* integrates method and wisdom, or quiescence and insight, so that those contemplations are able to unite naturally. That is said to be *contemplation*.

The Tantra of Inconceivable Mysteries, among the earlier translations, and *The Tantra of the Great River of Āli and Kāli*, among the later translations, state:

> With the majestic *samādhi* of the lion's contemplation, consciousness is clarified with single-pointed, unwavering limpidity, and one is awakened solely by self-arisen, primordial wisdom. With firm patience the suffering of the miserable states of existence is eliminated.

Yang Gönpa says:

> First there is the single-pointed contemplation of remaining in the one state, and the *samādhi* of remaining there is quiescence alone. Here, *contemplation* must entail the union of quiescence and insight. Subtle and coarse thoughts are calmed right where they are. Then the experience of insight is the arising of nonconceptual consciousness that ascertains the luminous emptiness of the mind, vividly present like the realm of transparent space.
>
> Meditation in which quiescence and insight are integrated entails nonconceptual consciousness when the meditation goes well. Remaining in a state of radiant, vivid, unmediated, bliss and clarity is seeing the essence of bliss and clarity. Sometimes this may not happen when you meditate, and sometimes it may happen even when you are not meditating. This is due to not gaining mastery of *samādhi*, just as a novice craftsman may be negligent due to having little concentration.
>
> Mahāmudrā meditation begins from this point. This is to be introduced by an experienced spiritual mentor, and at this point it is said that the meditative state arises.

The Great Instructions states:

> The small degree of single-pointedness entails the cessation of manifest, dispersing thoughts when the mind is placed in meditative equipoise without modification. Having entered a state of joy, clarity, and nonconceptuality, the attention is maintained single-pointedly.
>
> Due to not yet having mastered *samādhi*, sometimes this does not occur while meditating and sometimes it does occur even while not meditating. At times there is clarity, and at times, not. During that period, realization is not gained, and no great ascertaining consciousness arises. But this can lead to limpidity, this begins to open up primordial wisdom, and this is just the beginning of the path. These single-pointed experiences are like seeing the crescent moon on the first day of the lunar month.
>
> By leaving the mind without modification, it remains in a state of vivid joy so that you do not want it to dissolve. But even if you do not dissolve it, it will dissolve anyway, and no authentic meditation will take place. Without blocking thoughts, recognize the lack of inherent nature of all thoughts that arise, and determine this with certainty.

– It is natural to want to hold onto this state of vivid bliss, but if you try to hold onto it you, this will impede your own progress. You need to let go of it, because this is only one phase of the practice. How do you move through this stage, so that further realization arises without blocking thoughts? At this point, ascertain the arising of thoughts, the release of thoughts, and the simultaneous arising and releasing of thoughts. –

> While there is a small degree of single-pointedness, you may recognize the mind of clarity and emptiness and a sense of joy. When thoughts arise from that state, they are naturally dispelled, and there may arise a mentally fabricated certainty that this is meditation. Thoughts of substantiality will arise towards subsequent appearances; thus, there will be the sense of regarding most pleasant appearances as being substantially existent. Due to grasping onto thoughts with the notion, "This is emptiness and the appearance of the mind," there will be a little greater clarity of your dreams, but no other progress.

– As long as you are prone to grasping, when various delightful appearances arise, you grasp onto them as being substantially existent. This pitfall will retard progress in the practice. As long as you continue to grasp onto these things, the only benefit you will receive is that your dreams will become a bit clearer. –

> By entering into meditative equipoise with the thought that the meditative state sometimes does not arise, there may be many delights and fluctuations, and reverence, pure visions, and compassion may increase.

– Sometimes the meditative state occurs and sometimes it doesn't. Do not sit down to meditate with the expectation that meditative equipoise will arise. Know that sometimes it just doesn't happen, and continue practicing anyway. Your meditation will vacillate, and various qualities may emerge from it. Allow them to arise without grasping and without fixation. –

Gyalwang Chöjé says:

> The concentrated single-pointedness explained here is single-pointed stability in which distracting thoughts have been calmed.
>
> Single-pointed freedom from conceptual elaboration is the nonobjectification of the elaborations of signs, which occurs while in that state.
>
> This is the single-pointed experience of *the one taste*: with respect to the elements of nonconceptuality, joy, and clarity, the threefold sense of joy, clarity, and nonconceptuality are merged into one taste.
>
> Single-pointed non-meditation entails achieving stability in that, then remaining in it day and night.

Then within the context of these public teachings, it would be enough not to explain anything beyond this. In this tradition, in terms of this single-pointedness, quiescence is most important, but not quiescence by itself. If quiescence is not integrated with insight, it is not included within the set of the four contemplations. According to the general Kagyü tradition, including the Zurmang Kagyü, when one is introduced to this alone, this opens the way to further practices without differentiation. Even though one knows the distinctions among them, one may not know how to articulate them, so it is difficult to make those differentiations.

There are pitfalls within the context of quiescence, but once you have been introduced to insight, there are no pitfalls. You begin with single-pointedness, then set out on the path of Mahāmudrā. So you may practice this yourself without giving up, and there will be no need for you to draw on anything else to enhance your practice. Reverence and supplications alone are enough. There is no need for questioning others or making any modifications, for by making supplications with intense reverence, your spiritual mentor will dissolve into you. And by observing the mind, whatever thoughts arise, there will be no hindrances or pitfalls. There is no need to be introduced to that. Proceeding along the stages and paths due to experiential realizations arising from the power of reverence is the Mahāmudrā of reverence that was bestowed upon Gö Tsangpa by Dorje Pagmo.

– To begin meditating and progress to the point of gaining genuine realization, it may be enough simply to receive quintessential instructions. However, even though your meditative realizations may be quite good, if your meditative practice is not supported by a thorough study of the material, it will be difficult to articulate your realizations to your spiritual mentor.

Once you have been introduced to insight—which means not simply hearing the teaching, but actually gaining realization—you are free of pitfalls in your meditative practice. –

CHAPTER EIGHT

Atiyoga

Homage to Avalokiteśvara!

These are the profound practical instructions of Avalokiteśvara, precepts that open the eyes of primordial wisdom by visual observation. These Great Perfection, clear light instructions on the Leap-over have a strong connection to the essential instructions of Avalokiteśvara. King Songtsen Gampo says, "This Dharma of Avalokiteśvara is also the Great Perfection," and he discusses this point at length. *The Clear Expanse* states, "Narratives are told for the sake of belief." These are to be taught in accordance with the lineage tracing back to the glorious Samantabhadra. *The Tantra of the Union of the Sun and Moon* states:

> Then narratives are to be explained. If the meaning of the narratives is not explained, there will be the problem of disbelief in this teaching in which the great mysteries are ascertained.

In order to instill belief, to receive blessings, and to bring about ascertainment, the great qualities of the lineage are explained.

In the beginning, when there was no distinction between the Buddha and sentient beings, the glorious Samantabhadra was a Buddha who had never experienced delusion. Until then there had been no other Buddhas, so this being is called the *Original Buddha,* and this is the predecessor of all the Buddhas. Because sentient beings do not know their own nature, they wander in the cycle of existence.

Samantabhadra then arose from the empty state of the Dharmakāya in embodiments as:

[1] Vajradhara
[2] Acintyaprabhāsa
[3] Akopyabhāsā
[4] the Revealer Bhayatrāṇa
[5] the Revealer Kumārakrīḍāvikrīḍamāna
[6] the Revealer Vajradhara
[7] the Revealer Kumāravīrabalin
[8] the Revealer Ṛṣi Krodharāja
[9] the Revealer Suvarṇabhāsottama
[10] the Revealer Kṛpākrīḍābuddhi
[11] the Revealer the Senior Kāśyapa
[12] the Revealer Ṣamyaksaṃrāja
[13] the Revealer Śākyamuni[57]

The twelve Revealers who have already appeared taught sixty-four hundred thousand sets of Atiyogatantras. These were taught by Vajrasattva to Garab Dorje of the land of Orgyen, who fathomed their meaning and wrote them down. Garab Dorje explained them to the Chinese Vidyādhara Śrī Siṅha, and the Indian Vidyādharas Mañjuśrīmitra and Mānavaka, which gave rise to the acclaimed three Atiyoga traditions, including the Mānavaka tradition.

– Garab Dorje was eight years old when he received these teachings during a visionary encounter with Vajrasattva. Having received the teachings, he told the king that he wanted to debate with five hundred *paṇḍits.* Quite a commotion ensued because of his young age, but eventually the debate took place, and he defeated his rivals. The *paṇḍits* praised his accomplishment, declaring, "The Buddha has returned." It was at that time that he was given the name Garab Dorje. "Garab" means superb happiness, which is exactly what the young prodigy brought to everyone.

The Chinese Vidyādhara Śrī Siṅha received these teachings from Garab Dorje. He was prophesied in China by Avalokiteśvara, who spoke of him as a great being who would frequently walk one cubit above the ground. Leaving China, he went to India, and received the complete teachings on Atiyoga. This text states that he received the Atiyoga teachings from Garab Dorje, but elsewhere it is said that he received them from Mañjuśrīmitra. So we can conclude that he received the teachings on Atiyoga from both those masters. Eventually, he returned to China and brought 700,000 disciples to the state of enlightenment. A more detailed account of his life is found in the biography of Padmasambhava and in *The Nyingma School of Tibetan Buddhism* by His Holiness Dudjom Rinpoche. –

Śrī Siṅha explained [the Atiyoga teachings] to Padmasambhava, Paṇḍit Gyalwa Yeshe Do, and Vimalamitra. Vimalamitra traveled to Tibet and taught them to Nyang Ting-nge-dzin Zangpo, Vairocana, and so on. *The Pith Instructions of Vimalamitra* and *The Mask of Vairocana* and so on comprise the textual Atiyoga.[58] Orgyen concealed as treasures innumerable works such as *The Pith Instructions of the Ḍākinīs, The Pith Instructions of the Clear Expanse, The Pith Instructions of Vajrasattva, The View of the Vast Expanse,* and *The Unimpeded Contemplation.* Until now there have appeared more than two hundred and fifty Treasure Revealers, and Atiyoga is included in each of the treasures.[59]

In general, it is said there are sixty-four hundred thousand sets of Atiyogatantras, but most remain as hidden treasures. Some have been promulgated in the lands of humans. The seventeen Atiyogatantras, the seventeen young son *tantras, The Tantra of the Blazing Clear Expanse of the Ḍākinīs,* the seventeen mind teachings on the mother and child, the seven *sūtras* on magical displays, and so on are known as the *sūtras, tantras,* and mind [teachings].

In general, this Great Perfection, including *The Heart Blood of the Ḍākinīs* and *The Dharma of Practical Instruction,* is the pinnacle of the nine *yānas.* Because of the presence of the Protectors of the Teachings, such as the Mamo, Za, and Damchen, it is inappropriate to teach these publicly. They are to be taught only to individual students, otherwise there is great danger. Among the treasures of Karma Lingpa, there are the common Dharmas, including *The Peaceful and Wrathful Lotus Avalokiteśvara* and *The Natural Emergence of the Peaceful and Wrathful from Enlightened Awareness.* Among the *Six Transitional Processes,* there is *The Natural Liberation of Conscious Awareness: the Identification of the Six Lamps,* and *The Natural Liberation of Seeing: the Identification of the Transitional Process of Reality-itself.*[60]

Among the thirty-two introductions, the fifth, which is *An Introduction to the Light Rays of the Sun and Moon,* introduces the pure realm of the three embodiments. That should be taught, for since it is a Dharma for the benefit of sentient beings, it is appropriate to teach it as public Dharma. But for such a teaching it is necessary first to receive an empowerment that is related to the Great Perfection. If that is not received, it is not appropriate even to listen to these teachings, let alone to practice them without such a Mantrayāna empowerment. As it is said:

> How can a boatman with no paddle go across? Once one has received empowerments, the entire Secret Mantra[yāna] may be accomplished.

– In Tibet a boat of yak skin is often used to cross a river or large body of water. Practicing Atiyoga without an empowerment is said to be like crossing a body of water in a boat with no paddle. Not only must one receive the empowerment and the teachings, but one must also keep the *samayas*, or tantric pledges. –

And:

> Teaching Tantra to those who have not received empowerment, and taking up a burden without regard for its weight are both causes of failure.

– If you load a yak without paying attention to the weight of the load, eventually, the yak will break down and die. Similarly, if you teach *tantra* to those who have not received empowerment, you plant causes for rebirth in the lower states of existence for eons without any chance for liberation. These days the Geluk, Sakya, and Kagyü traditions tend not to teach Atiyoga. The reason for this is that they consider it inappropriate to give these advanced teachings without a suitable foundation. However, the Lamas of the Nyingma lineage, drawing from the prophecies of Guru Rinpoche, take a different approach. Guru Rinpoche prophesied that as the Dharma falls into decline, sentient beings would be suitable vessels to receive Atiyoga teachings. This implies that they can be given more and more freely. On one occasion, H.H. Dudjom Rinpoche commented that he thought it was quite plausible that Atiyoga teachings could be given fairly openly in these times and specifically to Westerners. Similarly, after receiving very extensive Atiyoga teachings, Yangthang Rinpoche was told by his primary spiritual mentor that he was to teach them relatively freely and without any reservations. Moreover, he was told that if peculiar people—like Westerners—requested these teachings, he should go out of his way to teach them because they would be suitable vessels. Upon hearing this, if you respond by thinking that you are very special, you are only laying a foundation for rebirth in a lower state of existence. –

Those who have already been granted an empowerment related to Atiyoga are permitted. The time is taught in *The Clear Expanse*:

> It is best to teach at the time of the autumnal equinox and spring equinox.

The best times are in the autumn and spring, when the sky is limpid, but if that does not work out, the introduction should be given right at sunrise or at sunset.

Here the preliminaries to the main practice will be explained. *The Primary Tantra on the Penetration of Sound* states:

> Exercise in the preliminaries. Explain how to distinguish between *saṃsāra* and *nirvāṇa* in terms of the body, speech, and mind. If the distinction is not made between *saṃsāra* and *nirvāṇa*, you will not cut the connection between *saṃsāra* and *nirvāṇa* in terms of the body, speech, and mind. So distinguish between *saṃsāra* and *nirvāṇa*.

– Because of confusion, we find it hard to distinguish between *saṃsāra* and *nirvāṇa*. Due to attachment and grasping, we cling to the objects of our desire as if they were pure. Therefore, we respond to the cycle of existence as if it were a pure land. Similarly, when practicing the stage of generation, including the cultivation of divine pride, many people simultaneously grasp onto their personal identity and cling to the real identity of phenomena. This is the source of more confusion. Why do some people who have received many empowerments and oral transmissions still not find much benefit? This is solely due to not understanding and pondering the Four Thoughts that Turn the Mind. If you meditate on them, faith will arise, fear will arise, compassion will also arise, and so will patience and enthusiasm. As you build a foundation through the Four Thoughts that Turn the Mind, you lay the foundation for the first five of the Six Perfections. Without this foundation, the sixth Perfection, wisdom, cannot arise. Therefore, the Four Thoughts that Turn the Mind are indispensable. –

Nirvāṇa Traces states:

> In order to perform the physical preliminaries, engage in the behavior of the six types of sentient beings and in the behavior of the Three Jewels.
>
> In order to perform the verbal preliminaries, speak the languages of the six types of sentient beings, and experience the various kinds of sounds of the peaceful and wrathful beings and of the elements.
>
> In order to perform the mental preliminaries, bring to mind the suffering of the six types of sentient beings. Afterwards investigate your consciousness.
>
> Because this body is produced by ignorance, the seeds of rebirth as the six types of sentient beings are present in it.
>
> Because awareness is the actual three embodiments, the three embodiments arise as the three syllables. Exercise the power of those syllables and differentiate among them.

– In order to perform the physical preliminaries, engage in the behavior of the six types of sentient beings and the Three Jewels. This means mimicking the behavior of those beings and the objects of refuge. After doing so, examine the nature of your own mind. To perform the verbal preliminaries, mimic the sounds of each of the states of existence, including animals, hell beings, and so on. Then articulate the sounds of peaceful and wrathful beings and the elements. Again examine the nature of your own mind. Next, to perform the mental preliminaries, bring to mind the suffering of the six types of sentient beings.

This is a very practical way to establish a foundation in the Four Thoughts. Imagine the sufferings in each state of existence, from the hells to the god realms, and at each point look into the very nature of that which you have brought to mind. From one perspective, this body seems to be merely a receptacle for seeds of rebirth in all the six states of existence because it is produced by delusion. Yet, from a pure perspective, awareness is none other than the three embodiments. The three embodiments arise as the syllables *Oṃ*, *Āḥ*, and *Hūṃ*. –

Here is the meaning. With your body, speech, and mind meditate on the following objects: Imagine that your own and all other sentient beings' sins and obscurations that lead to birth in the hot hells dissolve into a black syllable *Duḥ* on the sole of your right foot, causing it to transform into the eight hot hells, like reflections appearing in a mirror. Imagine yourself being put into them and experiencing immeasurable suffering. Recite "*Raṃ na ra ka*" seven or three times. Now observe the mind of the person imagining that. It is not established in an essence of any kind.

Now imagine that the sins and obscurations that lead to birth in the cold hells dissolve into a black syllable *Duḥ* on the sole of your left foot, transforming it into the cold hells. Imagine yourself being put into them, experiencing extreme cold and the cracking of your body. Recite "*Khaṃ na ra ka*" seven times. Observe the essence of the mind of the person imagining that.

Imagine that the sins and obscurations that lead to birth as a *preta* dissolve into a red syllable *Preḥ* at your genitals, transforming it into the realm of the *pretas*. Imagine yourself being put there so that you experience immeasurable suffering of hunger and thirst. Recite "*Sarva pretaka*" seven times. Now observe your mind.

Likewise, imagine that the sins and obscurations that lead to birth as an animal dissolve into a dark red syllable *Triḥ* at your navel, transforming it into the realm of animals. Imagine that you are stupid and mute, and recite seven times "*Sarva tiryaka.*" Now observe your mind.

Imagine all the causes for birth as a human dissolving into the syllable *Nriḥ* at your heart, transforming it into the human realm with its four world-sectors. Imagine the sufferings of birth, aging, sickness, and death, and recite seven times "*Sarva aṇuṣe.*" Then observe your mind.

Imagine all the sins and obscurations that lead to birth as a demigod dissolving into the yellow syllable *Suḥ* at your throat, transforming it into the combative realm of the demigods. Imagine yourself being put there and experiencing the fearful suffering of combat. Recite "*Sarva asura*" seven times, then observe the mind of the meditator.

Imagine the causes for birth as a god dissolving into the white syllable *Aḥ* on the crown of your head, transforming it into the divine abodes of the six classes of gods of the desire realm and so on. Imagine yourself being brought there, then experiencing the misery of falling from that state. Recite "*Sarva deva*" seven times, then observe the mind of the one who is meditating like that.

Those miseries of the six types of existence are the mind, and the mind is emptiness. In emptiness so-called *joy* and *sorrow* are unestablished. Such meditation is the practical means for closing the door to rebirth in the six types of existence. Now chant in unison this *mantra* for closing the door on rebirth: "*Aḥ aḥ śaḥ saḥ maḥ haḥ.*"[61]

– We have accumulated causes for every type of rebirth. Hatred, jealousy, pride, and so on operate in our minds, and as we engage in activities motivated by those mental afflictions, we continue to sow seeds for all types of rebirth, including rebirth in the hot hells. It is a mistake for any of us to think we are beyond reproach, believing that we are not accumulating further causes for lower rebirth. Unless they are purified by means of the Four Remedial Powers, inevitably those poisons will give rise to lower rebirth. Imagine being in the different states of existence. Vividly bring to mind the suffering that originates from the mental afflictions and nonvirtuous actions. Then imagine that it is you who is experiencing this suffering. On that basis, you will develop the four immeasurables, including compassion, for sentient beings in the miserable states of existence. In each instance, conclude by observing your mind.

The miseries of the six types of existence are the mind. It is your mind and not your body that takes rebirth in and experiences those six states. But do not forget that the nature of the mind is emptiness, and within emptiness, it is impossible to be benefited by joy or afflicted by sorrow. –

Now imagine a white *Oṃ* on the crown of your head, a red *Āḥ* at your throat, and a blue *Hūṃ* at your heart. Imagine the blessings of the body, speech, and mind of all the Buddhas dissolving into them, igniting them with the five-colored flame of primordial wisdom. The six channel centers in the body incinerate the abodes of the six types of existence together with their seed syllables. Imagine the domains of the six types of existence to be empty. Chant in unison "*Oṃ Āḥ Hūṃ*" once.

Then imagine you are the monk Ajita, of the nature of the Jewel of the Saṅgha, and recite three times "*Namo saṅghāya.*" Now imagine you are *The Perfection of Wisdom Sūtra*, the great Mother, of the nature of the Jewel of the Dharma, and recite three times "*Namo dharmāya.*" Now imagine yourselves as the embodiment of the Jina Śākyamuni, and recite three times "*Namo buddhāya.*" Now imagine yourselves as the peaceful embodiment of Avalokiteśvara, and recite the six syllables[62] three times. Imagine yourselves as the ferocious Hayagrīva, and recite three times "*Oṃ Hayagrīva hūṃ phaṭ.*"

Think that this body is made up of the five elements, and that even the outer elements are displays of awareness, or the mind-itself, and recite three times "*E yaṃ raṃ baṃ laṃ.*" *The Primary Tantra on the Penetration of Sound* states:

> By sitting in the *vajrāsana*, such physical exercise is of benefit to the mind. Maintaining the verbalization of *Hūṃ*, speech is sealed and exercised, and by entering the path of flexibility, such verbal training is of benefit to the mind.

Now sit with your body erect in the *vajrāsana*, and join your palms at the crown of your head. Imagine this body as a golden, five-pointed *vajra* marked in the center with a blue syllable *Hūṃ*. From it a string of blue *Hūṃ*s emerges from your mouth, and the entire universe is filled with blue *Hūṃ*s. Drawing them back in, imagine in space a blue *Hūṃ* the size of one cubit. Imagine the whole interior of your body also filled with many blue *Hūṃ*s, and chant three long *Hūṃ*s, and chant in unison one short *Hūṃ*. *Hūṃ Hūṃ Hūṃ Hūṃ Hūṃ Hūṃ Hūṃ.* That way of differentiating the three realms of the cycle of existence is a precept to cease wandering in the cycle of existence.

– Imagine your own body as a five-pointed golden *vajra* marked in the center with a blue syllable *Hūṃ*. Join your palms at the crown of your head. From the blue *Hūṃ*, visualize that a string of blue *Hūṃ*s comes out and strikes everything in the universe, including stones, mountains and trees. The entire universe is filled with *Hūṃ*s. Imagine that as they strike the entire animate and inanimate contents of the universe, all true existence is destroyed. By so doing, your tendency to grasp onto the inherent existence of phenomena is counteracted. Then draw the *Hūṃ*s back in.

This practice is said to serve the same function as the wheel of protection in the stage of generation practice. It also helps to make the mind flexible and supple. Counteracting the grasping onto substantial existence by drawing the *Hūṃ*s back corresponds to the stage of completion practice.

Next, visualize in the space in front a *Hūṃ* the length of one cubit—the distance from your elbow to your finger tips. Imagine the interior of your body is filled with many *Hūṃ*s. Chant three long *Hūṃ*s. Then as you chant the series of seven *Hūṃ*s, each *Hūṃ* is quite short. –

A *tantra* states:

> Once you have differentiated the six types of existence, you do not return to the state of the cycle of existence, and the ability to serve the needs of sentient beings arises in the manner of a [wish-fulfilling] jewel.

The Blazing Lamp states:

> Once you have differentiated between *saṃsāra* and *nirvāṇa*, your body, speech, and mind settle in their natural state.

Let your body be in any posture you like, say nothing with your speech, and let your mind be undistractedly in a state free of thoughts and expressions.

– Although the text states "let your body be in any posture you like," there are limitations. Choose a comfortable posture, such as the *vajrāsana*, the *ṛṣi* posture, or the supine position. Then relax completely, like a bundle of sheaves with its cord cut loose. In that state of total relaxation, observe whatever thoughts arise, whether they are good or bad, pertaining to the past, present, or future. Whatever thoughts arise, observe them like a great river flowing out to sea. Know that whatever flows down that river can neither harm you nor benefit you. Simply sever the cord of your speech, and let your mind settle in an undistracted state, free of thought and expression. –

Nirvāṇa Traces states:

> Then become adept at settling your body, speech, and mind in their natural state.

The advantages of settling them in their natural state are taught in *The Clear Expanse*:

> By settling in the natural state, the conditions leading to illnesses in which the vital energies are disturbed are pacified, and grasping is released naturally. Let your body, speech, and mind be self-liberating.

And:

> Remaining in the contemplation of the natural state, the original reality is realized.

Now I shall introduce the main practice of the six lamps in a way that is easy to understand. The essence of the lamps is the essence of your own awareness. The nature of the lamps is emptiness. The characteristic of the lamps is nondual luminosity and emptiness. Those have already come up in the introductory instructions, so there is no need to explain them here. This is the connection: abiding in the *sugatagarbha*, the universal ground, is the fundamental lamp. Those [practices] are the basis of the Great Perfection called Breakthrough, which is identical to Mahāmudrā. That is the cycle of the Mind class of the Great Perfection. Once that basis has been realized, you proceed on the path of the Leap-over, which is called the Expanse class and Precept class of Atiyoga. This is said to be even higher than Mahāmudrā.

– The practice of the Breakthrough is the basis for the teachings and practice of the six lamps, and the six lamps constitute the path of the Leap-over stage of Atiyoga practice. This introduction to the essence, nature, and characteristics of the six lamps provides some theoretical context for practicing the Leap-over.

Dwelling in the *sugatagarbha*, or the Buddha-nature, is the first of the lamps, and this is accomplished through the practice of the Breakthrough, which is identical to Mahāmudrā. Among the three classes of Atiyoga, namely, the Mind class, the Expanse class, and the Precept class, the Breakthrough belongs to the Mind class. Once you have realized the *sugatagarbha*, you proceed on the path of the Leap-over, which belongs to the Expanse class. Among the three classes, the latter two—the Expanse and Precept classes—are said to be even higher than Mahāmudrā. –

The *citta* lamp of the flesh: In general the reality of the nature of existence is present in the body, specifically inside the heart. *The Tantra That Bestows the Introduction* states:

> Reality is present as great primordial wisdom in the heart in the center of your own body.

The Tantra That Synthesizes the Bindus states:

> In the center of the *citta*, which causes the mind to operate, is the essence of the mind, which bears three attributes.

– The essence of the mind, as the *citta* lamp of the flesh, is present inside the heart, though it is not identical to the physical organ of the heart. Likewise, the eyeball is not the same as the lamp of the eye, and the lamps of the channels are not the same as the many channels in the body. Rather, each of these lamps is located in the heart, the eye, and the channels respectively. –

Awareness that is located in the center of the heart is *the citta lamp of the flesh.*

The lamp of the white, tender channel: The channel that connects the heart with the two eyes is *the channel that is the faculty that clearly discerns good and bad qualities.* Inside there is an empty luminosity devoid of blood and lymph, and that is immutable awareness. That is called *the lamp of the white, tender channel. The Tantra That Synthesizes the Bindus* states:

> The king of channels consists of crystal tubes that penetrate inside the sun and moon.[63]

The Tantra of the Blazing Lamp states:

> Within the white conch of the skull is a channel in the shape of a snail's antenna that coils three times in a clockwise direction. Among the channels, this is the one that draws in the vital essence of the elements and causes the appearances of sense-objects. Thus, the pathway that transforms consciousness is called *the lamp of the white, tender channel.*

The fluid lasso lamp: Due to the fluid orbs of the eyes, there is the clarity of unimpeded vision.

– Just as a lasso draws in something from afar, so does this lamp, which pertains to visual perception, draw in things from a distance. –

The Primary Tantra on the Penetration of Sound states:

> From the appearance of primordial wisdom, the entrances called the *cakū*[64] emerge, which draw in all the nutritive and vital essences of the body.

The Tantra of the Self-arising Buddha states:

> Unimpeded primordial wisdom, which reveals itself in the embodiments of primordial wisdom, has for its basis one's own eyes. Its location is in the center of one's pupils. Its luminosity is the clarity of unimpeded vision. This infinite unimpededness in the center of one's pupils is the embodiment of the unimpeded primordial wisdom of the Buddhas.

And:

> This luminosity of the eyes seeing without impediment is called *the fluid lasso lamp.*

The Introduction to the Secret Path of the Supreme Light of the Primordial Wisdom of Avalokiteśvara states:

> Lord of Mysteries,[65] listen! The embodiment of the primordial wisdom of the Sugatas has as its basis the upper portion of one's own torso. Its location is inside the heart. Its pathway is a channel connecting the heart to the eyes, flexible like a white, silken thread, and devoid of blood and lymph. That is the pathway of primordial wisdom.

The Tantra of the Essential Meaning of Avalokiteśvara states:

> Thus, the basis of the experience of the clear light is *the fluid lasso lamp.*

The Natural Liberation of Seeing: the Identification of the Transitional Process of Reality-itself among the teachings of Orgyen states:

> In the morning and the evening when the sky and the rays of the sun are clear, all the students are to gaze at the sun while squinting their eyes, or they may have their gaze adjusted [by their mentor]. Children of good breeding, this essence of the sun is pure and clear without contamination. Likewise, know that the Dharmakāya, with its twofold purity, is originally pure and without contamination. The radiance of the sun possesses the five colors of the rainbow; it is not created by anyone, but is self-luminous. Likewise, know that from the originally pure radiance of the Dharmakāya there appears the spontaneous Sambho-gakāya, possessing the five definite attributes, bearing the five spheres of rainbow light, an undrawn body *maṇḍala* of the nature of clear light. Recognize its possession of the five colors of rainbow light as the nature of the five families of all the Buddhas.

– In this Leap-over practice, you do not gaze directly at the sun, for this will very quickly harm your eyes. Instead, look either above, beneath, to the left, or to the right of the sun. Do not focus your eyes directly on it. These introductory points of the definite attributes, the spheres, and the five types of light are laid out in much greater detail in more extensive teachings on the Leap-over. The five colors of rainbow light, which are the nature of the five Buddha families, are the same as those that appear in the transitional process, and they are very important. –

Recognize the unimpeded presence of space, which is not obscured or inhibited for an instant, as the corporeality of the Buddhas' primordial wisdom. This is an embodiment that appears but is without a self-nature, an embodiment without dimension, the indivisible embodiment of the absolute nature and primordial wisdom.

These are like the appearance of the [eye of a] peacock [feather] or like a round breastplate. Know that abiding within the five-fold arch of rainbow light is the lamp of the pure absolute nature of reality, and that is dwelling in the self-illuminating pure lands.

From those rays and brilliance, rays of light are emanated in all directions. Know that this illumination is the display of the Sambhogakāya, which possesses the five definite attributes, and is the Nirmāṇakāya, which possesses the five indefinite attributes, and which unceasingly serves sentient beings in every way.

Among those light rays are inconceivable spheres and minute spheres like fish eyes and like a net of pearls. Between them are interconnecting, moving patterns of lattice networks, and those profusions of appearances are the emanated embodiments of compassion. Know that these inconceivable trillions of embodiments ceaselessly serve the needs of sentient beings. They appear in different ways; but just as the sun and rainbow light, and the *bindu* and emptiness are innately indivisible, know that in reality the different modes of appearance of the three embodiments are in essence indivisible from reality-itself.

– A wide variety of appearances or visions may occur in this practice. They will not be the same for each person. People come with their own superior, medium, or inferior capacities, in accordance with which these visions arise. Of course, if you don't practice, no visions will occur. While the manifold appearances of the Dharmakāya, Sambhogakāya, and Nirmāṇakāya are mentioned as being distinct, in essence, they are indivisible with reality-itself. –

Introduction to the shafts of sun rays: When the sky is limpid and the rays of the sun are bright, the students are to gaze at the sun while squinting their eyes, so that the rays of the sun appear like aligned weapons, like parallel spears, and like parallel strings of yarn. That is like the rays of light in the transitional process of reality-itself, which seem like a downpour of weapons penetrating into oneself. Those are not weapons, but are clear rays of primordial wisdom. Without being frightened of them, recognize them as self-appearing. If these appearances of five-colored lights are not recognized, they are the five poisons.

– When you actually experience the transitional process of reality-itself, it seems as if a multitude of weapons are penetrating into you, and you may be very frightened, feeling that you will be annihilated. However, if you recognize their nature, you will see them as displays of primordial wisdom. You will recognize them as your own appearances, and, with that recognition, you will be liberated from them. If you are not able to recognize them as displays of primordial wisdom and as your own appearances, this experience will be like having a nightmare. –

If the five lights are recognized, they are the five families of Buddhas. The dark blue light is Vajrasattva; the white light is Vairocana; the yellow light is Ratnasambhava; the red light is Amitābha; and the green light is Amoghasiddhi. If they are not recognized, they are the five aggregates. The dark blue light is the aggregate of consciousness; the white light is the aggregate of form; the yellow light is the aggregate of feeling; the red light is the aggregate of recognition; and the green light is the aggregate of compositional factors.

– Moreover, if the dark blue light is not recognized, it is the poison of hatred, the white light is delusion, the yellow light is pride, the red light is attachment, and the green light is jealousy. –

If the reality of the five lights is realized, they are the five consorts. The dark blue light is Ākaśadhātviśvarī; the white light is Buddhalocanā; the yellow light is the supreme consort Māmaki; the red light is the supreme consort Paṇḍāravāsinī; and the green light is Samayatārā. If they are not recognized, they are the five elements. The dark blue light is the element of space; the white light is the element of water; the yellow light is the element of earth; the red light is the element of fire; and the green light is the element of air.

If the five lights are known, they are the five families. The dark blue light is the *vajra* family; the white light is the *sugata* family; the yellow light is the *ratna* family; the red light is the *padma* family; and the green light is the *karma* family. If they are not known, they are the five elemental vital energies. The dark blue light is the vital energy of space, or expanse; the white light is the vital energy of water, or fluidity; the yellow light is the vital energy of earth, or matter; the red light is the vital energy of fire, or combustion; and the green light is the vital energy of air, or motility.

If the reality of the five lights is known, they are the five pure realms. The dark blue light is the realm of Akaniṣṭha[66]; the white light is the realm of Abhirati; the yellow light is the realm of Śrīmat; the red light is the realm of Sukhāvatī; and the green light is the realm of Karmaprasiddhi. If they are not known, the five lights are the five directions. Dark blue is the center, white is east, yellow is south, red is west, and green is north.

If the reality of the five lights is known, they are the embodiments of the five classes of blood-drinkers.[67] The dark blue light is Vajra Heruka; the white light is Buddha Heruka; the yellow light is Ratna Heruka; the red light is Padma Heruka; and the green light is Karma Heruka. If they are not known, they are the five *māras* of the mental afflictions. The white light is the *māra* Devaputra; the dark blue light is the *māra* Lord of Death; the yellow light is the *māra* of the aggregates; the red light is the *māra* of mental afflictions; and the green light is the *māra* of the deluded ignorance.

If the five lights are known, they are the five families of Ḍākinīs. The dark blue light is Vajra Ḍākinī; the white light is Buddha Ḍākinī; the yellow light is Ratna Ḍākinī; the red light is Padma Ḍākinī; and the green light is Karma Ḍākinī. Know them! Do not get confused! Do not be afraid! Recognize them!

– When we think of the five families of Buddhas, fear does not arise. In fact, we feel a sense of comfort and familiarity. Similarly, we should not feel afraid of the blood-drinkers, because they are none other than the wrathful aspects of the five Buddhas. –

Introduction to the fixed gaze of the ocean: By pressing both your eyes with the tips of the index fingers, spheres of light appear. Know that these are indications of a present, peaceful embodiment in the center of your heart, within a fence of rainbow light.

– In this passage *ocean* refers to the eyes. The spheres of light that appear when you press your eyes indicate something in your heart related to the different lamps. The *citta* lamp of the heart is connected with the second lamp—the connection between the heart and the eyes—and with the third lamp of the eyes. The appearance of the spheres of light arises due to the interdependence of these three, but its origin is in the heart. –

Introduction to the waves of the ocean: By pressing both your ears with the tips of the index fingers, a roaring sound occurs from above. This is an indication of the sound of reality-itself in the transitional process of reality-itself, like the rolling thunder of a thousand dragons.

Introduction to the rays of reality-itself: By pressing closed both your eyes with your index fingers for a long time, moving, flickering patterns of rays and spheres spread outwards. Know that in the transitional process of reality-itself appearances of rays arise, and these are indications of them.

Well then, what is the benefit in looking at this rainbow light? It has to do with *the lamps at the time of the transitional process.* In the transitional process of reality-itself, countless peaceful and wrathful embodiments arise among such appearances as rainbow light, spheres, and minute spheres. When that happens, by recalling the meaning of the present introduction, it is said one may be free of fear and take birth in a pure realm.

– At the time of the transitional process of reality-itself, first the peaceful deities arise, then the wrathful embodiments appear. At the time of your own transitional process of reality-itself, if you are able to recall these teachings and recognize the nature of the peaceful embodiments, you will take rebirth in one of their pure realms. Alternatively, due to maintaining that recognition as the wrathful embodiments appear, you will take rebirth in one of the wrathful pure realms. –

The introductory treatise *The Natural Liberation of Seeing: the Identification of the Transitional Process of Reality-itself* states: "At this point offer pure prayers for the path of light of primordial wisdom." So recite the following:

> Homage to the spiritual mentors, chosen deities, and Ḍākinīs.
> Please lead us to the path of great mercy.
>
> When I am wandering in the cycle of existence due to delusion,
> May the spiritual mentors of the oral lineage lead me
> To the radiant path of unwavering hearing, thinking, and meditation.
> May the assembly of supreme consorts, the Ḍākinīs, support me.
> Please liberate me from the terrifying narrow passage of the transitional process.
> Bring me to the state of truly perfect Buddhahood.
>
> When I am wandering in the cycle of existence due to strong hatred,
> May Lord Vajrasattva lead me
> To the clear, radiant path of mirror-like primordial wisdom.
> May the supreme consort Buddhalocanā support me.
> Please liberate me from the terrifying narrow passage of the transitional process.
> Bring me to the state of truly perfect Buddhahood.

When I am wandering in the cycle of existence due to strong pride,
May Lord Ratnasambhava lead me
To the clear, radiant path of the primordial wisdom of equality.
May the supreme consort Māmaki support me.
Please liberate me from the terrifying narrow passage of the transitional process.
Bring me to the state of truly perfect Buddhahood.

When I am wandering in the cycle of existence due to strong attachment,
May Lord Amitābha lead me
To the clear, radiant path of the primordial wisdom of discernment.
May the supreme consort Paṇḍāravāsinī support me.
Please liberate me from the terrifying narrow passage of the transitional process.
Bring me to the state of truly perfect Buddhahood.

When I am wandering in the cycle of existence due to strong jealousy,
May Lord Amoghasiddhi lead me
To the clear, radiant path of the primordial wisdom of accomplishment.
May the supreme consort Samayatārā support me.
Please liberate me from the terrifying narrow passage of the transitional process.
Bring me to the state of truly perfect Buddhahood.

When I am wandering in the cycle of existence due to strong habitual propensities,
May the heroic Vidyādharas lead me
To the clear, radiant path of innate, primordial wisdom.
May the assembly of supreme consorts, the Ḍākinīs, support me.
Please liberate me from the terrifying narrow passage of the transitional process.
Bring me to the state of truly perfect Buddhahood.

When I am wandering in the cycle of existence due to strong delusive appearances,
May the heroic Vidyādharas lead me
To the path of light of clear, inborn primordial wisdom.
May the supreme consorts, the assembly of Ḍākinīs, support me.
Please liberate me from the fearful passage of the transitional process.
Bring me to the state of truly perfect Buddhahood.[68]

When I am wandering in the cycle of existence due to five strong poisons
May the five families of Jinas lead me

To the path of light of the clear four combined primordial wisdoms.
May the supreme consorts, the five families of Ḍākinīs, support me.
Please liberate me from the fearful passage of the transitional process.
Bring me to the state of perfect Buddhahood.[69]

May the element of space not arise as my adversary,
And may I see the deep blue realm of the Buddha.
May the element of water not arise as my adversary,
And may I see the white realm of the Buddha.
May the element of earth not arise as my adversary,
And may I see the yellow realm of the Buddha.
May the element of fire not arise as my adversary,
And may I see the red realm of the Buddha.
May the element of air not arise as my adversary,
And may I see the green realm of the Buddha.
May sounds, lights, and rays not arise as my adversaries,
And may I see the realm of the multitude of peaceful and
wrathful deities.[70]

Oh, in the morning and evening when the sky is limpid, look continually and you will have many visions of rays of light. The sight of the five-colored lights is not like seeing a rainbow. Rather, it is directly seeing the five primordial wisdoms, so in reality it is not different from meeting the five families of Jinas. People of pure *karma* may directly meet many peaceful deities, including the five families of Jinas, Avalokiteśvara, and Orgyen, as well as many wrathful deities such as Hayagrīva. If you meet them, you should keep this secret, without telling anyone but your spiritual mentor and close Dharma friends. If you do not keep this secret, the Protectors of the Teachings, including the Mamo, Za, and Damchen will pose a great danger for you, resulting in illness and so on. So keep it secret!

– For this phase of the Leap-over practice, three physical postures and three gazes are assumed. In this way the inner qualities of your primordial wisdom are externalized. The text describes your ability to see the five primordial wisdoms, which are within you, but through the practice you are able to see their outer display. If you meet the five Buddha families, it is due to your pure *karma*. This meeting is a result of the purity of your practice. If you do meet them, tell no one but your spiritual mentor and close Dharma friends, and only if you have had an authentic experience, one that is not simply a product of your imagination. And certainly don't lie about your experiences. We tend to be fascinated with deception. In addition, we get really excited about the experiences that arise in our meditation, so much so that we just can't wait to burst out and tell someone. Instead of allowing the inner qualities of primordial wisdom to emerge, our mental afflictions come out, which compel us to broadcast our experiences to other people. Many physical, verbal, and mental obstacles within our Vajrayāna practice come because we speak openly about things that should remain secret. Instead of sowing the seeds for enlightenment, we sow seeds for taking a lower rebirth. So hold onto your freedom of speech and reap the benefits, and if you do meet the five Buddhas keep this secret, except to your spiritual mentor and close spiritual friends. –

This completes the introduction to the Great Perfection.

CHAPTER NINE

Sealing with the Dedication

Homage to Avalokiteśvara!

These are the profound practical instructions of Avalokiteśvara, the oral instructions of the Lord, and the seal by way of dedication. Even if you know the foregoing introductions on practice, if you do not put them into practice, they are of no benefit. A *sūtra* states:

> Without thoroughly meditating on Dharma, reality-itself will not be seen. By seeing and hearing water, but not drinking it, your thirst will not be slaked.

– As a result of hearing the Dharma, thinking about it, and practicing meditation, it is possible to attain Buddhahood. In fact, all the Buddhas of the past have attained enlightenment in exactly this way. Therefore, we dedicate the merit towards this end.

The major reason for making ourselves suitable vessels for Dharma—for the practices explained in the *sūtras* and *tantras*—is to achieve a lasting state of well-being. Within the Vajrayāna, Atiyoga is of paramount importance, for it is by such practice that we gain an unmediated realization of the mind of the Buddha. In order to gain such realization, we must seek to make ourselves suitable vessels. In this very lifetime, we have the causes for attaining enlightenment. Now is indeed the right time to practice. If we have this opportunity in hand and throw it away, this is like throwing away a wish-fulfilling gem, and then immediately looking for another one. When you find an authentic Dharma, practice it with clarity and purity, and carry through with it. As you practice, discard pride and boastfulness, for one of the qualities of enlightenment is humility. It is not enough just to hear the teachings on the outer and inner preliminaries, the stage of generation, quiescence, insight, Mahāmudrā, and Atiyoga. To derive benefit from the teachings, they must be put into practice. There are meditations to be practiced at all levels of the Dharma, from the Hīnayāna through Atiyoga, and if you fail to meditate, you will fail to see the essence of the Dharma. –

The Bundle of Stalks Sūtra states:

> Dharma without meditation is like dying of starvation even while you are giving food and drink to the multitudes. Dharma without meditation is like not getting even a smile while you are counting up the many jewels in a treasure chest.

The Ornament Sūtra states:

> Dharma without meditation is like a deaf musician pleasing others with his music but not hearing it himself. Dharma without meditation is like a boatman carrying others across a river or an ocean, but drowning in the water himself.

The Bundle of Stalks Sūtra states:

> This authentic teaching of the Buddha is not accomplished merely by hearing it. Dharma without meditation is like those who die of thirst while being helplessly carried away by a great river.

The Sūtra of Bringing forth the Extraordinary Resolve states:

> Fools who think, "I am accomplished. What shall I do now?" experience misery at the time of death. By not having fathomed the depths, there is great misery. This is due to the obsession with talking.

– Those who learn about meditation and procrastinate in terms of actually putting it into practice will have only remorse at the time of their death. At that time, even if there are a hundred people around you, not one can be of benefit. Even if you beat your chest in dismay, it won't help. Why does this great remorse arise? It happens only because you have failed to find the essence of Dharma. –

The Great Mound of Jewels Sūtra states:

> Kāśyapa, it is like this: Just as some people are carried away by a great current in the ocean and perish from thirst, many religious devotees and brahmins learn and understand many Dharmas, but do not dispel their obsession with attachment, their obsession

with hatred, or their obsession with delusion. They are carried away by the ocean of Dharma, but they die of thirst due to their mental afflictions, and they go to miserable states of existence.

– In Tibet, there were certain Lamas with extraordinary erudition, and people thought no one had a better chance to attain Buddhahood than they. It is said that if you squeeze a snake, its limbs will protrude. In the same way, it was felt that if such a Lama were squeezed, you would find genuine knowledge. But when some of them were squeezed, it turned out that their immense learning, thinly veiled with a sheen of genuine Dharma, was only for the sake of the eight mundane concerns. When they were squeezed, the five poisons emerged instead of enlightenment. In reality, it was the Lamas' own mental afflictions that were squeezing them and exposing their true nature. In such cases, is the Dharma or the individual at fault? Although the practice of Dharma acts as an antidote for the five poisons, these individuals used Dharma to increase their own mental afflictions. As a result of their involvement with Dharma, their scholarly abilities led only to greater pride and greater delusion. –

The Sūtra of the Questions of Kāśyapa states:

> Like people who die of thirst in the ocean, many monks, upon filling themselves with learning, fail to eliminate their mental afflictions and are reborn in miserable states of existence.

– If you don't practice, the Dharma cannot act as an antidote for your mental afflictions. No push-button procedure can get rid of your mental afflictions. Nor can you wash them away. The very point of Dharma is to eliminate the afflictions of your mind. The Dharma really is medicine. If you go to a hospital filled with doctors and nurses but refuse treatment, you receive no benefit. Similarly, if you don't practice, you derive no benefit. –

The Tree Ornament Dhāraṇī states:

> One who does not practice after hearing much about Dharma is like an impoverished person who counts people's money for a living, but has none himself.

The Sūtra of No Arising states:

> If the nature of the mind is not thoroughly known, with faith in words you will not become enlightened as a Buddha.

The Moon Essence Sūtra states:

> If the meaning is not realized, there is no benefit in being learned in terminology. Cūḍapanthaka together with Kāśyapa achieved the state of an Arhat by realizing the meaning of each stanza of

> the verses on the Four Noble Truths. Ānanda knows how to explain all the collections of *sūtras*, but he has not achieved more than Stream-entry.[71]

Orgyen Rinpoche says:

> Thus, even though you recognize the nature of your own luminous, empty, vivid awareness, experience it directly. By practicing this, everyone is liberated, with no distinctions between those with sharp or dull faculties. Although milk is the cause of butter, if it is not churned and strained, butter does not emerge. Likewise, although all sentient beings are in reality the essence of the Buddhas, without practice, sentient beings do not become enlightened.
>
> If they do practice, even cowherds are liberated. Although they do not know how to describe it, they determine it experientially. While tasting sugar in your mouth, there is no need to describe its taste to others. Even scholars who have not realized this are confused. Even those who have become so learned that they know how to explain the nine *yānas* are like those who listen to distant tales that they have not witnessed. In the moment there is no distance between you and Buddhahood, and when this is realized, virtues and sins are self-liberating. As long as this is not realized, whatever virtues and sins are committed, there is no getting beyond the cycle of existence of the fortunate and miserable states of existence.

– All those who recognize and directly experience the nature of their own luminous, empty, vivid awareness can gain liberation. There are no excuses. You can't say you are not smart enough. Distinctions are often made in terms of people with superior, middling, and inferior faculties, but regardless of your ability, through this particular practice, liberation can be gained. Even cowherds, who are generally thought to hold a low position in society, can attain liberation. Even though they may be unable to articulate it, they know it experientially. When you have sugar in your mouth, you may not be able to describe it, but then there's really no need to describe that taste to others. –

Siddha Orgyen says:

> Thus, if experience is not sustained in terms of appearances and the mind, even those who can intellectually teach the four difficult points on the basis of their learning will not have the aid of escorts in the intermediate state. Even though they have in hand many volumes of profound instructions, they will not be able to reach the escorts in the intermediate state. They are like those

> whose experience of the taste of sugar is visual and mental, while what is needed is to experience the taste of sugar with the tongue. Likewise, all the profound meanings of the texts need to be applied to your own mind. To a person who is on the verge of starving to death during a famine, there is no benefit in saying, "You may eat food," and it does not satisfy his hunger to say, "This food is made of parched barley flour." What is needed is to parch some barley, grind it, and to eat it after preparing it as food. Similarly, to win the battle of the cycle of existence, you must bring all appearances into essential practice pertaining to awareness.

– Even though you have studied the quintessential teachings, if you don't apply the practice to appearances and the mind, at the time of the intermediate state, they will be of no benefit to you. Enlightenment will not be attained. Beginning with the preliminaries, and going through each of the stages that have been discussed, you must apply them to the central aim of the practice, which is the nature of awareness. –

Gyalwa Yang Gönpa says:

> It's not enough for the Dharma to be Atiyoga; the individual must become an Atiyogi. I see that while the Dharma discourse may be worth the price of a horse, the value of the individual is often not even that of a dog. There's no benefit simply in knowing the words of Dharma and having an intellectual understanding. All shuffling of dry words by those who have grown old while focusing solely on rhetoric is no different than the chattering of a parrot and the chirping of a songbird. Dharma does not reach their own mind-streams. Without mixing the flour and water of the mind and Dharma, the arrogance that separates Dharma from the individual is simply not removed. The Dharma remains like bits of lung floating in soup, and their speech is spurious.

Now it is important that you put into practice these points that I have explained, and apply them to the level of your understanding, be it great or small. The benefits of practicing like that are stated in *The King of Samādhi Sūtra*:

> There is greater merit in taking seven steps towards the wilderness out of an aspiration to realize phenomena as identityless than there is in bringing all sentient beings of the three worlds onto the path of the ten virtues.

– The Tibetan word *gönpa* (*dgon pa*) has the dual meaning of wilderness and monastery. Originally, it meant a place of solitude where there are few disturbances. In this solitary place, one could apply oneself single-pointedly to spiritual practice. At times, some solitary practitioners would join a loose community in the wilderness, and that came to be called a *gönpa*. Eventually, more and more practitioners gathered together for spiritual practice, but even when they numbered ten thousand, their abode was still called a *gönpa*. In such large spiritual communities in Tibet, some truly abandoned *saṃsāra* and genuinely applied themselves to practice. They were indeed living in a *gönpa*. If not, they were simply living in a city of monks. Even though two monks might be living next to each other, one might be living in a *gönpa*, the other dwelling in a city. This is because truly living in a *gönpa* is a matter of mental, rather than physical, solitude. –

The Ornament Sūtra states:

> Simply uttering the words "sugar is sweet" does not yield the experience, but if it is eaten its taste is found to be sweet. Likewise, simply uttering the word "emptiness" does not yield the experience, but through meditation its taste is experienced.

The Revelation of Thatness Sūtra states:

> Śāriputra, one's merit increases more by meditating on the reality of thatness for the duration of a finger snap than by listening [to Dharma] for ten eons. Śāriputra, therefore by all means teach this *samādhi* of thatness to others. Śāriputra, all the Bodhisattvas following the Buddha's teaching abide in this *samādhi*.

The Sūtra of Great Realization states:

> Entering the gateway to meditative stabilization just once is more meaningful than sacrificing your life for all the people who fill the three worlds.

The Sūtra of Inconceivable Mysteries states:

> Bodhisattvas who wish to achieve supreme enlightenment swiftly should not devote themselves to words. Those who wish to strive on the path to enlightenment should take up the essence of the practice.

The Synthesized Essence of the Intended Meaning states:

> Nowhere in the ten directions of the universe is the perfect Buddha to be found, for the mind-itself is the perfect Buddha. Do not seek the Buddha elsewhere.

The Sūtra of the Great Illumination states:

> You who wish to repay the kindness of the Jina when this Dharma is declining, the merit of cultivating meditative stabilization by meditating for a single instant is greater than that of sacrificing your life for the sentient beings who fill a thousand worlds.

The Sūtra of Entering the Sublime states:

> There is a greater collection of merit from meditating on emptiness for a single session than from providing the necessities of life to all sentient beings for the duration of their lives.

A *sūtra* states:

> By meditating on emptiness, even the Lord of Death cannot injure you, and even a billion Māras can never bring you harm.

The Perfection of Wisdom Sūtra in Twenty-five Thousand Stanzas states:

> There is a much greater increase of merit through cultivating this perfection of wisdom for the duration of a finger snap than there is in satisfying with generosity all the sentient beings who dwell in the billionfold world-system and in establishing them in ethical discipline, *samādhi*, wisdom, liberation, the vision of liberating intuition, Stream-entry, and the enlightenment of a Pratyekabuddha.

The King of Samādhi Sūtra states:

> One who maintains this supreme *samādhi* achieves the Ten [Bodhisattva] Grounds of the Very Joyous, the Stainless, the Luminous, the Radiant, the Difficult to Overcome, the Approaching, the Gone Afar, the Immovable, the Fine Intelligence, and the Cloud of Dharma.

The Great Mound of Jewels Sūtra states:

> Those living in an inferior era will not even have any doubts concerning this Dharma. Even the arising of a doubt causes cyclic existence to deteriorate.

– In degenerate times, people will not have any doubt about the Dharma. Instead of doubting it, they will reject it totally, without considering even for one moment that Dharma might be possible. Even the slightest uncertainty as to the possibility that Dharma might be true causes your own *saṃsāra* to begin deteriorating. –

The Kṣitigarbha Sūtra states:

> If *samādhi* is not achieved, no accumulated virtuous *karma* will be meaningful; the mind and the events arising from the mind will be poor.

The Vajra Uṣṇīṣa Tantra states:

> If you settle your awareness evenly in primordial reality, there are no *samayas*, no *mantra* practice, no need to hold a *vajra* and bell, and you accomplish the result of freedom from those ten.

The Great Uṣṇīṣa Sūtra states:

> There is greater merit in meditating for one day on the meaning of reality-itself than in hearing [Dharma] for many eons. Why? Because it distances one from the path of birth and death.

A Commentary to the Praise of Śaṃvara states:

> As a result of genuine meditation on Mahāmudrā, the great contemplative achieves omniscience of the nature of immutable bliss. In this life Buddhahood is attained.

The Tantra of the Lotus of Great Power states:

> *Siddhi* does not exist by itself; in reality it refers to the Spirit of Awakening. *Siddhi* refers to the manifestation of accomplishment and realization.

Tilopa says:

> Even the darkness that has gathered during a thousand eons is dispelled by a single lamp. Likewise, in an instant the clear light of your own mind dispels the ignorance, sins, and obscurations that have been accumulated for eons.

The King of Samādhi Sūtra states:

> One who maintains this serene *samādhi* has no difficulty in acquiring the excellent symbols and signs of a Buddha, the eighteen qualities of a Buddha, and the powers, fearlessness, and activities [of enlightenment].

The Great Tantra of Sampuṭa states:

> In short, the Buddhahood that is achieved after countless millions of eons may be achieved in this lifetime by you who experience sublime bliss. You may achieve the state of Vajradhara, or of a World Emperor, or the eight great *siddhis*. Furthermore, you may attain your heart's desire.

The Sphere of Primordial Wisdom states:

> Or, as soon as this body is left behind, [enlightenment] is accomplished even without effort.

Thus, there are incalculable benefits in engaging in practice. The optimal case is to become a Buddha in one lifetime and with one body, or else to become a Buddha as a Dharmakāya at death, when the outer breath ceases. The middling case is to recall the meaning of the unified stages of generation and completion of one's present meditation at the time when one's body and mind separate, resulting in becoming a Buddha in the intermediate state as a Sambhogakāya, indivisible from one's chosen deity. There are said to be twenty-one ways to achieve the result of Buddhahood, corresponding to the specific faculties of individuals. The very least of them is called *resting in a Nirmāṇakāya pure realm*. It is said that by making prayers to take birth in a Buddha realm, you will be reborn there. In this regard Machik Labdrön says:

> Apart from Sukhāvatī, one cannot take birth in the supreme pure realms without having reached the eighth [Bodhisattva] Ground. For the middling pure realms, one must have achieved at least the Path of Meditation on which the subtle afflictive obscurations have been eliminated; without that, one will not take birth there. For the five pristine abodes such as Akaniṣṭha and Aṭakāvatī, one must have achieved the Path of Seeing, on which the truth of reality-itself is seen after having severed the root of self-grasping; without that, one will not take birth there. However, without having reached the Path of Seeing, if one is without even the slightest infraction of one's *samayas* and vows and applies oneself to prayer and to virtue alone, it is just possible to take birth in a small pure realm such as Tuṣita, but it is difficult. Therefore, it is utterly hopeless for an individual with mental afflictions to take birth in a Buddha realm.
>
> However, the Protector Amitābha himself has promised that one may take birth in his pure realm due to the power of his prayers. Thus, you should strive with your body, speech, and mind in prayer to be born in the realm of Sukhāvatī. Ridding yourself of doubt, uncertainty, and spiritual sloth, with great and swift certainty and enthusiasm bring to mind the splendor and benefits of the realm of Sukhāvatī, and pray. Sukhāvatī is superior to the realms of other Buddhas in these ways: it is greater because it is possible for ordinary individuals with mental afflictions to be born there. And if you take birth there, all that you wish for is accomplished as soon as you think of it; you are not tainted by even subtle mental afflictions; and you may go from there to the realms of other Buddhas. Thus, it is superior. Sukhāvatī is endowed with inconceivable benefits, including the swifter attainment of Buddhahood there than in other pure realms. There is no other pure realm within closer reach than Sukhāvatī, so it is extremely important to strive in prayer to be reborn there.

– To take birth in the most sublime pure realms, one must have reached the eighth Bodhisattva Ground. For the middling pure realms, one must have already eliminated the coarse and subtle afflictive obscurations. To be born in the pristine abodes, one must have stopped grasping onto a personal identity and the identity of phenomena. If one has not committed any infractions of one's vows and one makes pure prayers, it is just possible that one may take birth in Tuṣita. As Atiyoga practitioners, you must keep your *samayas* and continue practicing until you attain the point of *the extinction into reality-itself,* which is the ultimate realization of the Great Perfection. Until then, you must continue practicing hearing and thinking about the Dharma, maintain your meditation practice, and attend to the nature of actions and their consequences. You must also continue to cultivate mindfulness, introspection, and conscientiousness.

For individuals with mental afflictions, there is a loophole that can enable them to take birth in a Buddha realm. The Protector Amitābha promised that one may take birth in his pure realm due to the power of his prayers. Thus with your body, speech, and mind focus on this goal; it is good to offer prayers from the *sūtras* and hidden treasure teachings to be reborn in Sukhāvatī. Many such prayers are found in each of the four orders of Tibetan Buddhism, as well as in the Chinese Buddhist tradition. Like prepared food and drink, they are ready to be eaten and drunk.

With complete certainty and enthusiasm, bring to mind the benefits of the realm of Sukhāvatī and pray to be reborn there. While you may find that you have a lot of energy for mundane things, you may still be totally overcome by spiritual sloth, which comes from grasping onto a personal identity. We think that we are important. We consider everything we do to be important. We may even say that our activities are for the sake of sentient beings, while they are truly for our own gratification. Then we cover up this self-centeredness by glossing it with the phrase, "This is altruistic; it's for the sake of the teachings and for sentient beings." This is like dumplings stuffed with rotten meat.

If we look to the Buddhas, *paṇḍits, siddhas,* and *yogis* of India, China, and Tibet, we find that they all have engaged in a gradual practice of Dharma, by finding and maintaining their own appropriate level of practice. The Buddha taught 84,000 collections of teachings, but he did not say that we should each try to practice them all. Rather, in this vast ocean of teaching, we need to determine what is appropriate for ourselves. We need to seek out which aspect, when put into practice, really alleviates our mental afflictions.

The moment you take birth in the pure realm of Sukhāvatī, you can instantaneously visit any other Buddha realm. Once there, you can listen to Dharma as well as engage in the practice of Dharma in other pure realms. Then you can travel back home to Sukhāvatī and resume your practice there. –

Thus, *The Splendor of Sukhāvatī Sūtra, The Great Mound of Jewels Sūtra, The Splendor of Amitābha Sūtra, The [Holy Dharma of the] White Lotus Sūtra, The Spell of the Sound of the Drum,* and the teachings of Orgyen

Rinpoche are all in agreement that unless you have committed any of the five acts of immediate retribution or abandoned the Dharma, if you single-pointedly pray to be reborn in that pure realm, you can take birth in the realm of Sukhāvatī. Moreover, it is said that you will be born there after earnestly praying ten times. That is due to the power of prayer of Buddha Amitābha, so it is crucial to make prayers for that pure realm.

– There is a Tibetan aphorism that it is very hard to sew with a double-pointed needle. Similarly, it is hard to get anything done if your mind is two-pointed. Therefore, as long as you have not committed any of the five deeds of immediate retribution or abandoned the Dharma, if you pray with the total focus of your prayer to be reborn in Sukhāvatī, you will be. Although it says that this will happen after praying earnestly ten times, do not let this be an excuse for succumbing to fickleness in your prayers or your Dharma practice in general. Continue to pray not just once, or ten times, but rather pray at all times.

There was a Lama from Yukho, a region of Tibet, who had thousands of monks under his guidance. Many of them devoted themselves very diligently to meditation and remained in retreat. One day a crazy monk from southern Amdo came to meet with him. Lama Chadral asked the monk what practice he was doing. The monk replied, "Prostrations."

Then he asked him, "What practice do you do along with the prostrations?"

The monk continued, "I have done many hundreds of thousands of prostrations. Sometimes I do them together with prayers to Guru Rinpoche or Amitābha. At other times I prostrate and recite the *mantra* of Avalokiteśvara or the Vajrasattva One-Hundred-Syllable *mantra*. But I am a little bit concerned about my practice because when I am doing the Guru Rinpoche prayer, I wonder what Amitābha and Vajrasattva think. Then I think I'll console Vajrasattva and petition him for awhile, but I think that Guru Rinpoche is getting irritated with me for being fickle."

Was this person practicing? Yes, but his practice was not genuine, because even though he was trying hard in his practice, he did not recognize the essence of Dharma. In short, there is a danger in being prone to a fickle attitude. Perhaps, if we were guaranteed a very long life, there might be time for a smorgasbord approach to Dharma. But in fact, our lives are very short. In truth our own death can come at any time. Many circumstances, such as illnesses and accidents, can lead to our very swift and unexpected demise. When we look back at our life, we wonder where the time has gone and what we have accomplished as a result of all our exertions. It seems as if we were born just a moment ago, but time passes swiftly by. It is unrealistic to depend on long-term plans, which cause us to chase after one project and then another. Meanwhile, we continually postpone the practice of Dharma. But unfortunately, eventually our lives will be over.

Look at the beggar Dharma practitioners of China, India, and Tibet, who lived in utter simplicity and complete devotion to Dharma and attained enlightenment. On the other hand, for all their exertions, smart and talented people who thoroughly suffuse their Dharma with their own yearnings for fame, praise, and influence may simply be destined for *vajra* hell. Recognizing the pathetic situation of sentient beings, Amitābha, with great compassion, made prayers that beings who are still suffering from the mental afflictions may be reborn in Sukhāvatī.

Look at our sense of self-importance, our sense of pride, conceit, and arrogance. What is the basis for this? If we really look at our situation, in terms of the degree to which we are subject to our own mental afflictions, there is no basis for pride. In fact, there is reason to weep, and there is little cause for rejoicing. So, it is crucial to make prayers to be reborn in Sukhāvatī. –

Dedication is like the reins that direct the steed of prayer. Dedication entirely accomplishes your own ends and the ends of others.

– Practicing Dharma is like riding a horse. Dedicating the merit of one's practice is like using a bridle and reins to direct the horse, or to use a more current analogy, turning the steering wheel of a car. When you want to make a turn, it's important that you don't wait until it's too late. If your horse is heading directly for the edge of a cliff, don't wait until it's falling over the cliff before you rein it in. You must anticipate beforehand where you want to turn. Similarly, if you put off the practice of Dharma and think that you will do it just before you die, it will be too late. Until you are on the verge of death, if you only engage in nonvirtuous activities and do not practice Dharma, you will be swept away by your nonvirtuous acts. They will take charge and propel you to places you would rather not go. Right now we have the opportunity to practice Dharma and to prepare for the transition of death. Right now we possess the five personal and five public endowments of a precious human life. Right now we have the eight types of leisure. Therefore, it's of the greatest importance to make use of this opportunity and not put it off until it's too late.

There was an accomplished and talented monk who lived in Canada, and three years ago he discovered that he had cancer. Since that time, his disease has become progressively worse so that now he is only able to ingest liquids. Although he has been very ill throughout these years, he has continued his Dharma practice. Some people felt very badly because he was on the verge of death. On second thought they said, "Wait a minute; he has recognized the value of Dharma and has a genuine practice. Moreover, he will die with a pure practice of Dharma." People should rather feel sorry for any of us who are still fooling around with other priorities and have no genuine Dharma practice. In fact, who knows whether we will die before he does?

At the start of a practice, the foremost motivation to be cultivated is the Spirit of Awakening. Then with this motivation engage in the main body of the practice, and at the culmination of the practice make prayers of dedication. By this means, you accomplish benefit for yourself and others. –

The Great Mound of Jewels Sūtra states:

> Bodhisattvas, after performing an act of generosity, if this is dedicated towards enlightenment, this benefits all sentient beings, and it is incalculably effective in accomplishing your own ends.

– If you engage in a virtuous activity followed by a burst of hatred or jealousy, this is like dropping a lit match on a dry grass house. It just explodes in flames. Just an instant of hatred or a burst of wrath can extinguish the seeds of virtue that have been stored in your mind-stream as a result of your virtuous activities. In contrast, if you place a single drop of water in the ocean, you cannot say that the drop evaporates until the ocean totally vanishes. Until that time, the drop that has merged with the ocean is safely stored there. Similarly, when you dedicate the merit of your activities, you preserve and protect the root of virtue that you have stored. –

The Sūtra of the Questions of Sāgaramati states:

> Just as a water drop that falls into the ocean does not evaporate until the ocean evaporates, so is virtue dedicated to enlightenment not exhausted until enlightenment is reached.

The Splendor of the Realm of Mañjuśrī states:

> All Dharmas converge at the point of aspiration in accordance with conditions. Results occur according to the prayers that are made.

– The dedication of merit towards the fulfillment of our aspirations for our Dharma practice has a very powerful impact on what, in fact, results from our practice. For example, when we engage in Dharma practice, if in our innermost hearts we wish to become so powerful that we can destroy anything we don't like, the prayer may be effective. Therein lies the problem. If we engage in Dharma practice with such a motivation, it will lead in that direction. Therefore, it is of utmost importance to bring forth a pure motivation, uncontaminated by the eight mundane concerns, such as practicing solely for the sake of your children or for your own material wealth and influence. The moment you finish any practice or any enactment of virtue, dedicate the spiritual power of that for your own enlightenment and the enlightenment of all sentient beings. Also, dedicate it in a general way, praying: "However the Buddhas of the past have dedicated their merit, may the spiritual power of my practice be directed likewise." –

Āryadeva says:

> That which is dedicated is not exhausted, but bountifully multiplies.

– Do not ignore even the smallest virtue that you perform. Even one recitation of *oṃ maṇi padme hūṃ* or one prostration can be dedicated. In the same manner, do not ignore the small nonvirtuous deeds that you do. That is as much a mistake as forgetting to dedicate small virtues. Watch out for even small nonvirtues with great conscientiousness and avoid such activity. Just as a single match can start a blaze that can torch an entire forest, so can a seemingly insignificant nonvirtue lead to very great problems. –

As a result of dedication, even a small virtue will not be exhausted until Buddhahood is achieved, and with the passage of each day it develops and increases. Thus, that which is small becomes great, and ultimately it turns into the fruition of Buddhahood; so this is extremely important.

If dedication is made without distraction from the nature of the mind, it becomes a dedication of a genuine agent, action, and object of action, which brings forth extraordinary benefits.

– This is a very lofty type of dedication. In the context of Atiyoga realization, this dedication takes place without grasping onto the agent, action, or the object of action. It is said to be a nonobjectified dedication, and it is the highest dedication. Even if we don't have that degree of realization and are unable to have such a sublime form of dedication, nothing prevents us from dedicating the spiritual power of our practice so that it may work in accord with the prayers of the Buddhas of the past. –

The Ornament for Higher Realization states:

> Distinctive dedication is the supreme enactment of that. This has the aspect of nonobjectification and it has the characteristic of validity.

The seal of dedication at the conclusion of any virtuous activity is like making supplications to a wish-fulfilling gem, for it accomplishes all that you desire.

– If you do not make the dedication, you are like a person with a wish-fulfilling gem in your house who fails to polish it, make offerings to it, or direct wishes to it. You just keep it there. If you don't possess a wish-fulfilling gem, there is no point in putting requests to it. Similarly, if you have no virtue, there is nothing to dedicate. You may recite *mantras* for hours, but if your mind is dominated by the five poisons, your verbal activity is not imbued with a virtuous motivation. In that case, the recitation is pointless. Moreover, you have nothing to dedicate. Then there are no results, and you have only wasted your time. For this reason, motivation is of the utmost importance.

Once again, from the beginning check your motivation. It is the motivation that makes a practice virtuous and genuine. Day and night, we faithfully devote ourselves to the five poisons. We attend very closely to enhancing our hatred, jealousy, and so on. Given our preoccupation with serving these masters, don't you think that spending an hour of actual Dharma practice with good motivation would be okay? If we ignore the issues of motivation and dedication and only go through the motions of Dharma practice, we are not even able to accomplish our own ends. Really, then, what is the point? Whether you are a Lama, a monk, a tantric practitioner, a man, or a woman, you may feel that you are special. You may think you are a Tulku, a Buddha, or an incarnation of Guru Rinpoche. If you have such thoughts, put them to the test. Look at your mental, verbal, and physical behavior. Look at your motivation. Are these the behavior and motivation of enlightened beings? Only when you attain enlightenment in this lifetime can you make any such claim. If not, your thoughts of being special amount to nothing. –

The Primary Treatise on the Fivefold Practice states:

> If the wish-fulfilling gem of the two collections is not polished with prayer, the fruits of your desires will not be accomplished. So at the end apply yourself to this dedication.

Therefore, whatever virtue you perform, do it with the excellent intention of the Spirit of Awakening, thinking, "I shall perform this virtue for the sake of all sentient beings." During the main practice, bear in mind the difficulty of achieving a human life of leisure and endowment, death and impermanence, causal actions and their consequences, and the problems of the cycle of existence. During each session focus on taking refuge, the Spirit of Awakening, Vajrasattva, the *maṇḍala* offering, and *guruyoga*. Then imagine yourself as Avalokiteśvara, and visualize on the crown of your head the form of Amitābha as the embodiment of all spiritual mentors. Imagine inviting all spiritual mentors and their dissolving into Amitābha, who becomes the embodiment of them all. Imagine inviting all chosen deities, who dissolve into yourself, so that you become the embodiment of all of them. At your heart imagine the syllable *Hrīḥ* surrounded clockwise by the six-syllables upon a moon-disc, which is the synthesis of all secret *mantras*, knowledge *mantras*, and spell *mantras*. Those are profound practical instructions for actualizing all deities by means of one deity

– Whatever your background within Tibetan Buddhism, with whatever chosen deities you have a connection, imagine that they dissolve into you and that you arise in the form of Avalokiteśvara as the synthesis of them all. Visualize the syllable *Hrīḥ* at your heart with *oṃ maṇi padme hūṃ* circling it clockwise. This is like a wish-fulfilling gem or a master key that opens up every door. –

Imagine rays of light emanating from your heart, transforming the physical universe into the pure realm of Sukhāvatī, and transforming all sentient beings into the form of Avalokiteśvara. That is transforming appearances into divine embodiments. Imagine their chanting leader rising up and all of them chanting the six syllables. That is transforming sounds into divine speech, so it is a teaching that causes many hundreds of millions [of *mantras* to be recited] in an instant. Whatever good and bad thoughts arise in the mind, observe their nature without rejecting or affirming them, and leave your mind without modification. That is transforming thoughts into the divine mind, and it is the practice of Mahāmudrā and the Breakthrough to the ground of the Great Perfection. Without supplementing those three with anything, they comprise a superb practice of the union of the stages of generation and completion. At the very least, you should never be parted from those three.

– In your mind, you transform your home, your city, your state, and the entire earth into Sukhāvatī, and all sentient beings appear as Avalokiteśvara. Imagine the great roar of these many, many people reciting the six-syllable *mantra* in unison. Now observe the nature of whatever thoughts arise in your mind. Neither reject nor affirm them, but leave your mind without modification. Transform all forms into divine embodiments, all sounds into divine speech, and all thoughts into the divine mind. Moreover, do not practice in a fragmented fashion, as if each is a distinct phase. Practice them indivisibly and with the recognition that they are of the same essence. This is the time to implement all that you understand in terms of your Atiyoga practice. To perceive indivisibly all forms as divine embodiments, all sounds as divine speech, and all mental activity as enlightened mind constitutes the union of the stages of generation and completion. –

At sunrise and at sunset, attend to the meaning of the clear-light Great Perfection Leap-over. Every morning at dawn and every evening at twilight, practice without fail a session of Sending and Receiving. When you are preparing for sleep, consider, "By whatever virtuous actions I have done today, may all sentient beings achieve Buddhahood. For that purpose, I shall manifestly become a Buddha; in order to achieve Buddhahood swiftly without interference, as soon as I pass from this life may I be born in the realm of Sukhāvatī." If you know how, recite a dedication to be reborn in Sukhāvatī, *The Sukhāvatī Prayer*, and *The Prayer of the Activities of Samantabhadra*. If you do not know them, it is enough to say, "May I be reborn in Sukhāvatī."

– At sunrise and at sunset practice the gazes of the Leap-over stage of the Great Perfection. At dawn and at twilight without fail practice a session of Sending and Receiving (Tib. *gtong len*) in conjunction with the cultivation of the four immeasurables: compassion, loving-kindness, empathetic joy, and equanimity. Then as you prepare for sleep, dedicate the merit of your virtuous activities to the achievement of Buddhahood for yourself and all sentient beings.

In Tibet, people measured the progress of their practice with white and black stones. During the day, if you engaged in something virtuous, you would add a white stone to the pile of white stones. Conversely, if you engaged in something nonvirtuous, you would place a black stone on another pile. In the evening, you would see how many white stones you had accumulated. You would then rejoice in the accumulation of your virtuous activities and dedicate the merit. Next, you would count the pile of black stones and confess your nonvirtuous activities in order to purify them. Normally, at the outset of such a practice, you would probably find that the black pile was much larger. But as you progress in the practice, the pile of white stones should increase as the number of black ones decreases. In the course of the practice, it is very important to realize that you are your own teacher; you are the guide for your own practice. In this way, as you take responsibility for your own practice, you will know that no one else is telling you to engage in virtue and there is no one to whom you can complain.

Given our present state, we need to recognize that although we may aspire to serve the needs of all sentient beings, we cannot effectively do so at present. After recognizing this limitation, aspire to attain Buddhahood. You may say something as simple as, "May I be reborn in Sukhāvatī. May I then attain enlightenment and by achieving enlightenment, may I serve sentient beings until everyone is liberated." However, it is enough to have a virtuous motivation and just to say, "May I be born in Sukhāvatī." –

Be utterly certain that you will be reborn in Sukhāvatī when you die. The certainty of being reborn there unless you have committed any of the five crimes of immediate retribution or have abandoned Dharma is due to the power of prayer of the Buddha. Killing one's father, mother, primary spiritual mentor and *vajra* master, or an Ārya Arhat, and attempting to murder a Buddha are crimes of immediate retribution. None of you have done such things, have you? If you abandon Dharma, you will not be reborn there, but I reckon you are people who have not abandoned Dharma and are doing what you can to practice. It is wrong to doubt whether or not you will be reborn there. It is said that if you doubt this, even if you are born in that pure realm, the flower in which you are born will not open for a long time, which postpones your encounter with the Buddha. So do not doubt whether or not you will be reborn there.

– Our faith must be unwavering. Together with this firm conviction and the power of the prayer of Amitābha, Sukhāvatī is exactly where we will be born. In fact, there have been many people in Tibet who have had this type of faith, and they indeed took rebirth there. However, bear in mind that this type of certainty is not enough. It must be coupled with the cultivation of virtue. If you devote yourself to the cultivation of virtue, pray to Amitābha, and do not commit any of the five deeds of immediate retribution, you may have total confidence in taking rebirth in Sukhāvatī. If you do have doubt, even if you are born in that pure realm, the lotus flower in which you are born will not open for a long time. In that case, your meeting with the Buddha will be postponed. For that reason alone, cast aside all doubt. –

What good is it to be born there? There is no suffering in taking birth in that realm, for your body is instantly brought forth in miraculous birth in the midst of a flower. Everyone without exception who is born there has a golden-colored body adorned with the signs and symbols of enlightenment and possesses incalculable extrasensory perception and paranormal abilities. In that realm you never even hear of the sufferings of illness, harmful spirits, enemies, famine, and so on. Whoever is born there is free of the five poisons of attachment, hatred, delusion, pride, and jealousy. The duration of one eon in our world is the equivalent of one day in the realm of Sukhāvatī, and even in a quadrillion of its years there is no death, no illness, and no aging. Whatever you desire in terms of food, clothing, enjoyments, and things to offer to the Buddha comes spontaneously with the mere thought of such things. There is no need to acquire them with effort, to preserve them, or make a living. Without needing to experience the suffering of the ripening of all your present sins and obscurations, they are purified by encountering Amitābha, making prostrations, circumambulations, and offerings, and by listening to the Dharma. Due to your unimpeded paranormal abilities and extrasensory perception, you may go to all the Buddha realms, meet the Buddhas, listen to Dharma, and with these connections serve as a guide to sentient beings. In the evening there is nothing to obstruct your paranormal ability to return to Sukhāvatī.

In such a state of bountiful joy and happiness, you may listen to the Dharma from the Buddha, make offerings, and by exercising the power of *samādhi* over countless eons, you accomplish the Ten Grounds and Five Paths of the *sūtra* tradition, the Thirteen Vajradhara Grounds of the *mantra* tradition, and the Sixteen Grounds of supreme primordial wisdom of the Atiyoga tradition. It is said that finally, as soon as you pass away from that life, you become a Buddha, with your body, speech, and mind indivisible from all the Buddhas. Therefore, having received this teaching, even though you do not remember the words, if you bear in mind the primary meanings and practice with enthusiasm, there is no doubt that you will be reborn in Sukhāvatī. The *sūtras, tantras*, and the teachings of Orgyen bear testimony to this.

– Through these teachings, we have been introduced to the cultivation of quiescence and insight, but because our lives are too busy or we are subject to spiritual sloth, we don't accomplish them. In this lifetime if we don't find much hope of achieving quiescence and insight and of gaining deep realization in Mahāmudrā and Atiyoga, there is still hope of taking birth without great difficulty in Sukhāvatī. We are not living in a realm of spiritual famine, as it were. Through the great kindness of Karma Chagmé and Amitābha, we are given a very viable possibility of taking birth in Sukhāvatī. If you apply yourself to virtue, avoid nonvirtue, and pray to Amitābha and Karma Chagmé, this is accessible to you. Conversely, if you ignore the cultivation of virtue, you will have no spiritual practice and certainly no growth or realization.

For two types of people there is no need to practice Dharma. One type is people who don't really fear suffering, even though they wish to be free of it. They don't fear the experiences that follow this life. Therefore, they are complacent and have no interest in the Dharma. It is all right if such people do not practice. The second type is people who have already achieved Buddhahood. They don't need to practice Dharma either. For the rest of us, Dharma is necessary.

It is said that Buddha Śākyamuni practiced for three countless eons before he became a fully enlightened Buddha. In his final life he went through great austerities and applied himself with extreme diligence and dedication to practice for six years, after which he gained the culminating experience of enlightenment. Similarly, Guru Rinpoche with great dedication and earnestness purified his mind-stream of any nonvirtuous imprints and accumulated spiritual power and knowledge through engaging in Dharma practice. If you looked at the life stories of the great adepts of India and Tibet, do you think you would find any who attained enlightenment by just hanging out and not applying themselves to Dharma?

The most famous life story in the history of Tibetan Buddhism is that of Milarepa. By reading his biography, you can ascertain the degree of diligence and depth of dedication that he applied to his practice of Dharma, which culminated in the attainment of enlightenment. When you think of the greatest teachers, Lamas, and contemplatives in the Kagyü tradition, are there any who attained enlightenment without totally dedicating themselves to the practice of Dharma? Can you point to a single one in the Geluk, Sakya, or Nyingma traditions? Are there any within the broader range of Hīnayāna, Mahāyāna, and Vajrayāna who have achieved enlightenment while practicing a lifetime of nonvirtue? If so, then these teachings are mistaken. But if they are not mistaken, then for all of us who are still within this cycle of suffering and discontent, the practice of Dharma is essential. Therefore, we must work to purify our minds and engage in virtue, thereby accumulating merit. –

Upon compiling this manual of teachings, I, Rāga Asey, asked, "Will it serve the needs of sentient beings?" I made single-pointed prayers to Avalokiteśvara, 108 times I offered the *ganacakra,* offerings, and *maṇḍala;* then that evening I examined the signs. In a state bordering visionary experience and the dream-state, there occurred a prophetic vision in which I was told, "Seven hundred million will go to Sukhāvatī." And when I was writing this down, the Dharma lord primordial wisdom Ḍākinīs assembled, and many dream signs of blessing also occurred. So there are also fine, beneficial precedents for you students of this teaching.

Previously I have received an eighteen-day teaching in the presence of Drungchen Kün-ga Namgyal. That was the first of the teachings I received, so in accordance with that precedent, these primary teachings on *The Essential Instructions of Avalokiteśvara on the Union of Mahāmudrā and Atiyoga* have also been completed in eighteen sessions. The supplementary teachings include all the *sūtras* and *tantras,* so they are limitless.

Maṅgalam[72]

The stages of instruction on Mahāmudrā, Atiyoga, mind training, and so on accord with the lineage of essential instructions I have received and with my experiences through meditating and teaching. Nowadays most superior and inferior lay and ordained people have received many sequential teachings bearing such great names as Mahāmudrā, Atiyoga, the Path and Its Fruits, the Six Dharmas, and the Six Yogas; they have received a myriad of empowerments and oral transmissions of the new and old traditions, and there are even those who have many times received great teachings in which a single instruction lasts more than three years. Yet apart from the mere benefit of receiving them, they do not bear in mind even a fragment of the practices themselves. Let your practice settle solely on the meditation and recitation of Avalokiteśvara and on attending to the essence of the mind.

Although there are many kinds of essential instructions of Avalokiteśvara, I have not explained anything more than the primary words. Thus, with regard to the essential instructions of Avalokiteśvara, this foundation of the great teaching on the union of Mahāmudrā and Atiyoga makes no distinction between the instructions and practice; and by practicing the meaning there is benefit to everyone.

Therefore, without desire for erudition or fame, and with pure *samayas*, you students should hold Avalokiteśvara as your chosen deity, and you will have fine experiential realizations of Mahāmudrā and Atiyoga.

Although there are many who are capable of teaching others, due to little intelligence and lack of study there are few who can explain the textual citations. Even when citations are understood, it is difficult to determine where they fit appropriately and how long to make each Dharma teaching session. So, without concealing anything, this may be read by those who are literate and have received the oral transmission, but no advanced scholars or adepts will listen to this. So I have composed this with the thought that many old mendicants and recluses may accomplish their eternal longing for happiness.

Since I have the limitation of being an ordinary person and lack the eyes of Dharma, whatever faults and inconsistencies of composition and spelling I have made—including the contamination of mistakes and revealing that which should remain hidden—I confess them all to the assembly of the Three Roots, the Dharma Lords and Protectors, and to those endowed with the eyes of wisdom. May they not contribute to interferences in this life or to obstacles to the Grounds and Paths in the hereafter, but may those beings view me with compassion and grant me their blessing.

At the beginning of each of these eighteen Dharma sessions there are many citations which may satisfy scholars, and those with understanding and intelligence will come to certain knowledge. At the end are concise stages of meditative practice that are easy to understand. Experiential realization will arise in all but the deaf.

On the first evening after you depart, offer a white *torma* and with the offering of the *torma* bless your environment. As a circumstance for inspiring virtue, bestow the *cundha* empowerment. Expel forces that are harmful outwardly, inwardly, and to the public, and establish the borders of your retreat place. For protection from infectious diseases, bestow the Loma Gyönma empowerment. Then in the morning and afternoon, etc., grant each of the permissions to the public. In the evening teach Dharma to your students, then meditate until the next day. Thus, the main body of the teachings takes eighteen days, and on the day on which you are about to finish, make the commitment to virtue, perform a celebratory *ganacakra*, grant a life empowerment, perform the dedication, and toss grain while chanting extensive auspicious prayers. In that way the great teaching is completed in twenty-one days. If a quick instruction is desired, by lecturing twice a day, this teaching may be completed in nine days. If empowerments are needed, grant them in the afternoon.

Due to the roots of virtue from writing this, may I and all those who have gained a connection with me and all those who have gained a connection with this manual of instruction experience in this life longevity, freedom from illness, and the growth of experiential realization. As soon as we pass away from this life, may we miraculously be reborn in the realm of Sukhāvatī, and never be separated from Amitābha.

May the Mamo and Gönpo Guardians of the Mahāmudrā *tantras*, the Protectors Jarogma and Seng-gey-dong, and the five gods of longevity guard this Dharma. May the Maning, Chamdral, Sogdrup Nagmo, Mamo, Za, and Damchen guard this Atiyoga Dharma in accordance with their earlier *samaya* and cause it to flourish. May the Nyurdzey Protector and Draggön Dungdzin cause this Dharma of essential instructions to flourish and grow. May the eighty white Jodrom guardians of the teachings and the twelve lamps dwelling in this world cause the meaning of these stages of the path of mind-training to flourish. May the eighty thousand minor deities who protect *samādhi* cause this Dharma of *samādhi* to flourish. Since you all are general guardians of the teachings, do not let this important Dharma decline, but let it flourish.

In particular, this Dharma treasure is entrusted to the keeping of Dorje Yudrönma, the Lady of Avalokiteśvara, the Guardian of the Dharma, the Mistress of all extrasensory perception, paranormal abilities, and *siddhis*, who fulfills the longings of practitioners. This teaching is turned over to you; please cause it to flourish, grow, and remain for a long time.

This was done in my sixty-first year, in the year of the eagle,[73] from the last day of the month of the monkey until the seventeenth day of the month of the bird. The scribe was Gelong Tsöndrü. There have been many regular ritual practices for which I have commitments, my body is unwell for it is afflicted by illness, and I have needed to perform regular ceremonies for the longevity of the king; so there have been many distractions from the empowerments, oral transmission, and so on. There may be errors in the order of some of the citations, so I ask scholars to forgive me. Since this is a fresh composition, there may be misspellings, which should be corrected by later scribes.

Maṅgalam bhavantu![74]

Notes

1. The spiritual mentor, the chosen deity, and the Ḍākinī.

2. The signs of warmth are indications of success in one's spiritual practice.

3. This is the lineage devoted primarily to meditative practice rather than elaborate scholarly learning.

4. Those with good karmic fortune have very good habitual predispositions. In other words, something good was carried over from a previous lifetime.

5. Trans. by Sangye Khandro (Ithaca: Snow Lion, 1988).

6. Meditative stabilization, reading, and action.

7. Killing your father, your mother, an Arhat, maliciously drawing the blood of a Buddha, and creating a schism in the Saṅgha.

8. These qualities are discussed in detail in *Generating the Deity* (Ithaca: Snow Lion, 1996) by Gyatrul Rinpoche.

9. VIII, 4. *A Guide to the Bodhisattva Way of Life*, trans. Vesna A. Wallace and B. Alan Wallace (Ithaca: Snow Lion, 1997).

10. VIII, 1.

11. V, 16.

12. V, 1.

13. V, 5.

14. V, 18.

15. V, 2.

16. V, 3.

17. V, 22.

18. V, 23. The Derge edition of the Tibetan reads in translation: "I appeal to those desiring to guard their minds: always diligently guard your mindfulness and introspection."

19. V, 108.

20. The mental afflictions.

21. Beings who have an unmediated, nonconceptual realization of emptiness.

22. This is a natural equanimity that occurs due to not grasping onto the joy that is experienced. Ordinary equanimity, in contrast, arises due to various external conditions, and in this sense is artificial.

23. These refer to the abodes of the gods of the desire realm, form realm, and formless realm.

24. These are the instructions given by Avalokiteśvara to Min-gyur Dorje (Mi 'gyur rdo rje).

25. The meaning here seems to be that the correct posture is not the normal, relaxed posture; rather, it must be learned and practiced.

26. *Grahas, pārthivas, nāgas, mātṛkās,* and *kṣamāpatis* are all classes of entities that may be malevolent to human beings.

27. Literally, a knife with a blade of bell metal, known for being exceptionally sharp and brittle.

28. This is an element of "inner heat" meditation (*gtum mo*).

29. The seven attributes of Vairocana.

30. VIII, 34-35.

31. Cf. *The Tibetan Dhammapada: Sayings of the Buddha,* trans. Gareth Sparham (Boston: Wisdom Publications, 1986), p. 102, v. 7.

32. Ibid., p. 103, v. 11.

33. Ibid., p. 103, v. 12.

34. Ibid., p. 114, v. 2.

35. Ibid., p. 114, v. 3.

36. V, 62-63.

37. Quoted from the section entitled "Engaging in the Search for the Mind" in *Natural Liberation: Padmasambhava's Teachings on the Six Bardos,* by Gyatrul Rinpoche, trans. by B. Alan Wallace (Boston: Wisdom Publications, 1997).

38. Ibid.

39. *Ci yang ma yin pa'i phung gsum sho re mi 'ong bas.* Trans.: This phrase is not clear to me.

40. This is the earliest of the three Nyingma (*rNying ma*) lineages to appear in the eastern region of Tibet known as Kham (*Khams*). The next to appear was the Palyül (*dPal yul*) lineage, to which this text belongs, and the third was the Dzogchen (*rDzogs chen*) lineage.

41. Tibetan monks who have completed a long, rigorous, academic training in Buddhist doctrine, metaphysics, and logic.

42. *A Guide to the Bodhisattva Way of Life*, IX, 17.

43. The sole *bindu* is the primordial essence and indivisible mode of being of both *saṃsāra* and *nirvāṇa*.

44. Quoted from the section entitled "Identifying Awareness" in *Natural Liberation: Padmasambhava's Teachings on the Six Bardos*, by Gyatrul Rinpoche, trans. by B. Alan Wallace.

45. The phrases in parentheses appear in the Tibetan text as annotations (*yig chung*).

46. The consort of the primordial Buddha Samantabhadra.

47. This corresponds closely to the theme of all appearances arising as emptiness. Thus emptiness is form, and form is emptiness.

48. Quoted from the section entitled "Meditative Equipoise of the Threefold Space" in *Natural Liberation: Padmasambhava's Teachings on the Six Bardos*, by Gyatrul Rinpoche, trans. by B. Alan Wallace.

49. Ibid.

50. The power of remorse, the power of applying antidotes, the power of reliance (on refuge and the cultivation of compassion), and the power of resolving to avoid sinful actions in the future.

51. The facsimiles of these ten signs are similar to the types of visions that occur in the Leap-over practice of the Great Perfection.

52. Tib. *byis pa nyer spyod kyi bsam gtan*, Skt. *balopacārikadhyana*.

53. Tib. *don rab tu 'byed pa'i bsam gtan*, Skt. *arthapravicayadhyāna*.

54. Tib. *de bzhin nyid dmigs bsam gtan*, Skt. *tathatālambanadhyāna*.

55. Tib. *kha gting med pa*.

56. The joy, clarity, and nonconceptuality that arise due to the cultivation of quiescence.

57. This is the lineage of the Great Perfection tradition.

58. This refers to the Kama (*bka' ma*) tradition of Atiyoga.

59. This refers to the Terma (*gter ma*) tradition of Atiyoga.

60. Padmasambhava's teachings on the six transitional processes revealed by Karma Lingpa are translated with Gyatrul Rinpoche's commentary in *Natural Liberation: Padmasambhava's Teachings on the Six Bardos*, by Gyatrul Rinpoche, trans. by B. Alan Wallace.

61. Karma Chagmé presented these teachings to an assembly of disciples, whom he is here leading in a group practice of chanting and meditation.

62. *Oṃ maṇi padme hūṃ*.

63. The sun and moon are the two eyes.

64. *Cakū* literally means "eye."

65. Vajrapāṇi

66. The Tibetan term given here is *sDug po bkod pa,* rather than *'Og min,* which is the direct translation of *Akaniṣṭha.*

67. "Blood-drinkers" are wrathful deities.

68. In *Natural Liberation: Padmasambhava's Teachings on the Six Bardos,* from which this prayer is extracted, this stanza reads: "When I am wandering in the cycle of existence due to strong, delusive appearances,/ May the assembly of blood-drinking wrathful deities lead me/ To the clear, radiant path that eliminates fear and terror./ May the assembly of wrathful Ākaśadhātviśvarīs support me./ Please liberate me from the terrifying narrow passage of the transitional process./ Bring me to the state of truly perfect Buddhahood."

69. In *Natural Liberation: Padmasambhava's Teachings on the Six Bardos,* this stanza reads: "Alas! When I am wandering in the cycle of existence due to the strong five poisons,/ May the Jinas of the five families lead me/ To the clear, radiant path of union with the four primordial wisdoms./ May the five great consorts of the absolute nature support me./ Please liberate me on the radiant path that transcends the six impure states of existence./ Please lead me to the five supreme pure realms."

70. Quoted from "The Prayer for Liberation through the Narrow Passage of the Transitional Process" in *Natural Liberation: Padmasambhava's Teachings on the Six Bardos,* by Gyatrul Rinpoche, trans. by B. Alan Wallace.

71. Cūḍapanthaka and Kāśyapa were disciples of the Buddha. Stream-entry is the first of the four stages on the path to Arhatship.

72. "May there be virtue."

73. Tib. *mkha' lding rgyal po.* This corresponds to the year of the bird.

74. "May there be virtues!"

Glossary of Terms

absolute nature of reality	chos kyi dbyings	dharmadhātu
actual primordial wisdom	don gyi ye shes	
afflictive obscuration	nyon mongs pa'i sgrib pa	kleśa-āvaraṇa
awareness	rig pa	vidyā
Breakthrough	khregs chod	
chosen deity	yi dam	iṣṭadevatā
conceptual elaboration	spros pa	prapañca
consummate awareness	rig pa tshad phebs	
contemplation	rnal 'byor	yoga
cycle of existence	'khor ba	saṃsāra
display of awareness	rig pa'i rtsal	
embodiment	sku	kāya
Expanse class	klong sde	
extinction into reality-itself	cho nyid zad pa	
Five Purifications	mngon byang lnga	pañcābhisambhodi
four contemplations	rnal 'byor bzhi	caturyoga
Four Remedial Powers	g.nyen po'i stobs bzhi	
Four Thoughts That Turn the Mind	blo ldog rnam bzhi	
extrasensory perception	mngon shes	abhijñā
habitual propensity	bag chags	vāsana
ideation	rnam par rtog pa	vikalpa
insight	lhag mthong	vipaśyanā
intermediate state	bar do	antarābhava
knowledge *mantra*	rig sngags	vidyāmantra
Leap-over	thod rgal	
meditative stabilization	bsam gtan	dhyāna
mental afflictions	nyon mongs	kleśa

Mind class	sems sde	
mind-itself	sems nyid	cittatā
obscuration	sgrib pa	āvaraṇa
original reality	ka dag don	
paranormal ability	dngos grub	siddhi
Precept class	man ngag sde	
primordial wisdom	ye shes	jñāna
propitiatory practice	bsnyen pa	
quiescence	zhi gnas	śamatha
reality-itself	chos nyid	dharmatā
secret *mantra*	gsang sngags	guhyamantra
Sending and Receiving	gtong len	
sense-base	skye mched	ayātana
sin	sdig pa	pāpa
Six-phase Yoga	sbyor ba yan lag drug	ṣaḍaṅgayoga
spell *mantra*	gzungs sngags	dhāraṇī
Spirit of Awakening	byang chub kyi sems	bodhicitta
stage of completion	rdzogs rim	sampannakrama
stage of generation	bskyed rim	utpattikrama
swift-footedness	rkang mgyogs	
Three Techniques	cho ga gsum	
total-ground	kun gzhi	ālaya
total presence of awareness	rig pa cog bzhag	
transitional process	bar do	antarābhava
vital energy	rlung	prāṇa
vows of dwelling in devotion/ of the devotional state	bsnyen gnas kyi sdom pa	
wisdom	shes rab	prajñā
yoga of instant total recall	skad cig dran rdzogs kyi rnal 'byor	

Glossary of Names

Chakya Chenpa
Phyag rgya chen pa

Cherbupa
gCer bu pa

Chö Yülwa
gCod yul ba

Chödrak Gyatso
Chos grags rgya mtsho
(The Seventh Karmapa)

Chökyi Wangchuk
Chos kyi dbang phyug

Chöying Dorje
Chos dbyings rdo rje
(The Tenth Karmapa)

Dadak Metri
mDa bdag metri

Dagpo Rinpoche
Dvags po rin po che
(Also known as Gampopa,
sGam po pa)

Déwé Gönpo
bDe ba'i mgon po

Dezhin Shegpa
De bzhin gshegs pa
(The Fifth Karmapa)

Dönden Zhap
Don ldan zhabs

Döndrup Tsenchen
Don grub mtshan can

Dong Kachöpa Saraha
gDong mkha' spyod pa sa ra ha

Dorje Pagmo
rDo rje phag mo

Dragkarwa
Brag dkar ba

Dragpa Gyaltsen
Grags pa rgyal mtshan

Drikung Könchok Trinley Namgyal
(Drikung Dharmarāja)
'Bri khung dkon mchog phrin las
rnam rgyal

Drogön Chöpak
'Gro mgon chos 'phags

Dromtön
'Brom ston

Drubgyü Tenpa Namgyal
sGrub rgyud bstan pa rnam rgyal

Drugchen Karma Tenpel
'Brug chen karma bstan 'phel

Drung Gampopa
Drung sgam po pa

Drungchen Kün-ga Namgyal
Drung chen kun dga' rnam rgyal

Düdül Dorje
bDud 'dul rdo rje

Düsum Kyenpa
Dus gsum mkhyen pa
(The First Karmpa)

Dzog Chenpa
rDzogs chen pa

Dzongtö Kandroma
rDzong stod mkha' 'gro ma

Garab Dorje
dGa' rab rdo rje

Gelong Tsöndrü
dGe slong brtson 'grus

Geshe Jayülpa
dGe bshes bya yul pa

Gö Tsangpa
rGod tshang pa

Gyachakri
rGya lcags ri

Gyalsey
rGyal sras

Gyaltshap Dragpa Chog-yang
rGyal tshab grags pa mchog dbyangs

Gyalwa Chö Dingwa
rGyal ba chos lding ba

Gyalwa Yeshe Do
rGyal ba ye shes mdo

Gyalwang Chöjé
rGyal dbang chos rje

Gyalwang Jé
rGyal dbang rje

Gyaré
rGya ras

Gyatön Chökyi Zangpo
rGya ston chos kyi bzang po

Jampal Zangpo
'Jam dpal bzang po

Jamyang Khyentse Lodrö Tayé
'Jam dbyangs mkhyen rtse blo gros mtha' yas

Jigten Gönpo
'Jig rten mgon po

Jigten Sumgön
'Jig rten gsum mgon

Kache Paṇchen
Kha che paṇ chen

Kachö Wangpo
mKha' spyod dbang po

Kangkawa
Kang ka ba

Karma Lingpa
Karma gling pa

Karma Pakṣi
Kar ma pak ṣi
(The Second Karmapa)

Karma Trinley
Karma phrin las

Katog
Kaḥ thog

Katogpa Jampa Bum
Kaḥ thog pa byams pa 'bum

Kenchen Chödrup Seng-ge
mKhan chen chos grub seng ge

Könchok Yenlak
dKon mchog yan lag

Kumché
sKu mched

Kün-ga Namgyal
Kun dga' rnam rgyal

Lama Drung Yigpa
Bla ma drung yig pa

Lama Zhang
Bla ma zhang

Legshé Drayang
Legs bshad sgra dbyangs

Lodrö Dragpa
Blo gros grags pa

Lodrö Rinchen
Blo gros rin chen

Machik Labdrön
Ma gcig lab sgron

Mahāsiddha Masey
Grub chen rma se

Maitrīpa
Mitrajvaki

Marpa Lhodrak
Mar pa lho brag

Mé-nyak Gomring
Me nyag bsgom ring

Mikyö Dorje
Mi bskyod rdo rje
(The Eighth Karmapa)

Mikyö Zhap
Mi bskyod zhabs

Milarepa
Mi la ras pa

Min-gyur Dorje
Mi 'gyur rdo rje

Mipam Padma Karpo
Mi pham padma dkar po

Namké Dorje
Nam mkha'i rdo rje

Natsok Rangdröl
sNa tshogs rang sgrol

Ngadak Nyang
mNga' bdag nyang

Norbu Gyenpa
Nor bu rgyan pa

Norbu Lingpa Déwé Dorje
Nor bu gling pa bde ba'i rdo rje

Nyang Ting-nge-dzin Zangpo
Nyang ting nge 'dzin bzang po

Nyima Beypa
Nyi ma sbas pa

Nyima Tsal
Nyi ma rtsal

Orgyen Rinpoche (Padmasambhava)
O rgyan rin po che

Özer Seng-ge
'Od zer seng ge

Padma Ledreltsal
Pad ma las 'brel rtsal

Pagmo Drüpa
Phag mo grus pa

Paljor Döndrup
dPal 'byor don grub

Patrul Rinpoche
dPa' sprul rin po che

Payül Chogtrul Rinpoche
dPal yul mchog sprul rin po che

Pomdrakpa
sPom brag pa

Rāga Asey
Rā ga a sras
(Karma Chakmé, Kar ma chags med)

Rangjung Dorje (Rangjungwa)
Rang byung rdo rje
(The Third Karmapa)

Ratna Lingpa
Ratna gling pa

Rechenpa
Ras chen pa

Rigdzin Longsel Nyingpo
Rig 'dzin klong gsal snying po

Rinchen Könchok Paljor
Rin chen dkon mchog dpal 'byor

Rolpey Dorje
Rol pa'i rdo rje
(The Fourth Karmapa)

Sakya Paṇchen
Sa skya paṇ chen
Sa skya Paṇḍita

Sampa Künkyap
bSam pa kun khyab

Sangye Gön
Sangs rgyas mgon

Sangye Nyenpa
Sangs rgyas gnyen pa

Sangye Zhagchenpa
Sang rgyas zhag chen pa

Serlingpa
gSer gling pa

Sey Lama Yeshe Dorje
Sras bla ma ye shes rdo rje

Sharawa
Sha ra wa

Situ Chökyi Gyaltsen
Si tu chos kyi rgyal mtshan

Songtsen Gampo
Srong btsan sgam po

Taglung Tashi Paldrup
sTag lung bkra shis dpal grub

Tonglen Rinpoche
gTong len rin po che

Tongwa Dönden
mThong ba don ldan
(The Sixth Karmapa)

Tsangpa Gyarey
gTsang pa rgya ras

Tsombupa
Tshom bu pa

Tsuglak Trengwa
gTsug lag phreng ba

Wangchuk Dorje
dBang phyug rdo rje
(The Ninth Karmapa)

Yagdey Paṇchen
g.Yag sde paṇ chen

Yang Gönpa
Yang dgon pa

Yungtönpa
g.Yung ston pa

Zhi Jepa
Zhi byed pa

Index of Texts Cited by the Author

The Account of Bhikṣu Mahādeva 20
dGe slong lha chen po'i lo rgyus

Avalokiteśvara's Collected Essential Instructions 146
Thugs rje chen po'i tshom bu dmar khrid

Avalokiteśvara's [Instructions on the] Natural Liberation from the Miserable States of Existence 24
Thugs rje chen po ngan song rang grol

Avalokiteśvara's Teachings to Maitrīpa 130
sPyan ras gzigs kyis mi tra dzva ki la gdams pa

The Bhadrakarātri Sūtra 83
mTshan mo bzang mo'i mdo

Birth Accounts 34, 36
sKye rabs
Jātaka

The Blazing Lamp 179
sGron me 'bar ba

The Bodhisattva Corpus Sūtra 34, 165
Byang chub sems dpa'i sde snod kyi mdo
Bodhisattvapiṭakasūtra

Buddhahood in the Palm of Your Hand: Instructions on the Great Perfection 25
rDzogs chen gyi khrid sangs rgyas lag 'chang

The Bundle of Stalks Sūtra 192
sDong po bkod pa'i mdo
Gaṇḍavyūhasūtra

The Chapter on Breakthrough: The Mode of Being in Which the Mind and Awareness Are Integrated 127
Sems rig pa bres nas yin lugs khreg chod pa'i le'u

The Clear Expanse 171, 173, 179
kLong gsal

A Commentary on the Spirit of Awakening 104, 106
Byang chub kyi sems kyi 'grel pa
Bodhicittavivaraṇa
by Nāgārjuna

A Commentary on Verifying Cognition 87
Tshad ma rnam 'grel
Pramāṇavārtika
by Dharmakīrti

A Commentary to the Dohas 133
Do ha'i 'grel pa

A Commentary to the Praise of Śaṃvara 198
bDe mchog bstod 'grel

The Compendium on Hearing 33
Thos pa'i tshom

The Complete Synthesis of the Three Roots 26
rTsa gsum kun 'dus
by Rig 'dzin blo gsal snying po

The Condensed Perfection of Wisdom 21, 107
Shes rab kyi pha rol tu phyin sdud pa
Prajñāpāramitāsañcayagāthā

The Descent into Laṅkā Sūtra 157
Lang kar gshegs pa'i mdo
Laṅkāvatārasūtra

The Dharma of Practical Instruction 173
Man ngag gi chos

Dreams of Secret Activity 26
gSang spyod rnal lam ma

Dreams of the Spirit of Awakening 26
Sems bskyed rmi lam ma

The Eight Treasuries of Dohas 25
Do ha mdzod brgyad

The Essential Instructions of Avalokiteśvara 23, 25, 27, 210
Thugs rje chen po'i dmar khrid

The Essential Instructions of the Bodhisattva Dawa Gyaltsen 24
Byang sems zla ba rgyal mtshan pa'i dmar khrid

The Essential Instructions of the Mahāsiddha Maitrīpa 23, 78
Grub chen mi tri'i dmar khrid

The Essential Instructions of the Palmo Tradition 24
dPal mo lugs kyi dmar khrid

The Essential Instructions of the Tsembu Tradition 24
Tshem bu lugs kyi dmar khrid

The Essential Instructions on the Refreshment of the Mind-itself 23
dMar khrid sems nyid ngal bso

The Extensive and Concise Elucidations of the Primordial Wisdom of Milarepa 25
Mi la'i ye shes gsal byed rgyas bsdus gnyis

Five Dharmas of Maitreya 22
Byams chos sde lnga

The Five Stages 28, 29
Rim lnga

The Fivefold Practices 25
lNga ldan
by Drikung Dharmarāja

The Great Instructions 68, 69, 167
Khrid chen

The Great Instructions on the Ocean of Definitive Meaning 24
Khrid chen nges don rgya mtsho

The Great Introduction 25
Ngo spyod chen mo
by O rgyan rin po che

The Great Lion's Roar of Maitreya Sūtra 31, 32
Byams pa'i seng ge'i sgra chen po'i mdo
MaitreyamahāSiṅhanādasūtra

The Great Mound of Jewels Sūtra 30, 33, 104, 192, 197, 200, 203
dKon mchog brtsegs pa'i mdo
Mahāratnakūṭasūtra

The Great Perfection Aro Oral Lineage of Yagdey Paṇchen 23, 144
rDzogs chen a ro snyan rgyud gyag sde paṇ chen gyi lugs
by Yagdey Paṇchen

The Great Perfection of the Supreme Mind 23
Sems mchog rdzogs pa chen po

The Great Perfection Quintessence of the Ḍākinīs 24, 25
rDzogs chen mkha' 'gro snying thig

Great Reverence 25
Mos gus chen mo
by rGod tshang pa

The Great Tantra of Sampuṭa 39, 82, 89, 198
Sampuṭamahātantra

The Great Uṣṇīṣa Sūtra 198
gTsug tor chen po'i mdo
Mahoṣṇīṣasūtra

The Guhyasamāja Tantra 40, 129
gSang ba 'dus pa'i rgyud

A Guide to the Bodhisattva Way of Life 65, 87, 89
Byang chub sems pa'i spyod pa la 'jug pa
Bodhicaryāvatāra
by Śāntideva

A Guide to the Middle Way 22
dBu ma la 'jug pa
Madhyamakāvatāra
by Candrakīrti

The Heart Blood of the Ḍākinīs 173
mKha' 'gro'i snying khrag

The Hevajra Tantra 59, 68, 129
Kye' rdo rje'i rgyud
Also known as bTags gnyis

The Holy Dharma of the White Lotus Sūtra 30, 44, 200
Dam chos pad ma dkar po'i mdo
Saddharmapuṇḍarīkasūtra

The Hundred and Eight Names of Avalokiteśvara 45
sPyan ras gzigs dbang phyug gi mtshan brgya rtsa brgyad pa
Avalokiteśvaranāmāṣṭaśataka

The Hundred Thousand Teachings 25
bKa' 'bum
by rGya ston chos kyi bzang po

Identifying the Three Embodiments: Essential Instructions of the Great Compassionate One 23
Thugs rje chen po'i dmar khrid sku gsum ngo spyod

Instructions on Parting from the Four Cravings 26
Zhen pa bzhi bral gyi khrid
by Kun dga' snying po

An Introduction to the Light Rays of the Sun and Moon 173
Nyi zla 'od zer ngo sprod

An Introduction to the Secret Path of the Supreme Light of the Primordial Wisdom of Avalokiteśvara 182

Thugs rje chen po'i ye shes 'od mchog gi gsang lam ngo sprod

An Introduction to the Three Embodiments 25
sKu gsum ngo sprod

The Jewel Ornament of Liberation 25, 66, 83
Thar pa'i rgyan
by sGam po pa

The Jewel Radiance of the Ḍākinīs 130
Ḍā ki ma nor bu'i 'od can

The Kadam Volume 43
bKa' gdams glegs bam

The King of Samādhi Sūtra 32, 83, 87, 195, 197, 198
Ting nge 'dzin rgyal po'i mdo
Samādhirājasūtra

The Kṣitigarbha Sūtra 197
Sa'i snying po'i mdo

A Lamp on the Path of Enlightenment 18, 64
Byang chub lam sgron
Bodhipathapradīpa
by Atīśa

A Lamp on the Three Avenues 39
Tshul gsum gyi sgron ma
Nayatrayapradīp

The Manifestation of Vairocana 77
rNam snang mngon 'byung

The Mask of Vairocana 173
Vai ro ca na'i 'dra 'bags

The Moon Essence Sūtra 193
Zla ba'i snying po'i mdo
Candragarbhasūtra

The Moon Lamp Sūtra 29
Zla ba sgron me'i mdo

The Natural Emergence of the Peaceful and Wrathful from Enlightened Awareness 25, 173
Zhi khro dgongs pa rang grol
by Padmasambhava

The Natural Liberation from the Miserable States of Existence 25
Ngan song rang grol
by Padmasambhava

The Natural Liberation of Conscious Awareness: the Identification of the Six Lamps 173
sGron ma drug gi ngo sprod shes rig rang grol
by Padmasambhava

The Natural Liberation of Seeing: the Identification of the Transitional Process of Reality-itself 173, 182, 186
Chos nyid bar do'i ngo sprod mthong ba rang grol
by Padmasambhava

The Nine Collections of Concentration 72
Ting nge 'dzin tshogs dgu
by Bodhibhadra

Nirvāṇa Traces 175, 179
'Das rjes

The Ocean of Definitive Meaning 158, 159, 161
Nges don rgya mtsho

One Word of Essential Teachings 25
sNying gtam tshig gcig
by Rang byung rdo rje

The Oral Transmission of the Lineage of the Siddhas 158, 159, 161, 165
Grub thob brgyud pa'i zhal lung

The Ornament for Higher Realization 204
mNgon rtogs rgyan
Abhisamayālaṃkāra
by Maitreya

The Ornament for the Sūtras 17
mDo sde rgyan
Mahāyānasūtrālaṃkāra
by Maitreya

The Ornament Sūtra 192, 196
Phal chen gyi mdo
Avataṃsakasūtra

The Path and Fruition 24
Lam 'bras
by Virūpa

The Peaceful and Wrathful Lotus Avalokiteśvara 173
Thugs rje chen po padma zhi khro

The Perfect Expression of the Names of Mañjuśrī 20
'Jam dpal gyi mtshan yang dag par brjod pa
Mañjuśrīnāmasaṃgīti

The Perfection of Wisdom Sūtra in One Hundred Thousand Stanzas 87, 131
Yum
Śatasahasrikāprajñāpāramitā

The Perfection of Wisdom Sūtra in Seven Hundred Stanzas 68
Shes rab kyi pha rol tu phyin pa bdun brgya pa
Saptaśatikāprajñāpāramitāsūtra

The Perfection of Wisdom Sūtra in Ten Thousand Stanzas 77
Khri pa
Daśasāhastrikāprajñāpāramitāsūtra

The Perfection of Wisdom Sūtra in Twenty-five Thousand Stanzas 66, 197
Shes rab kyi pha rol tu phyin pa stong phrag nyer lnga pa
Pañcaviṃśatisāhastrikāprajñāpāramitāsūtra

The Pith Instructions of the Ḍākinīs 23, 116, 173
mKha' 'gro snying tig

The Pith Instructions of Vajrasattva 173
rDor sems snying tig

The Pith Instructions of Vimalamitra 26, 173
Vimala snying tig

The Pith Instructions on the Clear Expanse 25, 26, 91, 116, 173
Klong gsal snying tig

Pointing Out the Dharmakāya 25, 95, 120
Chos sku mdzub tshugs
by dBang phyug rdo rje

The Prayer of the Activities of Samantabhadra 206
bZang spyod smon lam

The Precepts of the Four Contemplations 166
rNal 'byor bzhi'i gdams pa

The Primary Tantra of Kālacakra 40
Dus 'khor rtsa rgyud
Kālacakramūlatantra

The Primary Tantra of Mañjuśrī 76
'Jam dpal rtsa rgyud
Mañjuśrīmūlatantra

Primary Tantra on the Penetration of Sound 91, 175, 178, 181
sGra thal 'gyur rtsa ba'i rgyud

The Primary Treatise on the Fivefold Practice 61, 205
lNga ldan rtsa ba

The Primary Words 84, 117
rTsa tshig

The Primary Words of Essential Instructions of the Great Compassionate One 57
Thugs rje chen po'i dmar khrid rtsa tshig

The Primary Words of the Great Instructions 84
Khrid chen rtsa tshig

Questions and Answers Between Lord [Atīśa] and Drom Tönpa 122
Jo 'brom zhus len

The Rainbow Treasure: A General Synthesis of the Jewels of the Great Perfection 24
'Ja' tson pa'i gter kha rdzogs chen dkon mchog spyi 'dus

The Refreshment of the Mind-itself 25
Sems nyid ngal gso

A Refutation of Objections 114
rTsod bzlog
Vigrahavyāvartanī
by Nāgārjuna

The Revelation of Thatness Sūtra 196
De kho na nyid nges par bstan pa'i mdo

The Sadhana of Jinasāgara, the Great Compassionate One 49
Thugs rje chen po rgyal ba rgya mtsho'i sgrub thabs

The Set of Aphorisms 88
Ched du brjod pa'i tshom
Udānavarga

The Seven Seeds of Dharma: Essential Instructions of Avalokiteśvara 25
Thugs rje chen po'i khrid chos 'bru bdun pa

The Single Meaning of the Vajra Speech 22
rDo rje' i gsungs dgongs pa gcig pa

The Six Transitional Processes 173
Bar do drug

The Spell of the Sound of the Drum 200
rNga sgra'i gzungs

The Sphere of Primordial Wisdom 198
Ye shes thig le

The Splendor of Amitābha Sūtra 200
'Od dpag med kyi bkod pa'i mdo
Amitābhavyūhasūtra

The Splendor of Sukhāvatī Sūtra 200
bDe ba can gyi bkod pa'i mdo
Sukhāvatīvyūhasūtra

The Splendor of the Realm of Mañjuśrī 203
'Jam dpal zhing bkod

Stanzas on the Madhyamaka Root of Wisdom 89, 113
dBu ma rtsa ba shes rab
Prajñāmūlamadhyamakakārikā
by Nāgārjuna

The Sukhāvatī Prayer 206
bDe smon

The Summarized Meaning of the Equal Taste 25
Ro snyom dgongs dril

Support 25
rGyab skyor
by Yang dgon pa

The Sūtra of Ānanda's Instruction on Entering the Womb 64, 165
dGa' bo la mngal na gnas pa bstan pa'i mdo
Ānandagarbhavikrāntinirdeśasūtra

The Sūtra of Basket Weaving 46, 88
Za ma tog bkod pa'i mdo
Karaṇḍavyūhasūtra

The Sūtra of Bringing forth the Extraordinary Resolve 32, 192
lHag pa'i bsam pa bskul ba'i mdo
Adhyāśayasañcodanasūtra

The Sūtra of Cultivating Faith in the Mahāyāna 103
Theg pa chen po la dad pa rab tu sgom pa'i mdo
Mahāyānaprasādaprabhāvanasūtra

The Sūtra of Entering the Sublime 197
Dam pa 'jug pa'i mdo

The Sūtra of Great Realization 196
rTogs pa chen po'i mdo
Mahāsamayasūtra

The Sūtra of Inconceivable Mysteries 196
gSang ba bsam gyis mi khyap pa'i mdo

The Sūtra of Instructions on the Indivisibility of the Absolute Nature of Reality 90
Chos kyi dbyings dbyer med pa'i le'u
Dharmadhātuprakṛtyasaṃbhedanirdeśasūtra

The Sūtra of No Arising 193
'Byung ba med pa'i mdo

The Sūtra of the Cloud of Jewels 90
'Phags pa dkon mchog sprin
Āryaratnameghasūtra

The Sūtra of the Great Illumination 196

Thar pa chen po'i mdo
Mahābhricasūtra

The Sūtra of the Holy Golden Light 31
gSer 'od dam pa mdo sde'i dbang po'i rgyal po'i mdo
Suvarṇaprabhāsottamasūtrendrarājasūtra

The Sūtra of the Questions of Guṇaratnasaṅkusumita 86
mDo yon tan rin chen
Guṇaratnasaṅkusumitaparipṛcchāsūtra

The Sūtra of the Questions of Kāśyapa 90, 106, 193
'Od srung gis zhus pa'i le'u
Kāśyapaparivartasūtra

The Sūtra of the Questions of Maitreya 107
Byams pas zhus pa'i mdo
Maitreyaparivartasūtra

The Sūtra of the Questions of Nārāyaṇa 35
Sred med kyi bus zhus pa'i mdo
Nārāyaṇaparipṛcchāsūtra

The Sūtra of the Questions of Prince Candra 34
rGyal bu zla bas zhus pa'i mdo
Candraparipṛcchāsūtra

The Sūtra of the Questions of Ratnacūḍa 158
gTsug na rin po ches zhus pa'i mdo
Ratnacūḍaparipṛcchāsūtra

The Sūtra of the Questions of Sāgaramati 15, 30, 203
Blo gros rgya mtshos zhus pa'i mdo
Sāgaramatiparipṛcchāsūtra

The Sūtra of the Questions of Sāgaranāgarāja 31
Klu'i rgyal po rgya mtshos zhus pa'i mdo
Sāgaranāgarājaparipṛcchāsūtra

The Sūtra of the Questions of Siṅha 31
Seng ges zhus pa'i mdo
Siṅhaparipṛcchāsūtra

The Sūtra of the Questions of Śrīsambhava 36
dPal 'byung gis zhus pa'i mdo
Śrīsambhavaparipṛcchāsūtra

The Sūtra of the Samādhi Which is Established in the Presence of the Contemporary Buddha 83
Da ltar gyi sangs rgyas mngon sum du bzhugs pa'i ting nge 'dzin gyi mdo
Pratyutpannabuddha-saṃmukhāvasthitasamādhisūtra

The Sūtra of the Synthesized Meaning 23
mDo dgongs pa 'dus pa

The Sūtra of the Ten Grounds 27
mDo sde sa bcu pa
Daśabhūmikasūtra

The Sūtra of the Ten Wheels of Kṣitigarbha 77
Sa'i snying po 'khor lo bcu pa'i mdo
Kṣitigarbhadaśacakrasūtra

The Sūtra of Thirty-three Questions 90, 106
Sum cu rtsa gsum pa'i mdo
Trayastriṃśatparivartasūtra

The Sūtra on Possessing the Roots of Virtue 64
dGe ba'i rtsa ba yongs su 'dzin pa'i mdo
Kuśalamūlasaṃparigrahasūtra

The Sūtra on the Meeting of the Father and Son 63
Yab sras mjal ba'i mdo
Pitāputrasamāgamasūtra

The Synthesized Essence of the Intended Meaning 24, 196
dGongs pa 'dus pa'i snying po

Synthesized Words 132
Tshig bsdus

The Tantra of Fine Accomplishment 49
Legs par grub par byed pa'i rgyud
Susiddhikaratantra

The Tantra of Inborn Inconceivability 131
Lhan cig skyes pa bsam gyis mi khyap pa'i rgyud

The Tantra of Inconceivable Mysteries 166
gSang ba bsam gyis mi khyap pa'i rgyud

The Tantra of the Blazing Clear Expanse of the Ḍākinīs 125, 173
mKha' 'gro klong gsal 'bar ma'i rgyud

The Tantra of the Blazing Clear Expanse of the Great Perfection 90, 110
rDzogs chen klong gsal 'bar ma'i rgyud

The Tantra of the Blazing Lamp 181
sGron ma 'bar ba'i rgyud

The Tantra of the Charnel Ground Ornament 29
Dur khrod rgyan pa'i rgyud
Śmaśānālaṃkāratantra

The Tantra of the Equal Union with All the Buddhas 40
Sangs rgyas thams chad dang mnyam par sbyor ba mkha' 'gro ma sgyu ma bde ba'i mchog kyi rgyud phyi ma
Sarvabuddhasamāyogaḍākinījālasaṃvaranāmauttaratantra

The Tantra of the Essential Meaning of Avalokiteśvara 182
Thugs rje chen po'i don tig gi rgyud

The Tantra of the Full Enlightenment of Vairocana 90, 104, 106
rNam snang mngon byang gi rgyud
Vairocanābhisaṃbodhitantra

The Tantra of the Garland of Vajras 68, 83
rDo rje phreng ba
Vajramālatantra

The Tantra of the Great River of Āli and Kāli 166
Ā li kā li chu klung chen po'i rgyud

The Tantra of the Lotus King 43, 44
Pad ma rgyal po'i rgyud

The Tantra of the Lotus Net 69
Padma dra ba'i rgyud
Padmajālatantra

The Tantra of the Lotus of Great Power 198
Padma dbang chen gyi rgyud

The Tantra of the Net of Magical Displays 23, 29
rGyud rgyu 'phrul dra ba

The Tantra of the Orb of Primordial Wisdom 40
Ye shes thig le rnal 'byor ma'i rgyud kyi rgyal po chen po mchog tu rmad du byung ba
Jñānatilakayoginītantrarājaparamamahādbhuta

The Tantra of the Questions of Subāhu 48
dPung bzang gis zhus pa'i rgyud
Subāhuparipṛcchātantra

The Tantra of the Self-arising Buddha 181
Sangs rgyas rang chas kyi rgyud

The Tantra of the Synthesized Mysteries of Avalokiteśvara 23, 25, 136
Thugs rje chen po'i gsang ba 'dus pa

The Tantra of the Union of the Sun and Moon 171
Nyi zla kha sbyor gyi rgyud

The Tantra That Bestows the Introduction 180
Ngo sprod sprad pa'i rgyud

The Tantra That Synthesizes the Bindus 180, 181
Thig le 'dus pa'i rgyud

Ten Dharmas 25
Chos bcu

by sGam po pa

The Three Cycles of the Oral Lineage 24
sNyan rgyud skor gsum

The Three Hundred 16
Sum brgya pa
by Śākya 'od

The Three Treasuries of Dohas 25
Do ha mdzod gsum

The Three Treasuries of Mysteries 25
gSang ba mdzod gsum

The Three Zhijé Cycles 24
Zhi byed skor gsum

The Tip of the Vajra 40
rDo rje rtse mo

The Treasure of Siddhis: The Hundred Thousand Teachings on the Maṇi 23, 25
Ma ṇi bka' 'bum grub thob dngos grub kyi gter ma

A Treatise in Four Hundred Stanzas 114
bZhi brgya pa
Catuḥśatakaśāstrakārikā
by Āryadeva

The Tree Ornament Dhāraṇī 193
'Phags pa sdong po rgyan gyi gzungs
Ārya-gulmālaṃkāradhāraṇī

The Twenty Precepts 17
sDom pa nyi shu pa
Saṃvaravimṃśaka

Unimpeded Contemplation 173
dGongs pa zang thal

The Unsurpassed Innermost Secret of the Great Compassionate One 23
Thugs rje chen po'i yang gsang bla med

The Vajra Garland Explanatory Tantra 27
bShad rgyud rdo rje phreng ba

The Vajra Pavilion Tantra 42
rDo rje gur gyi rgyud

The Vajra Uṣṇīṣa Tantra 197
rDo rje gtsug tor gyi rgyud

The View of the Vast Expanse 173

lTa ba klong yangs

Worship of the Ultimate 181
Don dam pa'i bsnyen pa
Paramārthasevā
by Pad ma dkar po (Puṇḍarīka)

The Yellow Document 23
Shog ser ma

Zhijé Dreams 26
Zhi byed rmi lam ma

General Index

Amitābha 9, 15, 22, 57, 59, 78, 83, 184, 187, 199, 200-202, 205, 212
Atiśa 18, 23, 58, 122
Avalokiteśvara 7-9, 11, 15-16, 24-27, 39, 47-49, 61, 63, 79, 83, 85, 115, 125, 137, 149, 153, 171-172, 201, 205-206, 212
Breakthrough 103, 180, 206
Cherbupa 113
Chödrak Gyatso 22-23
Chökyi Wangchuk 22, 24
Chöying Dorje 24
Dadak Metri 130
Dagpo Rinpoche (Gampopa) 19, 138, 165
Déwé Gönpo 22
Dezhin Shegpa 22-24
Dönden Zhap 73
Döndrup Tsenchen 24
Dong Kachöpa Saraha 144
Dorje Pagmo 169
Dragkarwa 23
Dragpa Gyaltsen 138
Drikung Könchok Trinley Namgyal 25
Drugchen Karma Tenpel 25
Drung Gampopa 99
Drungchen Kün-ga Namgyal 97, 147, 210
Düdül Dorje 9, 25-26
Düsum Kyenpa 22-23, 69, 156
Dzongtö Kandroma 41
Expanse class 180
four contemplations 166
Four Thoughts That Turn the Mind 51, 75, 86, 118, 132, 135, 139, 146, 152-153, 175
Garab Dorje 172
Gelong Tsöndrü 212
Geshe Jayülpa 93
Great Compassionate One 15, 46-47, 50, 52, 56, 58
Gö Tsangpa 25, 139, 150, 156, 169
Gyachakri 23
Gyalsey 23
Gyalwa Chö Dingwa 164
Gyalwa Yeshe Do 173
Gyalwang Chöjé 168
Gyaré 166
Gyatön Chökyi Zangpo 145
Jampal Zangpo 22, 27
Jamyang Khyentse Lodrö Tayé 11
Jigten Gönpo 164
Kangkawa 23
Karma Lingpa 173
Karma Pakṣi 22-24, 42, 49
Karma Trinley 24

Katogpa Jampa Bum 23
Könchok Yenlak 22, 51
Kumché 23
Kün-ga Namgyal 7, 24, 97, 147, 210
Lama Drung Yigpa 25
Lama Zhang 71
Leap-over 70, 149-150, 163, 171, 180, 182, 188, 206-207
Legshé Drayang 24
Lodrö Dragpa 24
Lodrö Rinchen 22
Machik Labdrön 48, 199
Mahāsiddha Masey 24
Maitreya 22, 32-33, 37, 107
Mañjuśri 20, 22-23, 26, 36, 154
Marpa Lhodrak 71
Mé-nyak Gomring 157
Mikyö Dorje 22, 24
Mikyö Zhap 24
Milarepa 22-23, 209
Mind class 180
Min-gyur Dorje 8-10, 12, 24
Mipam Padma Karpo 165
Namké Dorje 133
Nāgārjuna 18, 22, 42, 87, 104
Natsok Rangdröl 11, 27
Ngadak Nyang 23
Norbu Gyenpa 24
Norbu Lingpa Déwé Dorje 133
Nyang Ting-nge-dzin Zangpo 173
Nyima Beypa 112
Nyima Tsal 112
Orgyen Rinpoche (Padmasambhava) 7-9, 15, 19, 23, 26, 43, 47, 73, 86, 94, 107, 112, 120, 134, 153, 172-173, 194, 200
Özer Seng-ge 24
Padma Ledreltsal 23
Pagmo Drüpa 26, 42, 105, 163
Paljor Döndrup 22-23
Patrul Rinpoche 14, 30
Payül Chogtrul Rinpoche 11
Precept class 180
Rāga Asey 22, 24, 26, 51, 156, 210
Rāhula 22
Rangjung Dorje (Rangjungwa) 23, 25, 92, 117, 163
Ratna Lingpa 7, 9, 23, 27
Rechenpa 22
Rinchen Könchok Paljor 25
Sakya Paṇchen 138
Sampa Künkyap 11
Sangye Gön 11, 27
Sangye Nyenpa 22
Sangye Zhagchenpa 24
Śāntideva 23, 73, 107
Saraha 22, 105, 112, 129-131
secret *mantra* 22, 39-41, 49, 174, 205
Sending and Receiving 206-207
Serlingpa 23
Sey Lama Yeshe Dorje 23
Sharawa 23
Situ Chökyi Gyaltsen 25
Six-phase Yoga 42
Songtsen Gampo 46-47, 115, 137, 171
spell *mantra* 205
Taglung Tashi Paldrup 25
Tonglen Rinpoche 21
Tongwa Dönden 22-23
Tsangpa Gyarey 26
Tsombupa 57
Tsuglak Trengwa 67, 146, 160, 162
Vajradhara 22, 40, 75, 172
Vajravārāhi 22, 57
Vimalamitra 23, 173
Wangchuk Dorje 22, 25
Yagdey Paṇchen 144
Yang Gönpa 25, 140, 166
Yungtönpa 22-23